D0421835

The Politics of Remediation

Pittsburgh Series in Composition, Literacy, and Culture

DAVID BARTHOLOMAE *and* JEAN FERGUSON CARR, *Editors*

The Politics of Remediation

Institutional and Student Needs in Higher Education

MARY SOLIDAY

UNIVERSITY OF PITTSBURGH PRESS

Published by the University of Pittsburgh Press, Pittsburgh, Pa., 15261
Copyright © 2002, University of Pittsburgh Press
Manufactured in the United States of America
Printed on acid-free paper
10 9 8 7 6 5 4 3 2 1

Library of Congress Cataloging-in-Publication Data

Soliday, Mary.
    The politics of remediation : institutional and student needs in
higher education / Mary Soliday.
      p. cm. — (Pittsburgh series in composition, literacy, and
culture)
Includes bibliographical references and index.
    ISBN 0-8229-4186-4
    1. English language—Study and teaching (Higher)—Political
aspects—New York (State)—New York. 2. English language—Study and
teaching (Higher)—New York (State)—New York. 3. Education,
Higher—Political aspects—New York (State)—New York. 4. English
language—Remedial teaching—New York (State)—New York. 5. Basic
writing (Remedial education)—New York (State)—New York. 6. City
University of New York. City College. 7. City University of New York.
I. Title. II. Series.
    PE1069.C47 S65 2002
    428'.0071'17471—dc21
                                                2002003127

To L. F. Hanley

Contents

Acknowledgments   ix

1   The Politics of Access and the Politics
of Representation   1

2   Remedial Traditions and Institutional
Crisis, 1870–1970   20

3   Looking for Mina:
Reforming Basic Writing, 1966–1980   65

4   Representing Remediation:
The Politics of Agency, 1985–2000   105

5   Writing between Worlds: Access as Translation   146

Notes   187
Works Cited   195
Index   213

Acknowledgments

My greatest debt goes to Larry Hanley, who, among so many things, brought me into the contemporary world of computers and helped with the research for every chapter of this book. Bill Herman, Mark McBeth, Susan D'Raimo, and Carol Smith generously gave me documents that I used to write chapter 3. Bill Crain deepened my understanding of access politics; he and his fellow activists continue to provide me with models of good academic behavior. Marilyn Sternglass, Ira Shor, and Joseph Harris have all provided intellectual and professional support—thanks.

The staff of the Cohen Library at City College—including interlibrary loan, the circulation desk, and the archivist, Sidney van Nort—were wonderfully helpful over so many semesters. Josh Wilner, Fred Reynolds, and Ellen Smiley have supported my various teaching and administrative ventures at City for several years. Thanks to Jean Ferguson Carr of the University of Pittsburgh Press for encouragement, especially early in the process. I also appreciate the remarks of the anonymous reviewers and Chris Schroeder, who read drafts of chapters 1 and 5. The Simon H. Rifkind Foundation for the Humanities and Arts at City College awarded me a release from one course in the spring of 2001 so that I could prepare the final manuscript. Finally: thanks to City College students and Writing Center tutors, whose drafts and essays and hundreds of conversations during, between, and after office hours clarified my ideas and motivated me to finish this book.

The Politics of Remediation

1

The Politics of Access and the Politics of Representation

▶ *THE POLITICS OF REMEDIATION* CHALLENGES THE PERVASIVE idea that remediation at the college level is a novel endeavor because students' needs are novel. This book argues that remediation exists also to fulfill institutional needs and to resolve social conflicts as they are played out through the educational tier most identified with access to the professional middle class. Each chapter explores one of those related beliefs that together sustain what Sharon Crowley calls the "discourse of student need": the special illiteracy of urban students of color, the agency of basic skills programs in promoting access to the B.A., and the equivalence between educational success and a writer's untroubled assimilation to a dominant intellectual culture. Above all, this discourse depends upon the belief that institutions' standards for writing do not change, only the students' abilities do.

The status of college writing instruction in general helps to determine the specific institutional fortunes of remedial English. For that reason, this book focuses chiefly but not exclusively on remedial college English. Indeed, remedial composition would not have evolved as an often silent but always persistent "other" in English studies if the freshman course, advanced composition, and writing across the curriculum (WAC) programs had not also been institutionalized in particular ways. The politics of remediation also illustrate those broader material and ideological conflicts surrounding literacy instruction within higher education. These conflicts have not been settled in all cases, especially within those mid-level institutions whose missions are less well defined than those that occupy either the top tiers, which are dedicated to research, or the lower tiers, which are dedicated to teaching. Composition teaching is a complex enterprise because writing programs often mediate the institutional and social class needs that tiering is designed to address: the need to offer democratic access to growing numbers of students while also protecting selectivity; and the need to generate enrollments while also promoting the research and development that attract corporate, state, and federal funding.

The time-honored solution to these dilemmas has been to differentiate higher education into sectors, a process that began in the late nineteenth century when colleges distinguished themselves from the public high school. Though differentiation marked the growth of higher education throughout the first half of the twentieth century, it intensified most markedly in the 1960s, which saw the emergence of the four-year comprehensive and a vocational mission for the two-year college.[1] In the post–'60s era, remediation's gradual alignment with these low-status tiers was a result of its institutional use as, to borrow Barbara Ann Scott's phrasing, a crisis management tool. Remediation serves immediate institutional needs to solve crises in growth—in enrollment, curriculum, mission, and admissions standards—as much as it does to serve students' needs.

This is not to say that remedial students don't "need" more intensive writing and reading instruction than other students. But, even at the risk of overstating my case, I want to stress that, since the 1920s, a sizeable portion of the undergraduate population has completed remedial coursework or participated in some form of ad hoc remediation. Since the socioeconomic status of students enrolled in most four-year colleges has not changed dramatically over the last century, we cannot confidently attribute their needs to their backgrounds anymore than we can reasonably view remediation to be extraordinary. We must look elsewhere for an explanation of why at least half of all four-year institutions continue today to offer some type of remedial instruction to their predominantly white, middle-

and upper-class student bodies. We must look elsewhere for an explanation of why, over a century, faculty and administrators in every segment of private and public higher education have skirmished over writing curriculums, complained about student writing, and lamented the decline of standards.

Mike Rose observed in 1985 that the institutional memory of the need for writing instruction is exceedingly short-lived, so that the demand for it in the present always appears to be new. Why we forget what we once knew is largely a matter of institutional politics, which, particularly within the public sector, are shaped by cultural debates about the uses of education. The uses of education are intimately woven into American class politics, for, since the formation of the modern university in the late nineteenth century, the college slowly began to assume the premier role of educating a professional middle class. For complex reasons I touch on in chapters 2 and 3, higher education did not fully assume this role until the late 1960s. Remediation and its adjuncts—writing centers, proficiency testing, tutorials—had been well-entrenched in higher education since the turn of the twentieth century. However, college students' literacy did not become a subject of bitter conflict until the mid-1970s, while remediation at the college level did not garner national attention until the late 1980s. I argue in chapter 4 that the changing fortunes of remedial English teaching in this respect are partly a consequence of an increasing middle-class need to protect the exclusivity of an institution that, now more than ever, most defines its identity as a social class.

Under pressure to justify the existence of programs and students, while trying to stabilize a shaky identity in the academy, basic writing teachers, unsurprisingly, tend to dwell in an exigent present. For the sort of historical and political analysis I develop in this book has not been central to basic writing scholarship. Beyond Bruce Horner and Min-Zhan Lu's 1999 study of open admissions at the City University of New York, there is no sustained historical analysis of remedial English, and only a handful of books and articles documents the institutional politics of remedial writing instruction.[2] Aside from these and other notable exceptions, most research focuses on, even celebrates, the individual student and classroom pedagogy because basic writing scholarship has always been especially concerned to identify, and then meet, students' needs.

This tendency to focus on student need in the present tense is particularly significant now because of the national backlash against remediation in four-year schools, which I discuss in chapter 4. To counter this wave of critique, some scholars have called for more "hard data," while others assert that we ought to forgo culturalist critique and "return" to the individual case. In the field's most recent book, *Rethinking Basic Writing: Exploring Identity, Politics, and Community in Interaction,* Laura Gray-Rosendale advances this position by focusing on how individual students represent their political and cultural identities through peer group talk. Gray-Rosendale opposes her ethnomethodological approach to cultural or institutional critiques by aligning the first with individual students, and the second with abstract analysis. She finds that "our own attachment to broad categories for analysis can and has already led us to often neglect the local context of interaction as a primary site for meaning and identity production" (14). While it makes sense to ground an issue like "identity" within a "local context of interaction," the study of a few memorable students does not result in a powerful analysis of those "extra-institutional bodies" that exert pressure on basic writing programs (165). Yet these "bodies," Gray-Rosendale worries, will jeopardize the type of summer bridge program she studied at Syracuse University. Commenting on how the struggles over remediation at the City University might affect these programs, Gray-Rosendale notes that New York's Republican politicians attack remediation "while having had little to no engagement in teaching these students and learning about their *specific needs*" (165, my emphasis).

Gray-Rosendale's focus on the political as individual students represent it also determines what she thinks needs most to be re-formed. One argument that runs throughout this book is that if we clarify what we mean by "political," we also identify what constitutes a meaningful avenue for reform. Gray-Rosendale ends her study with three lists of specific reforms. The first offers suggestions for developing process pedagogy, while the second offers suggestions for involving more full-time faculty in programs without displacing the adjunct professorate responsible for most first-year composition teaching. The third calls for more "microlevel" as opposed to "macrolevel" research (170). The reforms contained in the first two lists aren't equivalent, however. By proposing a theory of literacy that engages with orality, the first list involves influencing the choices that an individual teacher makes in the classroom. But by focusing on "faculty roles," the second list would require substantial, even revolutionary, changes in institutional hiring practices. Gray-Rosendale doesn't explore the complexity of what she is advocating because the reform of hiring practices involves macrolevel, not microlevel, analysis.

In her book, Gray-Rosendale locates the "political" in microlevel "practices" and in ongoing, daily interactions (171). As she puts her case, "what might properly be said to constitute the political and the social within rhetoric and composition studies, and within Basic Writing scholarship" has "inevitably centered around political categories and theories such that the theoretical frameworks we use not only characterize but likewise partially constitute the nature of students' interactions" (171). There is little room in Gray-Rosendale's list of reforms for a more elaborate discussion of who teaches basic writing, and where, because this view of the political, centered on "meaning" and "identity," borrows heavily from a poststructuralist vocabulary.

In chapters 3, 4, and 5, I explore how the politics of meaning that Gray-Rosendale privileges is not equivalent to what I identify as a politics of access. In my view, the politics of access concerns how students gain entry to an institution and to the liberal arts, and the complex roles that remedial education could play in the process. By contrast, the politics of representation is more concerned with how students gain entry to traditional forms of academic knowledge, and with the identity conflicts writers may experience as a result. A politics of access also emphasizes institutional, rather than disciplinary, allegiances and concerns. In chapter 3, I will argue that this distinction is important because composition scholars tend to suggest that what is transgressive in the profession is equally so in a college or university setting.

In the first half of *The Politics of Remediation*, I historicize basic writing's institutional uses, in part by sketching out an abbreviated narrative of its evolution over the past century. From the perspective of institutional access that informs this part of the book, I locate reform within structures that would alter the conditions for learning that affect who teaches whom, and where. I use the history of higher education, revisionist scholarship on the history of composition, and the sociology of education as analytical frameworks to read historical documents, for instance surveys of composition teaching and archival sources from my institution. In the book's second half, I examine how remediation and remedial students have been represented in the post–open admissions era. Here I locate reform in curriculum development and in ways of writing about composition teaching. I use cultural studies, sociolinguistics, and the anthropology of education as frameworks for reading student writing, ideological debates, and literary and ethnographic accounts.

How we conceive of reform also reflects how we conceive of the responsibility for educational failure or success. Thus, while neither political focus—and its consequent emphasis upon reform—is more desirable than the other, it may be ideologically dangerous to conflate the two because neoconservative critics can use identity politics to dismiss a serious debate about the defunding of public higher education. As I document in chapters 4 and 5, critics can attribute the responsibility for educational failure to students' identity politics rather than to the very direct consequences of downsizing. While an analysis of the politics of representation and the border pedagogies that result from it should remain central to our enterprise, nevertheless we also have to acknowledge that a politics of language doesn't contest the academy's essential selective functions. Reforming curriculum does not necessarily reform the conditions for learning that organize teachers' and students' everyday experiences.

In the humanities, debates about the status of the politics of meaning illuminate the split I identify in composition studies. For instance, John Guillory argues that struggles over canon reformation have not resulted in a critique of the social effects that would result from cultural or educational change. He writes in *Cultural Capital*, "The question is rather what social effects are produced by the knowledges disseminated in the university, and by the manner of their dissemination" (50). From this perspective, which is informed by Pierre Bourdieu's sociology, it's not just the kinds of texts that matter, but who assigns and reads them, and where. Analyzing the relationship between PC debates, multiculturalism, and the Gulf War, Carol Stabile, a professor of communications, concludes that "'Politics' (as in the currently fashionable image of the multicultural university) was isolated from 'economics,' and the conflict was duly transformed into struggles over language, now safely removed from larger political and economic battles" (117).

The relationship between the politics of meaning and freshman writing courses has long preoccupied composition's left wing, per-haps best illustrated in Ira Shor's work on pedagogy, institutional differentiation, and culture war (1980, 1986, 1997, 2000). This long-standing interest owes to composition's historic role in helping stu-dents move between different social worlds, and, perhaps as one consequence of this mediation, to its equally historic role in provid-ing the economic base for a scholarly industry absorbed with the problems of meaning. James Slevin succinctly stated the case in 1991: "Those in composition are stained by their immersion in history, by a preoccupation with social practice, and by a concern with the uses of language that refuses to privilege canonical texts and forms. This conceptual framework seems absolutely indispensable in order to maintain the current economic structure of the profession. If we didn't have it, we'd have to invent it" (6). Throughout, I emphasize that institutions realize and maintain the "current economic struc-ture of the profession" through various differentiation strategies that manage their growth.

In the first half of the book, I focus on how institutions use strate-gies of internal and external stratification to resolve the historic ten-sions that coalesce around first-year composition teaching. Internal strategies include using first-year courses or writing assessment to regulate students' entry into liberal arts courses, or deploying ad-junct labor to teach required composition so that a full-time faculty can teach electives and perform some research. External strategies include using writing assessment to regulate the boundaries be-tween liberal arts and vocational colleges, shifting remediation to the lower tiers, and raising admissions standards in the higher tiers.

The Writing Program Administrator (WPA) is an especially crucial figure in the reform efforts I describe, since she is the individual most able to contest the use of writing instruction to solve institutional needs. In chapter 3, I argue that Mina Shaughnessy offers an administrative legacy that reflects this sort of challenging bureaucratic politics.

First-year writing courses are usually institutionalized to prepare students to enter the liberal arts and professional schools or to enroll in elective courses. For this reason, a longitudinal perspective is critical in shaping a robust politics of access. However, because a long-term view of a student's (or teacher's) development would also include an examination of how nonlinguistic factors shape educational success or failure, remediation's agency is less important within the politics of access than it may be from a viewpoint shaped by the politics of meaning.

Remediation plays a far less prominent role in those few studies that seek to measure retention rates or document students' intellectual growth over the years. In *Time to Know Them*, a six-year study of students' writing and learning, Marilyn Sternglass reveals that, even though some students experienced important changes in their cultural identities, these changes did not affect their persistence in college. As I'll discuss in chapters 3 and 4, Sternglass does not award substantial agency to English teachers in preparing students to succeed in liberal arts classes: neither writing teacher nor composition course plays a prominent role in helping students to stay in school over the long term. In her list of reforms, Sternglass emphasizes those changes consonant with a politics of access. Along with her critique of mass assessment, she stresses the causal role that tuition increases, rising rents, and long commuting hours played in students' educational narratives.

Those who espouse a long-term view will consider how material considerations affect educational success as much or more than linguistic choices that students and teachers make. Linguistic choice is central to the politics of representation, which have informed both a theory of learning and classroom practices. From this perspective, which is shaped by poststructuralism, students' identity conflicts affect how they learn; the privileging of academic language constitutes a chief barrier to their academic success. In the most extreme view, identity politics are awarded the agency to affect retention rates. Since language use is also connected to ways of knowing that characterize a writer's membership in different social worlds, reform would focus on what we teach and how we construct ourselves and others through writing. To contest academic exclusivity, we would contest the role that language plays in sustaining it.

The 1974 *Students' Right to Their Own Language* most famously illustrates the central role of the politics of language use in composition studies. This is because writing courses have been institutionalized to initiate students into academic discourse; composition's primary institutional identity lies in its mandate to help students write between what are often culturally unequal worlds. In the '70s, that mandate was politicized within the context of access movements that were aligned with civil rights and related social reforms that, in turn, fostered the growth of women's studies and ethnic studies programs in the academy. With the advent of multiculturalism in the 1980s, which informed fields as diverse as linguistics, the anthropology of education, and literary studies, composition scholars problematized writing between worlds as a psychologically and politically complex issue, especially for minority students.

Within this critique, curriculum assumes more power to affect students' intellectual growth than it does in a more materialist analysis. In scholarship that's inflected by poststructuralist theory, remediation's role or agency may be said to be more significant in enhancing students' educational success than it is in a study like Sternglass's. My goal is not to favor one analysis above another or to privilege access to the university at the expense of the access to knowledge but to distinguish more fully than we have done so far between two views of what constitutes the political. In this way, I want to clarify the limits of what each can reasonably hope to accomplish.

Probably another reason that scholars urge a return to the individual case is that they are acutely aware that institutional location defines almost everything we do as teachers, researchers, or administrators. Terence Collins observes that basic writing isn't a monolith because "we all have created Basic Writing from our multiple perspectives in our multiple sites" (100). Gray-Rosendale, for instance, chooses an ethnomethodological approach because it promises to integrate the microlevel experience of institutional life with a broader macrolevel analysis of institutional politics. I tend to locate the teaching of writing in the sector with which I am most familiar, the midlevel public comprehensive that enrolls the lion's share of students in the four-year segment. I also lean on my own institutional experience because my purpose is to connect material struggles to ideological ones in very specific ways. I use the City University of New York (CUNY) and one of its senior colleges where I teach, the City College of New York (CCNY), as exemplars of remediation's fortunes as they developed over a century in an institution that, before the early '70s, was dedicated primarily to teaching. Throughout the book, I connect this specific case to larger national conflicts and historical shifts which have organized literacy instruction in American higher education for a century.

Using the local example to explore more global issues, I also focus in some detail on the relationships between material needs and ideological justification. I argue in chapter 3 that these relationships have not been richly explored in groundbreaking ideological critiques like Horner and Lu's *Representing the "Other."* Through a focus on remedial English at the City University, I link ideological discussion to specific struggles over material goods and the particular needs of social groups. I hope that a term like "ideology" can function less as an abstract category of analysis and more as a concrete set of arguments that affect our daily teaching lives within institutions. In chapter 4, for instance, I use the revisionist scholarship of literacy crisis to read a particular panic over student writing in New York City. In the 1990s, the always-new remedial student emerged as a potent justification of New York's need to restratify its municipal college system. The City University had rejected this strategy in 1969 but, like other mid-level comprehensives across the country, embraced it in 2000 with an immediate impact upon teaching and learning in the nation's largest public urban system.

The lack of a vigorous historical consciousness in basic writing is not just a scholarly matter, because the proponents of downsizing often rely upon a particular version of the remedial past to bolster their arguments in the present. The discourse of student need de-

pends upon a belief that standards for writing are universal and decline when new groups of students enter higher education. Consider, for instance, *Open Admissions and Remedial Education at the
City University of New York*, one of five reports on remediation that
were appended to *The City University of New York: An Institution
Adrift*. Made available to the public in the summer of 1999, *An Institution Adrift*, which I discuss briefly in chapter 4, claimed that remediation was the chief source of the City University's alleged decline.
Sally Renfro and Allison Armour-Garb, the authors of the hefty appendix *Open Admissions and Remedial Education*, frame their critique
with a condensed history of remediation in table form, "History of
Remediation in the U.S., 1800s'–Present." This table explains how,
by the 1920s, "Most four-year institutions stopped providing remediation. Two-year colleges absorbed most of the remedial student
population." By the 1950s, "The bulk of remediation shifted to two-
year institutions"; between the 1960s and '70s, "Two-and four-year
colleges expanded access and began offering some credit for remedial work" (10). As "access continued to expand" in the '70s, "remediation became institutionalized at the postsecondary level" (10).

The always-new student whose needs organized so much hostile
discourse in New York and elsewhere could not exist without also
believing that standards for writing were uniform before the 1960s,
but, as a result of open access movements, began rapidly to decline
in the 1970s. In the myth of transience, no group of students needs as
much writing instruction as the group that we currently serve. Renfro and Armour-Garb can't deny that remediation existed in the
American college before the twentieth century, but, as they note in
the body of their text, it did so to remediate students in subjects like
the classical languages (8). In any case, by the 1920s, remediation had
been shifted to two-year colleges, only to resurface in the four-year
college in the wake of '60s access movements. In Renfro and Armour-Garb's version of the past, the historical consequences of expanded access are symbolized in today's remedial programs that
serve students of color, perpetuate low standards, fail to differentiate between two-year and four-year schools, and provoke fiscal
chaos.

Chapter 2, "Remedial Traditions and Institutional Crisis,

1870–1970," examines the roots of this historical commonsense. Using Barbara Scott's analysis of institutional crisis management, I argue that remediation was used before World War II as a way to stratify internally. A college experience was not central to middle-class aspirations before the '40s in the way it is today; though enrollments grew during this period, declines were periodic and threatened institutional growth and stability. Surely this is one reason why most institutions offered remedial courses to large numbers of their students, often through highly organized ability grouping, in other places through ad hoc, barely acknowledged practices.

Though higher education had begun to stratify as early as the 1890s, when it began most clearly to distinguish itself as the top educational tier, and though in the '20s a handful of liberal arts schools began to emerge as exclusive, institutions did not, as a whole, differentiate externally until the 1960s. It wasn't until the '60s that external institutional differentiation by curriculum, standards, mission, and student body began to occur most markedly, a process that sharply accelerated in the '70s. Drawing upon archival sources at City College, I examine, for instance, the claim that writing courses declined in the '60s because of the high level of student ability, only to be reestablished in the '70s in response to the presence of students with lower abilities. This claim is weakened if we also consider how English departments created writing programs to generate enrollments during a period of social and fiscal crisis that marked the end of the most expansive years of their growth.

Strategies of external differentiation became key management tools in the post–'60s era to manage what is today our primary educational conflict: the struggle between access and excellence. Burton Clark had identified that conflict in *The Open Door College*: "What is to be done when the pressure on colleges from the state legislators, city officials, parents, and students is to open wide the doors, but when, at the same time, college staffs and some outside groups are determined to hold up and possibly raise the standards of admission and attainment?" (162) To mediate between these opposing group interests, Clark thought that public institutions within a state would do one of two things. Either a series of internal barriers would be established that "cool out" working-class students within an institution, or institutions would differentiate to create less selective colleges that siphon off students who may not fulfill traditional educational narratives. The use of internal barriers and the differentiation of public higher education institutionalize our historical ambivalence toward the uses of education to achieve class mobility. The unselective institution exists *in order to* maintain democratic access without damaging selectivity in a hierarchical system.

Similarly, adopting what Kevin Dougherty calls an "institutionalist" viewpoint, I stress that the vocational mission for the two-year college emerged to mediate this struggle in the '70s. As private liberal arts colleges and midlevel comprehensives experienced fiscal crisis, the two-year sector was the target of selective federal funding and political attention. This institutional differentiation prepared the grounds for ideologies that emerged in the late '80s, which, for the first time, aligned the remedial student with minorities, affirmative action, and a dominant discourse of student need. One could say that remediation never became as visible in the history of higher education as when it was attached to students of color, a population that has never been heavily represented in the four-year sector.

By the early '70s, midlevel institutions struggled to upgrade their status by shedding a pure teaching mission, offering more professional and graduate education, and requiring some research as conditions for faculty hiring or advancement. The conflict between teaching and research that is today most acutely felt in this middle sector was institutionalized during this period. I illustrate this conflict by charting remediation's fate at the site of its genesis from "bonehead English" to "Basic Writing"—the City College of New York. In chapter 3, "Looking for Mina: Reforming Basic Writing, 1966–1980," I examine the rise and fall of Shaughnessy's famous program through the lens of stratification. In this context, Shaughnessy's emphasis upon acculturating students to academic discourse also reflects a politics of access that challenges the tiering of higher education. The desire to integrate a working-class population into a traditional liberal arts institution contested those plans for tiering that would align nontraditional student bodies with vocational education, and more traditional liberal arts curriculums and middle-class students with the upper tiers.

The subject of much lively controversy since 1980, Shaughnessy is an ambivalent figure because she embodies a friction between the two kinds of politics I identify in this book. By historicizing Shaughnessy's work, I don't gloss over the problems inherent in her formalist pedagogy. But I distinguish between the politics of language use and the politics of basic skills programs by highlighting the considerable administrative work that preoccupied her for several years. Today, Shaughnessy's work provides us with a robust version of a WPA who contests the low status of a remedial program by trying to improve the everyday conditions for working and learning.

Perhaps unfortunately, Shaughnessy did not wrestle with those essentialist attitudes toward language teaching that have helped to justify the weak intellectual status of all first-year writing courses. This is partly because she privileged academic language, but it is also because she was more interested in how language and meaning are segregated institutionally. I offer examples of projects she developed that consistently challenged how teachers, students, and their courses are housed outside or beyond liberal arts courses. From her focus on sequencing, Shaughnessy called for longitudinal research that would complicate the gatekeeping functions of writing programs. Because she understood that remedial programs are often used to solve institutional crises, Shaughnessy also believed that these programs could not function as "the" avenue for access to a liberal arts education. If the agency of basic writing programs is thus downplayed, then not only does the responsibility have to be shared, we must also find different ways to sequence courses and to evaluate or assess that growth beyond a single program.

By the late '80s, remedial programs at the senior colleges in the City University of New York had lost their local autonomy and therefore much of their original insurgent qualities. Nevertheless, remediation became the subject of controversy and, throughout the '90s, the center of arguments to privatize, defund, and restratify the municipal system. Remediation assumed importance in these debates because it symbolized the central crisis of this period: how to protect the selectivity of a research tier without ignoring the aspirations of upwardly mobile working-class and lower middle-class populations. Representations of remediation are central to understanding basic writing's role in the post–'60s era because complaints about students' illiteracy at the college level become ideological.

In chapter 4, "Representing Remediation: The Politics of Agency, 1985–2000," I link the representation of remediation to efforts to restratify the four-year sector, both nationally and in New York. Since, as Clark had suggested in his case study research, stratification can't proceed without the consent of groups with opposing interests, the representation of remediation becomes ideological when it serves to build class coalitions. For instance, I focus on how a coalition of critics in New York City fomented a literacy crisis in order to create a class consensus to downsize public higher education. Though the State University of New York and CUNY were the focus of a fierce debate that spanned a decade and culminated in a series of reforms for both systems, remedial students at the City University played a central ideological role in all these struggles.

As these debates raged nationally, in New York remedial students emerged as members of a special urban underclass who were suddenly "discovered" by journalists like James Traub. Traub and others used these students to assign agency to the cultural deprivation they argued is typical of anti-intellectual, inner-city minorities. I use the analysis of culture war developed by Barbara Ehrenreich, Ira Shor, and John Trimbur to read several texts written by public intellectuals as well as composition scholars. I examine how intellectuals use the "poor" remedial student to reflect upon middle-class responsibility toward the "other" classes and, by extension, toward those institutions designed to remediate poverty. In writing about the student who is estranged from middle-class institutions, neoliberal intellectuals explore their own estrangement from the contemporary city.

Representing remediation becomes a political matter when writers assign agency for educational success or failure to a specific social group, program, or institution. In New York, these representations were often used to argue that, if remedial education fails, then so too does open access as a policy. From this perspective, remediation functions to transform students' literacy skills within one or two precollege courses. When these programs fail to accomplish this transformation, it has often been argued that part of the blame rests upon the shoulders of those students who resist assimilating to dominant intellectual cultures. In other words, during the New York City literacy crisis that I describe, critics frequently suggested that—in sharp contrast to previous generations—students' identity politics prevent them from assimilating to the mainstream.

This argument dangerously conflates the politics of access with the identity politics I associate with multicultural perspectives. In the politics of access, remediation plays a less crucial role in sustaining open access policies: more responsibility is accorded here to those larger shifts in higher education such as privatization strategies, which I describe in some detail in chapter 4. But for some neoliberal intellectuals, students' underclass cultures are assumed to be in irreconcilable conflict with traditional liberal arts knowledge.

Ultimately, representation is political when it serves to establish class coalitions. In New York, the organic intellectuals of the City University's past often express distance or alienation from those potential intellectuals of the city's future, many of them enrolled now at the City University. Yet these struggles over assimilation, as I note in chapter 5, "Writing between Worlds: Access as Translation," have shaped one strand of American intellectual autobiography, an argument that Min-Zhan Lu developed through her cogent readings of Du Bois and Irving Howe (1999). In progressive education, of course, intellectuals have also long questioned the uncomplicated status of melting pot imagery. Perhaps reflecting discussions by intellectuals like Randolph Bourne or Scott Nearing, Jane Addams had proposed in *Twenty Years at Hull-House* a "reciprocal" version of urban education where teachers and students would find new meaning and value out of the dynamic relationship between subordinate and dominant cultures. American society, she argued, does not benefit from the loss of ethnic identities and immigrant cultures. "I believe that we may get, and should get, something of that sort of revivifying effect and upspringing of new culture from our contact with the groups who come to us from foreign countries," she wrote in 1930 (279). One responsibility of urban education, Addams thought, was to transcreate competing cultures rather than value one above the other.

Anzia Yezierska, whose work I discuss in chapter 5, offers a similarly reciprocal perspective upon education and literacy as the means to assimilate to a dominant culture. A Jewish intellectual who published fiction and semiautobiography from the '20s to the '50s, Yezierska complicated the view that a working-class college student will embrace new knowledge by shedding a past identity, language, or cultural tradition. Like other writers who have moved from ethnic enclaves to elite institutions—Zora Neale Hurston offers one spectacular example—Yezierska does not lose one cultural allegiance in favor of the dominant one, but instead develops an imagery of bilateral travels between worlds as her characters struggle to live meaningfully between them by transcreating the values or languages embodied in each. In their essays, City College students represent their own intercultural encounters in these more complicated terms. Access to traditional knowledge or to dominant American cultures, they suggest, is not a matter of making a singular choice. Writers like Yezierska or my City College students challenge a politics of agency practiced by critics like James Traub, whose arguments for downsizing remediation often rest on the assumption that working-class intellectuals of the past assimilated smoothly to dominant discourses. But, of course, identity politics are no more novel than are remedial students; both have helped to shape the American cultural milieu since the turn of the century.

Writing courses are often institutionalized to prepare students to write someplace else in the academy. Therefore, many teachers question the value of experimental curriculums that they don't believe fulfill a course's institutional aims. Others will object that the writing I discuss in this chapter does not adequately challenge conventional academic styles. My local answer to these broader questions is to focus exclusively on familiar essay writing as one example of what I call translation pedagogy. Translation pedagogy attempts to negotiate between different discourses—those that students bring with them, and those that they may encounter in other academic situations.

The familiar essay is one among many forms where private and public languages intersect. It gives less-experienced writers the freedom to invent new styles while also imitating those of expert writers, and it allows them to fuse nonacademic languages and artistic forms with the conventional features of prose essays. Its success or readability depends on the writer's ability to present her experience as meaningful to another audience—it is a representation, not a chronicle, of personal events or feelings. Both conventional and experimental, familiar essays also give teachers a place to discuss those relationships that organize a writing course more generally: the connections between style and meaning, reading and writing, tradition, innovation, and audience. Many of the students whose work I examine do transcreate knowledge, identity, or style using a form whose hallmark is consonant with the broad goal of academic literacies—the development of secular critical thinking.

Public intellectuals often use the form of the familiar essay to comment on the issues of their time to a broader audience. In this regard, a pedagogy of translation aims to give student writers a place in the classroom to act and think as intellectuals who discuss issues significant to each other and to their families as well as to the academic representative, their teacher. We could develop a curriculum that serves solely to prepare students to write in academic contexts, as was the case in the mid-1980s; conversely, we could develop one that radically departs from its institutional mandate. I try to negotiate between these tensions by building upon the rich tradition already existing within composition studies whose goals are parodic. If we view parody as Linda Hutcheon defined it some time ago—as a "repetition with a difference"—then we could teach students to imitate dominant forms by inflecting them with their own accents. While this is not always possible, in the practice I sketch out, many writers can and do imitate forms with a distinct difference. Equally important, they and their teacher experience pleasure in the process of reading and writing, which is not always true for required composition courses.

Those issues that are central to identity politics in composition studies—the loss of self or authentic motives when accommodating readers who represent a more powerful culture—are also relevant to teaching writing in any context. Case study accounts suggest that expert academic writers also struggle not to betray their intentions in the process of translating their local research into forms that are readable for national audiences. On the one hand, the writing of the City College students that I discuss in this chapter provides a rich exploration of specific contemporary cultural conflicts. On the other hand, this writing also offers a more general portrait of what happens when writers are obliged to translate between different social worlds.

In 1992, Laura Rendón, a professor of higher education administration, published an autobiographical essay eloquently detailing her effort to translate herself between socially unequal worlds. Describing the identity conflicts she experienced as a Mexican American who traveled "from the barrio to the academy," Rendón concludes: "I contend that the most important lesson to be learned is *not* that higher education must increase access for new scholarship 'boys and girls' or must offer them better financial aid packages, more role models, and better counseling and mentoring. These standard solutions, while important, do not focus on the larger and more important issue, which is that higher education must begin to think in new ways about what constitutes intellectual development and about whether the traditional manner with which education prepares new students is appropriate for people of color as well as for white women and men" (60). *The Politics of Remediation* reflects Rendón's concern that we begin to "think in new ways about what constitutes intellectual development," especially in courses that continue to play an initiatory institutional role. But I am equally concerned with promoting these students' access to the liberal arts, especially for those who are not on "scholarship." While I embrace the view that a critique of knowledge is central to educational reform, I also take issue with multicultural perspectives that tend to assume that curriculum changes will challenge the academy's selective functions. To work against the discourse of student needs as that has defined our enterprise, we cannot afford to conflate two perspectives or to neglect one in favor of the other. In what follows, I distinguish between the particular power that each holds as a mode of analysis and reform for teaching and administration, for scholarly and activist work.

2 | Remedial Traditions and Institutional Crisis, 1870–1970

▶ IN *THE CHRONICLE OF HIGHER EDUCATION,* NATHAN Glazer recalled his undergraduate days: "When I entered City College, in 1940, admission was based solely on high-school grades, and it was taken for granted that those grades meant more or less the same thing in all the public high schools of the city. There was nothing like remedial education, at least in my recollection, unless we consider the required courses in 'speech,' whose only purpose seemed to be to eliminate any evidence of a New York accent or intonation. In contrast, the statistics on how many of today's incoming students require remedial education are awesome" (3). According to its *Bulletin* for 1940–41, the Department of English Language and Literature at Glazer's alma mater offered "Remedial English" for "the man who was deficient" in grammar and mechanics. This course had been offered since 1927, along with an upper-level remedial course, and an array of remedial evening courses, such as English C, "a quick review of high school English for matriculated students." For over forty years, the college regularly published in its bulletin specific remedies for writers "reported" as deficient in their courses. In 1963, the English faculty declared to the *New York Times* that they had judged a quarter of that year's freshmen—all averaging at least 85 percent in their high school work—as "too backward in spelling and grammar for the opening course in composition."

This considerable gap between memory and practice dramatizes the peculiar historical amnesia surrounding postsecondary remediation in American culture. This chapter concerns that always-forgetting and the consequences of forgetting for particular people. A distinguished sociologist and well-known public intellectual, Glazer writes about urban education in forums like the *Times* or *The Public Interest*, so his memories assume a special salience in public debates about admissions, standards, and remediation (1994, 1999a, 1999b). And since he often invokes the City College of New York as a specific example, Glazer's memories reflect—and help to sustain—the widespread assumption that urban students have a uniquely "awesome" need for remediation. In this chapter, I will complicate the persistent assumption that standards for writing are timeless, and weaken the ideologically damaging association between remediation and the open access policies of the 1960s.

Lost from both personal and institutional memory is a sentence like this one, from a one-paragraph placement essay, "The Kind of Books I Like," produced in 1912 at the University of Wisconsin. Edwin Woolley cited it as a remedial exemplar in the *English Journal*:

> I dont very often read a novel, but one in a while I will pick one up and read it, because is kind of give me a change but when I do read one I want one which deals with the happier thoughts in life and not one which makes a joke out of life as some of the authors do of the present day, which are written to sell and not to stay on the list of great writers. (244)

What lingers in the memory for many is a sentence like this one, also from a placement exam, produced in the 1970s by a City College student. Mina Shaughnessy cited it as an exemplar of basic writing in *Errors and Expectations*:

> I feel that if I *had go* on to college instead of to work as I did I would be more capable to simply communicate to my fellow employers in a more open-minded way and maybe they *would have realize* how close-minded they were. (103, emphasis in original)

These sentences underscore the profound consequences of the myth of transience in terms of the different ideological roles that remedia-

tion played at Wisconsin in the early twentieth century and at the
City University in the 1990s. For Diane Ravitch, an influential
scholar, former bureaucrat, and vocal opponent of the City University's open admissions policy, the fact that college students "dont
very often read a novel" is a contemporary phenomenon rooted in
the open access policies of the '60s (McGowan 31). For James Traub,
a journalist for the *Times* and prominent critic of remediation, it is
characteristic of black students' anti-intellectualism. In New York
State, as I indicated in chapter 1 and will describe further in chapter
4, the urban illiterate loomed large in the neoconservative imagina-
tion of the '90s as an exotic being never before encountered in college.

Yet remedial English has always been with us in various forms
because it has long acted as an ad hoc form of admissions within all
types of institutions. Remedial writing was used to stratify students
within institutions through the 1940s, and, beginning in the 1920s
and accelerating in the 1970s, more markedly to stratify the institutions themselves. I do not question the value of thousands of basic
skills programs that may have helped students gain access to the B.A.
But I do question the wisdom of using basic skills courses to fulfill
institutional commitments and to resolve educational conflicts in a
submerged or marginal form. Ultimately, we all need to question
remediation's anomalous status within institutions in order to imagine alternatives to it.

A rich body of scholarship has revealed that it was hardly inevitable or natural that English departments should degrade rhetoric
or oratory, once central to their mission, in favor of an aesthetic study
of canonical texts.[1] Similarly, it was not inevitable that remedial
English should be offered as a set of scattered, barely acknowledged
practices focusing mostly on teaching grammar, spelling, and mechanics. To study remediation's historical evolution is to study the
politics of institutions and to contest the commonsense assumptions
that standards for writing are universal and that, as a consequence, remediation exists only because students need to be remediated. By
studying remediation's past, we are more fully equipped to contest
the persistent, widespread practice of separating skills teaching from
the liberal arts in the present.

Remediation's uses shift over time because it is often used to navigate broader institutional changes in mission, enrollment, curriculum, standards, and admissions, all of which affect the status of English studies and composition teaching. Institutions use composition and remediation in more complex ways to fulfill their own, not just students', needs. Chief among these is the institutional struggle to balance the need to sustain enrollments with the desire to establish a particular mission. For this reason, I situate remedial English within a broader history of the gradual differentiation of American higher education. Barbara Ann Scott argues that institutions differentiated to survive in a fiscal context that was shaped by funding practices. She shows, for instance, how unorganized private gifts in the 1870s were replaced at the turn of the century by a more rationalized process of giving controlled largely by the Rockefeller and Carnegie foundations, both of which played major roles in shaping the admissions standards of selected institutions. By 1945, the federal government supplanted the private foundations in funding, especially in scientific research and development. In the nineteenth century, Scott writes, "The essential structural change that occurred was one of internal stratification within single, still-autonomous institutions. It was not until later that new applications of crisis management brought about a comprehensive stratification of multiple diverse institutions within a single academic system" (22). Institutions of higher education developed strategies such as admissions policies to cope with—increasingly, to rationalize—various crises that are a consequence of a capitalist economy: periodic cycles of boom and bust, fiscal growth and contraction, and the demographic shifts and aspirations that accompany these.

Crisis is also cultural, and within this economy it involves conflicting aspirations that higher education has addressed for a century: the desire to create a meritocratic culture through democratic access to the B.A.; and the desire to create an insular, exclusive research tier that promotes our spectacular economic and technological expansion. Stratification was a chief strategy that institutions developed to survive within this context, selectively tailoring their missions and admissions policies to fulfill particular needs.

In this and the next two chapters, I use Scott's analysis of institutional stratification as a crisis management tool to read a history of remedial English. English composition figures centrally in this narrative of differentiation because, with the decline of the classical curriculum in the late nineteenth century, it became a key subject demarcating the boundaries among a precollegiate, freshman, and liberal arts curriculum within a single institution. Throughout the next century, it would be used to distinguish the borders between increasingly stratified institutions.

From 1870 to the 1900s, institutions used remedial English to sharpen the blurry boundary between secondary and college education in a culture that had not yet firmly defined college as the top educational tier. In this period, remediation was a diffuse set of practices, located for instance in the idiosyncratic but nevertheless ubiquitous preparatory programs housed in most institutions of higher learning before the turn of the twentieth century. In an era when more systematic admissions policies were being developed, composition emerged as one means to stabilize and rationalize the process as colleges shed their classical curriculums and distinguished themselves from lower institutions.

In the interwar period of the next century, English departments assumed their identity as departments of literature, and they began to use remediation as an internal admissions mechanism. Exclusivity was only beginning to be attached to a college education, enrollments were relatively low, and differentiation was emerging as a way to manage the competition between institutions. Remedial English could be used to stratify students within, rather than among, institutions. Hence, with the further decline of strong composition programs and of the "forensic system," which suffused writing across four years of college, the system of ability grouping that emerged between 1900 and the 1920s was devised to "sectionize" students according to remedial, average, and superior abilities. Another practice was to offer ad hoc remedial instruction, usually through tutorials, clinics, extra credit hours, self-study workbooks, awkward squads, and so on. Such strategies enabled institutions to establish standards internally rather than to fix them absolutely at the beginning.

The 1960s and early 1970s were watershed years for composition teaching in the U.S., as English departments experienced a growth and popularity that not all would be able to sustain in the following decades. In the lush years that saw the hyperspecialization of English studies and exponential growth in every area, the crisis of institutions involved managing their expansion. In part, the decline of remediation in this decade correlates with the increased differentiation of higher education into distinct tiers. But its decline also correlates with the flowering of the English major and specialized literary study, and with a new emphasis on research in midtier public comprehensives. With the diminished vigor in many midlevel schools of flourishing humanities divisions after the severe fiscal crunch of the early 1970s, remediation and basic skills returned with a vengeance. Though I argue these programs served to sustain enrollments for English departments, they became ideologically associated with open access, affirmative action, and equal opportunity programs, and thus with students of color.

Here and in subsequent chapters, I use the City College of New York to illustrate the changing role of remedial English. I rely on City as a particular example because it has been the home of the most famous remedial English program, and because it has served first-generation college students since the early twentieth century. But most important, City College is a public comprehensive college, an institution that emerged in the 1960s to become one of the dominant sectors within higher education. Much of the history of writing instruction emphasizes how the research mission emerged in the late nineteenth century. This bias neglects the fact that at midlevel teaching institutions, which with the two-year college form the majority of all public institutions, research would not become part of an institution's mission until the late '60s, with specific consequences for writing instruction.

In the next two chapters, I will examine remediation's shifting structural and ideological roles over the past thirty years. Here I focus on its origins and growth before 1970 to argue that remediation is as much a function of institutional differentiation as it is of the specific needs of always-new students. If, in the twenty-first century, the subfield called Basic Writing is at a crossroads, we would do well to reflect upon its past uses in our era marked by its own philosophical, structural, and demographic shifts.

Preparatory English and the Dual Mission, 1870–1900

In his study of college life in the early 1980s, Ernest Boyer found that remedial programs were well entrenched in higher education, and that most faculty felt their students were underprepared, especially in reading and writing. Boyer cited two national surveys from the early '80s to support these assertions. The first showed that 84 percent of 250 institutions offered basic skills courses, while the second found that in 91 percent of institutions surveyed, over a third of students were deficient in writing (76, 74). Boyer concluded that, while "Remediation has a long tradition," yesterday's student received help in Greek, history, or literature, not in basic skills: "In contrast, remedial programs today teach incoming college students to read, write, and compute" (74).

Boyer's assumption sustains the historically anomalous status of writing courses and their teachers by suggesting that "today's" students are themselves anomalous. Indeed, remedial writing courses didn't appear in large numbers as separate courses as we understand them today until well into the second decade of the twentieth century. Andrea Lunsford finds that the first remedial course, offered at Wellesley College in 1894, was designed to "'remedy' academic deficiencies" (1987, 248). Harvard offered the first remedial writing courses in 1899, when it abolished its upper-level composition courses and created three remedial courses for those students who did poorly in English A, the freshman course (Russell 56). Otherwise, in his survey of thirty-seven eastern colleges and universities, John Wozniak dates the first remedial course for writing in the first decade of the twentieth century, at the University of Pennsylvania (130).

But remedial English didn't appear before 1900 in college catalogues not because students didn't need it but for reasons involving the development of English studies, and more broadly, the modern university. In the flux that characterized the last two decades of the nineteenth century, the dividing line between institutions—college, university, academy, and public high school—had not been firmly fixed. Because funding depended upon large but random gifts from private benefactors, enrollments were more closely tied to institutions' fiscal health than to their exclusivity. Consequently, admissions practices were still somewhat idiosyncratic. Moreover, composition had not yet become one of the primary points of demarcation between groups of students and different kinds of institutions. Within emergent English departments struggling to rid themselves of a classical curriculum, literary study had not yet emerged as the dominant force.

Since complaint about students' illiteracy echoes across the years,[2] an alternative interpretation to Boyer's contention that "basic skills" remediation is new is that other structures existed to remedy "deficiencies." Between the 1870s and the 1900s, there were three traditional approaches to literacy instruction that institutions used in lieu of remedial courses. The first was preparatory programs, which were housed within colleges, especially in land grant institutions or a municipal college like the City College of New York, and which offered subfreshman coursework to sustain enrollments. The second was the practice of conditioning in the few private schools that had already established relationships with designated feeder schools and so did not explicitly offer preparatory work. The third was the attempt to provide writing instruction throughout a student's four years, rather than settling it within one course. Taken together, these approaches allowed colleges to admit students the faculty might not consider fully fluent in the vernacular and to remediate their English continuously, often beyond the first year.

It was not, then, that some students didn't require remediation in writing, reading, or arithmetic (or Latin and Greek, for that matter), but that remediation was conducted in the preparatory programs contained within colleges and universities, whose difference from lower institutions wasn't as firmly fixed in the postwar era of emergent systems as they would be by the century's end. In 1936, R. L. Duffus commented that the "pioneers" of the period—presidents like Nicholas Murray Butler of Columbia—developed new admissions systems to "define a college and mark out a boundary between

the college and the secondary school" (52). In 1886, President
Charles W. Eliot of Harvard argued that the unorganized standards
for English composition illustrated a broader anarchy in entrance
requirements: "Some colleges demanded no English at entrance;
others required the candidate to write a short composition, but gave
no hint as to what the subject might be; others called for a knowledge of formal grammar and nothing else; others for both grammar
and composition. Some of the examination papers asked questions
which could not be fully answered without a minute knowledge of
prescribed texts, or of difficult points in grammar; others asked
questions suited to the capacity of grammar school, or even primary
school, pupils" (qtd. in Duffus 45–46). Two decades later, in 1908,
the Carnegie Foundation for the Advancement of Teaching focused
similarly on mathematics: "There was no real basis for secondary
schools as such, or for college courses: there was confusion; plane
geometry, history and elementary science were high school studies
as well as college studies" (45). Viewed in this light, the painstaking
dissection of student writing that Harvard's Committee on Composition and Rhetoric produced in successive reports in the 1890s reveals an effort to demarcate institutions through what, along with
mathematics, would become a key subject for articulation, English
composition.

Before the so-called Carnegie unit became a widely accepted
practice for admissions purposes, colleges relied on their own
preparatory programs to resolve the related problems of articulation and sustaining enrollments. These programs, as Frederick
Rudolph explains, "caught students at a tender age and insulated
them from the blandishment of rival institutions" (281). A fixture
within nineteenth-century institutions of higher learning, they probably also served to remediate students' reading, writing, and mathematics. In 1889, 335 out of 400 institutions of higher learning in the
U.S. supported a preparatory department (Wyatt 12). In 1865, the
University of Wisconsin, which created what may have been the first
preparatory department in 1849, enrolled 331 students, of whom
only 41 attended regular classes (11–12). In 1870, only five states in the
union—all in the northeast—did not offer such preparatory work
housed within their institutions of higher learning; and within these

states, there were only twelve colleges that didn't offer subfreshman coursework. "Everywhere else in the country," comments Rudolph, "the pattern of integral college preparation was well established" (281). In 1894, over 40 percent of the nation's 238,000 college students were enrolled in subfreshmen courses (*College Remediation* 3). As late as 1915, the U.S. Commissioner of Education reported that 350 institutions still housed these programs (Wyatt 12).

At the same time, however, colleges recognized that preparatory programs forced them to develop a dual mission. If they did not distinguish themselves from the lower tier, they could never upgrade their status as institutions of higher learning. A local institution, for instance, would operate simultaneously as "the classical academy as well as the college for the district that it served" (Rudolph 282). While private schools (especially in the northeast) continued to rely on an established network of feeder schools to prepare their students, and continued as well to admit students based on their own examination systems, the public colleges and universities moved ahead to pioneer a system that would gradually free them from the dual mission that distinguished their curriculums throughout the latter half of the nineteenth century. In 1870, the University of Michigan began admitting students on the basis of the certificate system, which allowed it to admit students from the public schools that the university had certified. In the next year, the University of Minnesota followed suit by announcing that a certificate system would result in a curriculum shift that would allow it to sustain a research mission: "it intended as soon as possible to shift the work of its preparatory *and* collegiate departments to the high schools and eventually to limit the work of the university to professional study and graduate study in science, literature, and the arts" (Rudolph 283–84). Admission by certification spread throughout the midwest and south: Indiana and Illinois adopted the practice in 1872, and Ohio in 1874; by 1900, 42 state institutions and 150 of the privates were using the certification system (284).

In 1895, while 40 percent of all college admits were still graduates of the preparatory departments, 41 percent possessed high school diplomas (Rudolph 284). "By this time," writes S. Willis Rudy, "colleges throughout the nation were being more sharply differentiated than ever from academies, high schools, and all other secondary schools, and were tending to demand four years of high school work as a preliminary to admission to college work" (231). In New York State, the Pavey bill of 1896 created a Board of Superintendents for New York City empowered to establish a full-fledged school system spanning K–12. The Board established three high schools for the city in the same year, thus formally ushering in the era of consolidated municipal high school systems (Rudy 230). At the same time, the New York State Board of Regents also ruled that, to claim the status of a college, institutions must offer a full four-year course in liberal arts and sciences, with grammar school and four years of high school as prerequisites (231).

As one result of this legislation, the City College of New York (which had itself begun in 1847 as the Free Academy), moved in 1899 to transform its preparatory program into a certified public high school, Townsend Harris Hall, housed within the college until 1942. But before that date, and well into the twentieth century, the preparatory program was a dominant feature of the institution, enrolling more than half its total number of students, and figuring centrally in the pages of its bulletins. This three-year program offered three subfreshmen classes—which enabled urban boys who had to work while studying to finish high school and college within seven rather than eight years. Alternatively, boys could, whatever their previous secondary education, enroll in the third subfreshman year (Class C) and finish both high school and college in a five-year prescribed college course. To be admitted to the City College, boys could finish the entire subfreshman course or just the last year and take exams that qualified them for entrance into the college proper.

These "subfreshmen" years offered courses ranging from Greek and Latin to American history, chemistry, and mathematics. And they included three years of composition, language, and literature. In the years 1901–2, the preparatory course for English included three years of composition, rhetoric, elementary philology, and literature. In the first year, along with an introduction to American literature, "The students receive a thorough training in English grammar and in the structure of the English sentence" (*Register* 1901–2, 19). For four hours a week, students used textbooks like Kittredge and

Arnold's *The Mother Tongue* and Carpenter's *Elements of Rhetoric,*
and they read *Masterpieces of American Literature.* In the second
year, students spent two hours a week on the "rhetorical study" of
diction, style, paragraphs, and whole compositions, along with an
introduction to British literature. They were expected to produce
short "fortnightly themes," four longer essays, and to hold conferences with their teachers (14). In the third year, they spent two hours
a week with "themes, essays, and conferences," in addition to reading texts like Burke's *Warren Hastings,* Macaulay's prose, Burke's
Speech on Conciliation, and selected Shakespeare plays (*Register*
1901–2, 19–20; 14–21).

The hazy line between subfreshman and freshman year studies
reflected the broader uncertainties about curriculum and standards
in an era when exclusivity wasn't tied to restrictive enrollments. For
instance, it was the distinction between high school and college that
formed the real battleground that the Harvard Reports waged over
literacy skills in the 1890s. In the opinion of the Overseers, public
school teachers should be responsible for writing in the vernacular,
and professors should take literature as their domain (see Brereton
27). In 1938, Arthur Palmer Hudson introduced "the perennial problem of the ill-prepared" in English composition by noting, "As early
as 1837 the University [of North Carolina at Chapel Hill] officially
complained of low standards of college preparation and of the competitive practices of certain other institutions in lowering standards
of admission to bolster enrollments [*sic*]" (723). This practice continued in many institutions through the early 1920s, and again in the
early '30s and early '40s, periods of depression and war that created
enrollment drops; between 1939 and 1944, enrollments declined nationally by 41 percent (Scott 44). As Walter Metzger points out, what
would become the top tier of higher education in terms of selectivity
had, at the turn of the twentieth century, the largest enrollments and
teaching staffs. In 1910, the University of Chicago, with 6,681 students, claimed the largest enrollment in the U.S., with Minnesota,
Illinois, Michigan, Pennsylvania, Harvard, and Columbia following
behind in numbers. Metzger observes, "immense enrollments and
elite pretensions were not seen as incompatible in this period: the
time had not yet come when an American university would gain

more prestige from the selectivity than from the magnitude of its admissions" (146).

Selectivity based on a student's academic preparation was not the stamp of this volatile period when many of the institutions that are now highly regarded faced crises in enrollments and funding, and adjusted standards accordingly. Well into the twentieth century, writes Laurence Veysey, "The private institutions which needed tuition income in order to survive always had a temptation to swell their admissions or cut corners on instructional expense. . . . Everywhere the size of enrollments was closely tied to admissions standards" (357). Consequently, crises in standards gripped some schools—at Harvard in 1875, when 223 students had to repeat courses, and 9 were deprived of degrees because of their poor records (358). By 1905, Yale's standards crisis resulted in the honors courses movement, an effort to upgrade the quality of work by stratifying groups of students within the institution (368). "Even more important," Veysey concludes, "the standard of work at leading institutions, despite the upturn of the years after 1905, remained extraordinarily low by the canons of the mid-twentieth century" (359).

Conditioning and the Forensic System

An alternative way to address students' lack of preparation was to require students to "remedy" the problem themselves over a specified period of time. In private schools that didn't use the certificate method but continued to examine their own students, there was a widespread practice of "conditioning" students, which meant they had a semester or a year to make up the condition of a failed subject, either by completing introductory coursework, retaking the failed subject exam, or pursuing independent study (Wechsler 121). At Columbia in 1907, the Special Committee on the Relations Between the College and the Secondary Schools discovered that two-thirds of the students admitted to the freshman class were given conditions, most commonly three conditions per student (122). Conditioning enabled private schools to cope with the problem caused partly by the gap between colleges' examinations and high school preparation, and partly by the growing stress upon English at the expense of classical languages.

Katherine Lee Bates, who taught at Wellesley College from 1885 to 1925, described how her department fulfilled its remedial needs through regular coursework and conditioning:

> Moreover, here, as at Stanford and Indiana, classes of condi-
> tioned Freshmen are a conspicuous feature of the Rhetoric
> Department, the training of secondary schools being griev-
> ously inadequate. Miss Hart of Radcliffe, and Miss Weaver,
> trained in England as well as in America, bend their united en-
> ergies to developing in the Freshmen the ability to write clear,
> correct, well-constructed English sentences. To have mas-
> tered the paragraph is to become, so far as the Rhetoric De-
> partment is concerned, a Sophomore; and to proceed, under
> guidance of Miss Willcox, whose preparation was in part re-
> ceived in an editorial office, to the structure of the essay.
> (144–45)

Colleges were coping with the disjunction between a student's ability to pay tuition and his or her preparation in the vernacular. To do
so, some, like Wellesley, developed college courses whose goals were
clearly to remediate their students' writing. "By 1905," writes Harold
Wechsler, "the use of conditions had become so widespread among
examining colleges that it began to draw considerable attention"—
most notably from the ubiquitous Carnegie Foundation, which initi-
ated a series of reforms in exchange for its largesse (123; Scott 36–41).

During a period of immense growth in knowledge and broad
structural change, the presence of large preparatory departments,
conditioning, and flexible admissions managed institutional change.
Moreover, composition had not yet become subordinate to literary
studies, as the comprehensive writing programs at Harvard and
Michigan most famously illustrate. Nor had writing yet become
clearly differentiated from literature in terms of status at all institutions. In 1934, Irving Feinstein, describing the history of the City
College English department, wrote, "Students of 1875 tell us that
their English composition work was not organized as it is at present.

Composition was then required once a month over a term of years, during which the teacher in class heard recitations from such books as Day's *Rhetoric* and Fowler's grammar." Though Feinstein celebrated a more modern approach, he also noted "there are those who prefer the old declamatory work to the modern courses" (72, 73). At City College and elsewhere, "the old declamatory work" included "themes, essays, compositions" in all four years and for different courses. Before it was divided into advanced writing courses, creative writing, and journalism, composition might be required during the sophomore or later years.[3] And students received much unofficial instruction in writing through their literary societies, debating clubs, newspapers, and competitions for prizes.[4]

The preparatory program and subfreshman year at City College that I described above emphasized heavy amounts of reading and writing in English; similarly, the next four years also oriented students toward rhetorical theory, philology, literature, composition, and oratory. In the nineteenth-century curriculum, there was no remedial course in a department devoted to language as well as to literature teaching throughout the four and five years of a student's career. At City, the Department of English Language and Literature was one of the first in the country to evolve from the Department of History and Belles-Lettres, in 1854 (Feinstein 15). Between 1852 and 1883, the curriculum, like that of many conservative schools (those not following Harvard's liberal lead in devising an elective system) prescribed oratory and composition throughout every term, required compositions in the first two years, and oratory in the junior and senior years. English etymology, rhetoric, and the history and philology of the English language were central to the curriculum in a college with a teaching, not a research, mission.

In 1894, when a chair of English described the goals of the prescribed curriculum at the City College of New York, he named composition as its first priority: "The course in English Language and Literature aims, in the first place, to stimulate and develop the student's power of expression and to enable them to say what they have to say clearly and correctly; secondly, to guide them in the study of the history of English and American literature, not only as a chronological outline of authors and their works, but also as a critical estimate of their writings; and, lastly, through the critical reading of some of the masterpieces of our language, to give the students a knowledge of literature itself and also the ability to appreciate it" (*Register* 1895–96, 25–26). Not until 1940 would the department officially reverse this priority when it listed literary study as its first obligation in the college bulletin. Through the '20s and early '30s, it would continue to offer several courses devoted to the study of language in a nonliterary context, along with a handful of remedial, freshman, and advanced writing and rhetoric courses that supplemented an array of required speech courses focusing on argument and public debate 5.

Robert Connors shows that, in many institutions, the responsibility for teaching public speaking and writing was a collective one, and City was no exception. By the last decade of the nineteenth century, City College students wrote orations that were corrected by a Professor of English Language and Literature, revised, and then given to an Instructor of Elocution, who after a conference with the student decided whether he would deliver it publicly to the faculty. The kind of civic, public rhetoric that Michael Halloran has described held writing and content more firmly together; the differentiation of subjects, and in the case of composition their stratification, had not yet been fully accomplished.

In 1899, the City College Department of English Language and Literature published *Hints on the Writing of an Oration*, which reflects this integration of reading, writing, and public speaking. Students were to write and type their orations of fewer than five hundred words, and then, if they were good enough, to deliver them to an audience of peers and faculty. All juniors and seniors were required to write and then deliver orations for four semesters as part of their required college work. Under THEME, the "Hints" informed the student that "The theme of an oration should be imperative; it should bear upon conduct or belief. You must have not only a subject, but an object, a purpose in view. You should be determined to make your hearers think as you do upon the topic chosen." Though a sophomore, Homer R. Collyer gave an oration on 10 May, 1899, titled "Education of the Masses." Collyer's topic resembled those Best English Prose Compositions that received City's Riggs

Medal between 1865 and 1896. The titles reflect the blurred lines between literature, history, political science, and composition that was
a common feature of coursework listed in catalogues that John Wozniak studied: "The Influence of the American Revolution on French
Politics" (1882); "Physical Science as a Means of Enlightenment"
(1884); "Shakespeare as a Historian" (1886); "Advantages and De-
fects of England's Colonial System" (1890); "Public Opinion and
Legislation" (1894); "William H. Seward as a Statesman" (1896)
(Feinstein 313–15).

A "prose composition" like "Shakespeare as a Historian" was designed to be both an oration and an essay, and it reflected a merged
sensibility between history, literature, rhetoric, and composition
that was characteristic of higher education in the years following the
American Civil War. Harvard adopted the freshman writing course
in 1885 (English A) but, as David Russell notes, "that change was
only part of a collegewide reform of composition instruction" (53).
Reformers like Adam S. Hill "originally saw the freshman course as
merely the beginning of a four-year program for developing students' writing, a program that retained the essential shape of the traditional rhetorical training" (51). By around 1870, John Wozniak
writes, "the sizeable number of combinations, twelve in all, which
joined rhetoric or literature and philosophy or history . . . points to a
still deeper advantage for such a collocation . . . namely, the increased material for themes to be derived from moral or intellectual
philosophy, political economy, and history" (51).

Russell describes these "combinations" as "the *forensic system,*"
which, in colleges that shifted to the elective system after 1869, was
designed to create "various collegewide writing requirements from
entrance to graduation" (51). This nascent form of writing across the
curriculum, which lasted until the 1920s, surely allowed institutions
to cope with literacy problems without resorting to the variety of
upper-level remedial practices that would become so widespread in
the twentieth century. Harvard's forensic system was the most
widely known and copied. But other institutions, like City College,
which did not adopt an elective system but clung tenaciously to a
prescribed course for different majors, adapted the forensic princi-
ple to their own peculiar environments. Rather than whittle writing

instruction down to a single course or insist that someone else do what Mina Shaughnessy later called "the dirty work," it was spread through multititled departments. In an era that was only beginning to stratify students, subjects, and institutions, composition hadn't yet become subordinated to literature and thus relegated to the bottom tier of study.

Subfreshman English and Testing Technology, 1920–1945

It is often said that freshman English became the universally required course at the turn of the century. But to be more precise, in the interwar period, because up to a quarter of students in some institutions were exempted from it, the "universal" course was required only for some freshmen. Moreover, there were many freshman Englishes, as the one course was split into several sections given different weights, contents, and requirements. In some institutions, students who were exempt from composition took a literature course, while others enrolled in a compulsory remedial course focusing exclusively on sentence structure. These remedial courses carried full, partial, or no credit.

Especially in those colleges that were beginning to reject applicants, English studies was more highly stratified. Here remediation assumed an ad hoc existence, especially at the upper levels, through composition conditions, reviews, repeats, tutorials, or writing clinic hours. These supplements could be attached to, and substitute for, a freshman course; later in a student's career, they might be required in preparation for a proficiency exam. The forensic system may have vanished, but the tradition of requiring "extra compositions" remained in the practice of requiring supplementary work from deficient writers. The difference, of course, was that this "extra work" wasn't in the form of public orations concerned with history, politics, and literature, but in the form of drills in grammar, punctuation, and spelling.

It is in the interwar period that remediation appears in college catalogues, in the pages of the *English Journal*, and, according to Robert Connors, in the grammar workbooks and handbooks designed specifically for the remedial student, which made their earliest appearance in Edwin Woolley's 1911 *Exercises in English Composition* (97). At the City College of New York, two courses for no credit—one for freshmen, and one for upper-level students—were offered in the *Register* for 1927–28. At Ohio State University in 1931–32, remedial courses were offered, for no credit (Lunsford 1987, 249). John Wozniak reports "a sharp rise in remedial work" in the decade 1920–30 at the four-year institutions he studied; seven colleges and universities variously awarded some, all, or no credit to remedial English, while the use of English Proficiency Exams was also increasing (184). By the following decade, ten more schools were offering remedial English, and writing clinics were being developed as well (186). Between 1920 and 1930, for example, Brown offered a full-credit remedial course for eleven terms, while for fourteen terms, Bucknell offered a remedial course for no credit (298).

Published in 1929, Warner Taylor's survey of 225 institutions reflects the official shift toward stratified coursework in composition. Taylor reported, for instance, that 56 percent of the institutions he surveyed offered both advanced and subfreshman English (16). By 1942, NCTE reported that, of the 292 four-year institutions replying to its national survey, thirty-four used a writing clinic for remedial purposes, while nine used it as a substitute for a remedial course. Well over half (67 percent) grouped students according to ability, reserving sections for the "poorest" students, and 194 offered some form of "follow-up" remediation to upper-division students. When answering the question what improvements they desired in their departments, ninety respondents said they wished for a better "follow-up system, including a proficiency test and remedial work" (585).

One reason for the development of different freshman courses serving different "needs" was that they acted as an internal admissions mechanism, a way to achieve articulation between institutions and between English departments and the content disciplines. Remediation, in other words, helped to solve the crisis inherent in defining what a college education was going to be, who was going to get it, and where it would be offered. Such questions weren't easily resolved when institutions were under further pressure from foundations to standardize entrance requirements, even as they experienced periodic enrollment declines in the early '20s, at the onset of the Depression and World War II, and again when G.I. Bill enrollments dropped in 1947 from 1.12 million to 388,000 in 1951 (Scott 50). Nor was college central to youthful aspiration in the way it is now. Historians like David Levine and Laurence Veysey stress that in the '20s, college was more popularly viewed as a social requirement for leisured youth, rather than as the means to upward mobility for the middle classes. Therefore, the sense of exclusivity urged on (and funded) by the foundations was only beginning to be keenly felt by a small group of schools, mostly Ivy League colleges.

The system of admissions, either the certificate method or that of a school's own examinations, helped to define what a college was, but it did not as clearly define the differences between colleges. In 1923, the Carnegie Foundation expressed the growing exasperation it felt with both methods. As the age of postwar progressive measurement dawned, the Foundation's report noted, "It is clear that neither the method of admission by certificate nor that of admission by examination has been satisfactory. . . . A way must be found to bring pupils face to face with sharp tests in a few fundamental subjects . . ." (Duffus 83). One of the "fundamental subjects" would be composition, which had been foreshadowed in the dire warnings about correct grammar in Harvard's catalogues of the late nineteenth century (see Brereton 33–44). The College Examination Entrance Board (CEEB) English exams would not dominate admissions policies for some years. That shift occurred after 1947, so that, by 1960, for the first time a majority (80 percent) of college applicants took entrance exams designed by colleges, states, or the CEEB (Traschel 111). But in 1926, colleges themselves were already deploying the "sharp tests" that the Carnegie Foundation yearned for, in part through the placement exams administered by their English departments. Such exams could help public institutions in particular to establish the measurement of English skills as a threshold between college and high school without having to turn away students, especially if those students were admitted by the certificate system or on conditions.

Before the rise of nationally standardized tests, one common strategy was to deploy a battery of English placement exams to stratify a population. In 1914, Edwin Woolley described in the *English Journal* the contents of the University of Wisconsin's *Requirements for Admission to the Freshman English Course*—a twenty-seven page bulletin addressed to students and their high school teachers that listed eighty-seven rules of correctness, along with lists of sentences that exemplified illiteracy (239). Like the early CEEB examinations that Mary Traschel describes, Wisconsin's handbook presents English as if it were a foreign language. Since "annually" 15 to 20 percent of the students hadn't mastered spelling, punctuation, or mechanics, Wisconsin was forced to create a "subfreshman" course that would be offered throughout the '20s and '30s (239; see Hughes). Composition had become one of the "few fundamental subjects" used to distinguish between groups of students. But because an institution like Wisconsin couldn't turn away a quarter of its students, these exams could be used as a sort of internal admissions mechanism, a way to resolve the ongoing conflict in American higher education between a selective research mission and democratic access within a single institution (see Trow).

In 1930, NCTE organized a Curriculum Commission to negotiate this complex situation of differentiation in terms of research and teaching, exclusivity and numbers. In the report that Oscar Campbell summarized, the commission listed a number of specific remedies involving stratification. These remedies included placement tests, to be developed collaboratively by high schools and colleges, and to be given to students in their senior year of high school. Once given, the tests in English should be used to fit composition requirements to the abilities of particular students. The commission recommended that freshman English be shifted to the second year, and it also formulated a remedial policy for the first year:

a.   All but those deficient in the minimum attainments should be excused from further work in composition. The deficient should be required to elect a course for which no credit toward graduation be given.

b.   Every student during his freshman year should receive instruction in composition fitted to the intellectual level which his entrance test shows him to have attained. (Campbell 26)

The commission hoped its report would foster collaboration between the university and the high school and thus ultimately reduce the need for remediation by clarifying the expectations of each tier. But as the first recommendation indicates, remedial courses for no credit could help institutions to negotiate standards internally for graduation, rather than require them at the start. Institutions used a host of placement exams to "section" students into levels of English to resolve the paradox of American higher education: how to bolster enrollments but also maintain standards, especially during those years when the consciousness of exclusivity was only beginning to be felt and to be expressed through the power of testing technologies. As the faculty of Syracuse's English department put the case in 1928: "If we cannot, at present, establish a minimum requirement in English for entrance, we can at least establish a minimum requirement which all students must meet for graduation" (Whitney 1928, 561).

The practice of "sectioning" further enabled English departments to stratify language and literature, as language increasingly meant "grammar, spelling, and mechanics," rather than the history of the language, the study of words or syntax, rhetoric, oratory, argumentation, or even nonfiction prose. In the dual or tripartite structures that often emerged, reading, writing, and grammar could be effectively ranked. Especially for large public schools, the more standard practice was to use a placement test to create the three-part structure that NCTE's Curriculum Commission recommended. Sectioning or classifying students according to ability helped to usher in the first official age of basic writing, in part because large remedial programs depend upon sophisticated mass assessment.

Chief among the trends that Warner Taylor identified in 1929 was the increased use of placement exams to "assign students to such divisions of Freshman English as will be most suited to their training and capacity" (15). Offering such a divided course was characteristic of—though never exclusive to—public institutions. This was the practice at Taylor's own institution, the University of Wisconsin (555; Hughes, 812). It was done at Syracuse, where, on the basis of a Minimum Essentials Test, 25 percent of the students were placed into Group C for two hours of college credit (Whitney, 1924). While Group A studied literature and Group B composition, Group C took a course focusing "largely" on sentence structure: "There are no

themes" (487). In 1932 at the University of Minnesota, the Minnesota College Ability Test, Iowa English Training Test, high school
ranks, and "scores on themes" were used to create three groups, the
lowest of which, "Sub-Freshman Rhetoric," had to be passed before
moving into the universally required Freshman English (Eurich 213).
The Iowa Test was also similarly used by North Carolina State to
identify three sections by ability (Clark). Purdue University used an
objective exam to assign about one-third of their most ill-prepared
students into a noncredit course (McKee, 1932, 1936). In 1935, a
three-part exam composed of objective questions about grammar
and diction, a summary exercise, and an impromptu theme was used
at the University of Illinois to create "special sections for the lowest
fourth of the students—sections in which there was extra instruction in the most elementary of fundamentals" (Jefferson, Glenn, and
Gettmann 38). At the decade's end, Chapel Hill used an objective
test to create three sections; C sections for about a quarter of the students were "devoted almost exclusively to the fundamentals of written expression—the elements of grammar, functionally considered,
sentence structure, punctuation, spelling, mechanics, reading, and
simple expository writing" (Hudson 725). By the late 1940s, credit-
bearing remedial courses and placement tests were, in Albert
Kitzhaber's estimation, standard in four-year institutions. He
thought that most also offered "a lengthy 'review' of grammar,
usage, and mechanics" in the freshman course, along with a writing
laboratory (1963, 93).

Ad Hoc Upper-Level Remediation

Another practice that emerges in this period was to create various
structures to remediate English in the upper division, perhaps filling
the void left by the old forensic system without surrendering credits
to English departments. In 1963, Albert Kitzhaber enumerated the
ad hoc policies that he thought were standard in the American college of the late '50s: conditions attached to students' transcripts,
withholding graduation credits, or giving incompletes that delayed
graduation; advanced courses that were really remedial courses for

seniors or transfer students; writing clinics, repeats, special tutoring, and the ever-present proficiency exam (119–27). In the late '30s and early '40s, Chapel Hill and Harvard created university committees to scrutinize the work of students designated by faculty outside of English as remedial (Hudson 727; Wozniak 196, n33). NCTE's 1942 report, which I mentioned earlier, also listed a host of similar practices under the category of the "'follow-up' of competence in writing" (585).

Kitzhaber illustrated the ironies of remediation by quoting from a memo written by a dean of liberal arts at an eastern university, which had a system of referrals:

> The Committee on Divisional Examinations in the Humanities has reported a shocking situation. Twenty-four out of the 337 papers written by the senior class last May were found by each of the two readers to be below minimum standards of literacy.
>
> This means that approximately seven per cent of the senior class has been awarded degrees by the faculty without being able to write a satisfactory paper of moderate length. (1963, 126)

Such complaints repeated across institutions point to the need to teach writing systematically, rather than to respond to the problem through scattered remedial practices. For, as David Russell points out, the emergent disciplines in the early twentieth century confronted a paradox that was never resolved. On the one hand, new professional disciplines required more time for in-depth study, but on the other, these disciplines also partly depended for their growth upon more specialized literacies to organize and perpetuate their knowledge (27–28).

One durable practice was to ask faculty to return students to the English department for a dose of remediation. This was especially common in those liberal arts schools like Yale, which did not require a universal writing course, but which apparently served deficient students. Up through the '40s, Yale required a year-long literature course, and assigned the problem "in the fundamentals of composition" to the vague realm of "extra work designed especially to fit [the] needs" of the deficient—who often met together in the well-known "awkward squads" (Johnson 3). In 1939–40, Harvard, responding to an internal literacy crisis expressed in various reports, mandated "special instruction intended to correct . . . deficiencies" in grammar, spelling, and clarity of ideas (Wozniak 196, n33).

During this period and well into the 1950s, dire warnings crop up in catalogues informing students that professors across the disciplines reserved the right to send them back to the English department for more remediation at any time during their educational career. I noted earlier that between 1927 and 1938, City College offered English 6, "prescribed for those students in the upper classes who are still weak in the technique of writing English." Also through these years, the *Bulletin* explained to students that credits in both English and speech were contingent on their performance in these courses. If found deficient in either, half the credits could be withheld until graduation. Then, in bold letters, the *Bulletin* further warned incoming freshmen: "The head of any department of the College who finds a student deficient in written or spoken English is required to report that fact to the Head of the Department of English Language and Literature or to the Head of the Department of Public Speech, as the case may require, and the student so reported shall be required to submit to such tests and to pursue such subjects or courses of study as shall satisfy the head of the department who shall have reported the deficiency that the same has been removed" (*Register 1927–28*, 62). Up until open admissions in 1970, the City College *Bulletin* would contain versions of this warning, even going so far in 1960–61 to warn students that they could be "dismissed from the college" if they were placed into but didn't complete the first remedial course, English 5. In its bulletin for 1930, Columbia described a similar practice. During the first six weeks of the semester, freshmen would be "given ample opportunity" to display their proficiency in writing. If proficient, they would be exempted from composition instruction "unless a relapse is reported by some college teacher"; if the delinquent were reported, "he is turned over to a member of the English staff for drill and instruction. This tutorial relation will continue until reasonable competency is achieved" (Wozniak 196, n28). A decade later, Lafayette College established a similar policy: "Students who are reported by any department as delinquent in English composition will be required to register in English 1–2 and to continue in the course until the English department is satisfied with their improvement" (197, n35). That schools felt compelled to issue regular warnings underscores the perpetual nature of student "relapse" within the American academy and considerably weakens the claims of critics who assert that the remedial needs of today's students are novel. Critics like Sally Renfro and Allison Armour-Garb, whose report on remediation I discussed briefly in chapter 1, use that historical claim to anchor their argument that today's remedial programs are anomalous in four-year schools.

The Always-New Student

The accretion of warnings in catalogues or the institutionalization of remedial courses in various guises occurred across institutions, so that it is safe to say that remediation does not historically cling to one particular group of students. This point is crucial because, again, it casts doubt on the belief that remediation exists *exclusively* to introduce a new generation of students to a shared body of standards. Before the 1940s, neither the race nor the social class backgrounds of students changed substantially; ethnicity changed only in those institutions that didn't practice "social" admissions. The social class background of the majority of students in four-year colleges, as I will argue here and throughout this book, has never changed significantly, and certainly never proportionately to represent the whole population of college-going youth. More lower-income students entered higher education in the 1970s, but the proportion was not great in terms of overall enrollments in four-year schools. When larger numbers of working-class students entered college, they did so at the time when the junior college was being differentiated into the community college, the public sector that would absorb most of these enrollments.

In the earlier interwar period, the great demographic shift in four-

year colleges concerned gender: by 1900, 40 percent of all students
were women (Veysey 272). Otherwise, the typical college student in
the 1920s didn't differ substantially in class, ethnic, or racial background from the Anglo-Saxon boy who attended Harvard after the
Civil War. At the turn of the twentieth century, students attending
the Big Ten and western universities were less stratified by income in
contrast to the general population than were students enrolled in
eastern schools. Nevertheless, even at an institution like Michigan,
only about 5 percent of all students had fathers who were skilled la-
borers (Veysey 291–92). In his analysis of studies conducted on class
stratification in the interwar period, David Levine concludes, "A
young man's socioeconomic background largely determined his expectations of college attendance in the 1920s and 1930s" (126). By the
mid-1920s, students with college-educated fathers were most likely
to attend a four-year school, a trend that only increased in the interwar period and was confirmed again by research in the early 1950s
(132). Without financial aid programs from either the colleges or the
federal government, less privileged students found it increasingly
unlikely that they would attend elite colleges in the '20s. "Every segment of American society participated in the enrollment boom
between the two world wars," Levine writes, "but the bulk of the
increase in attendance in the 1920s and 1930s was attributable to
young men from better-off and nonethnic homes" (133).

Since many colleges followed Columbia's practice of "social" admissions, developed during this period, the Anglo-Saxon character
of college students was further ensured, especially in colleges seeking to occupy an exclusive tier (e.g., see Wechsler's case studies). The
City College of New York earned its fame partly because it was an
oddity—a four-year college for working-class Jewish boys of eastern
European heritage. It is thus noteworthy that City College—which
offered remedial courses in writing, reading, speaking, and mathematics—enrolled one of the most select student bodies in the country. Before the creation of competitive state and municipal systems,
and with private competitors practicing "social" admissions that
excluded undesirables such as Jews, City skimmed off the cream of
the public high school system in New York City. Levine comments

that City College "deserved its reputation as 'the Harvard of the proletariat' because it was the most selective college in the country throughout most of the interwar period" (86).

So the remedial traditions that existed at City College and elsewhere through the 1950s cannot be explained as a response only to the shocking newness of students' "needs." Instead, institutions needed to bolster enrollments at a time when schools were also beginning to differentiate and to create a felt sense of exclusivity. Levine remarks: "As late as the second decade of the twentieth century, all American colleges were still seeking as many students as they could persuade to come, whatever their academic qualifications. The movement toward higher standards in admissions had only just begun at even the so-called best institutions on the eve of the war" (137). In 1920, a survey of the top forty schools revealed that only thirteen were rejecting applicants; Harvard turned down 229 during that year, and Yale none (139). Remediation's fragmentary but persistent presence in all types of schools is evidence of the strange bargain that institutions struck when confronting the increasing complexity of academic literacy. To achieve exclusivity— and thus, in many cases, to gain coveted funding from foundations that were the single greatest source of gifts before the '40s—colleges did not reject students but deployed various remedial traditions to establish standards after admission and before graduation.

The Decline and Rise of Remediation, 1960–1980

It is well known that the freshman writing course, as a universal requirement, declined in the 1960s, to be revived again in the wake of a full-blown literacy crisis of the 1970s. Similarly, remediation may have also declined throughout the '60s. In 1960, NCTE found that 55.6 percent of all four-year schools it surveyed provided some form of remediation (Wilcox 67). But in his survey of one hundred schools, Albert Kitzhaber reported that both remediation and English composition were on the decline, with less than half of the schools replying offering these courses (1962, 476). By 1973, Thomas Wilcox reported that only 27 percent of the four-year schools he surveyed were offering remedial writing courses (67). Ron Smith's survey of four-year schools, conducted in 1973 and published two years later, confirms Wilcox's findings that fewer schools were requiring one or two semesters of freshman composition. Remediation was still persistent, but less popular, as 44 percent of all the 491 colleges, public and private, reported offering at least one such course (140).

The resurgence of basic skills surely reflected the needs that institutions experienced in the '70s in the wake of enrollment declines and fiscal crisis. Lynn Q. Troyka reported that in 1979, the College Board and the American Association of Collegiate Registrars and Admissions Officers surveyed 1,500 institutions and concluded that only 8 percent could be called "competitive" (16). Indeed, Wilcox, who published his survey in 1973, added a cautionary note to the appearance of a downturn in remedial coursework. He noted that Dartmouth offered a remedial writing course in 1969, while "even in 1967," 470 departments in four-year schools still offered a course that stressed drill in mechanics, leading him to doubt it would quickly disappear altogether (67). By 1977, Andrea Lunsford thought that remedial programs were "rapidly reappearing"; she cited a 1974 survey of all accredited four-year institutions, which found that 71 percent either had or were creating basic skills programs (45). A survey she conducted in 1976 of 58 colleges showed that 90 percent either had or were planning to establish remedial English programs (45). In 1986, Christopher Gould and John Heyda reported that 77.4 percent of the 221 schools responding to their survey required remedial work from some of their students (11–12). A year later, Joseph Trimmer found in his survey of nine hundred institutions that 84 percent offered at least one basic skills course, of which 74 percent were housed in English departments (4).

This extraordinary decline and revival of remediation provides an especially stark moment for analysis of the politics of composition teaching as a crisis management tool. In part, a focus on this moment is significant because the late '70s saw the emergence of what in chapter 4 I call the ideology of access and the politics of agency—a belief that remedial writing programs fulfill institutional commitments to open access for a special group of students, minorities. For critics of remediation, this ideology derives strength from the belief that the '60s were a golden age of student ability, and that the '70s ushered in large numbers of remedial students as a consequence of open access and affirmative action programs. The discourse of student need that Sharon Crowley identifies grew out of this moment, for it is most vibrant when we use it to describe the needs of "at-risk" students.

But student need cannot be fully understood outside a bureaucratic context of institutional need and testing technologies. Ron Smith's data, for instance, tell an interesting story about the shifting uses of new placement exams, which were used to exempt students from both remedial and freshman courses. He reported that one reason for the decline in writing courses was that English departments were using a variety of commercially produced standardized tests to stratify their populations, exempting larger numbers from freshman writing than ever before. Notably, even those departments using the newly developed College Level Examination Program (CLEP) to make placement decisions established so many different cutoff points that Smith concluded, "the only thing certain is that there is no uniformity among the departmentally administered exemption tests," a conclusion that Wilcox had also drawn (145). Smith found that placement decisions in four-year schools were used within local contexts to mediate what he called "variables"—of enrollment, the presence of other writing courses, the school's mission, and the restrictiveness of its entrance requirements. For these reasons, he found huge differences in the use of CLEP cutoff points between institutions: CLEP was really used to negotiate institutional growth, not to stabilize a universal set of standards. In 1987, Joseph Trimmer further underscored the historical instability of standards in his survey of nine hundred schools, which he found used seven hundred different ways to determine who was remedial, with wide variations in the cutoff scores for the ACT, SAT, and TSWE (4).

In his expanded analysis of his 1960 survey in *Themes, Theories, and Therapy*, Kitzhaber offered several reasons for remediation's decline, which Smith's data on the use of placement exams recorded. Kitzhaber noted that remediation was often shifted into the upper levels: "Backsliding after freshman English has been completed appears to be universal in American colleges and universities"; he then goes on to detail in ten pages some of the "attempts at other colleges to maintain student literacy" that I summarized earlier (119). Possibly the increased focus in the high schools on composition teaching, for example, through AP programs and special efforts such as Project English, may have created more exemptions (1962, 479). But the main reason for the decline at the freshman level, Kitzhaber thought, was less a difference in student population and more a difference between institutions, which was growing more marked as colleges and universities coped with the crisis caused by surging enrollments and with the growing ability of some to establish selective entrance requirements. For the first time in its history, higher education would face larger enrollments than its capacity to serve rising numbers. Kitzhaber thought that even midlevel institutions could therefore—also for the first time—exercise academic selectivity by raising entrance requirements or establishing requirements they may never have had before (1962, 478).

Thus, Kitzhaber also ascribed the disappearance of some courses to "the proliferation of junior colleges throughout the nation." For this reason, he hastened to remind readers that "the disappearance of remedial English from four-year" institutions didn't represent a new population of unusual ability. Rather, "the students who used to populate remedial English courses in the colleges and universities are still with us, but most of them now appear to be going to junior colleges instead of to the more selective institutions" (1962, 478). As evidence, he cited NCTE's 1960 survey, which found that of the ten million dollars spent in higher education on remedial English in that year, half was spent at the two-year level (478).

Remediation and the Crisis of Growth, 1960s

Barbara Scott comments that historians agree "how unprecedented was the decade of the 1960s for the speed and concentration of the system's quantitative growth by every relevant index" (17). For instance, over a quarter of a million (226,000) full-time faculty were hired between 1960 and 1972 in the U.S. academy; of this number, more than half were hired after 1964, a watershed year for expansion (Finnegan 625).

Before the '60s, the crises had included shedding a classical curriculum, raising the prestige of a four-year degree, creating steady enrollments, and rationalizing funding. But in this decade, institutions had to manage a phenomenal expansion in enrollments, in professional schools and in the sciences, and also in capital improvements, the hiring of faculty, and graduate study. Increased differentiation into tiers marked by mission, curriculum, and student body would begin in the '60s and intensify in the '70s to manage the crisis of growth.

English departments in many four-year schools had also to manage global growth in their own local terms. They tended to stratify their curriculum as a means to manage the crisis engendered by enormous enrollments and student demand for more liberalized general education requirements. As Ron Smith commented, "the elimination or shrinkage of lower-division requirements" in many institutions contributed to the decline in the otherwise longstanding power of the freshman course (146). English departments may have been flexing their curricular muscles on campus in an era that saw unprecedented student interest in the humanities and the hiring of new faculty to staff English courses. From this perspective, the fortunes of remediation did not change in the '60s because students were more literate, or only because the less able among them were attending two-year colleges. Rather, the number of remedial courses declined also as a result of the response of English departments to a new crisis. Put more bluntly, the nature of the crisis allowed them to sustain their central enterprise—the teaching and study of literature—without having to rely on the economics of writing instruction.

In a period that saw the hyperspecialization of literary studies and an increased interest in research and graduate study, faculty could make literature requirements, electives, and graduate courses at the M.A. or Ph.D. level the center of their business. Nowhere was this truer than at the emergent public comprehensive: "From 1960 to 1980," writes Dorothy Finnegan, "more institutional change occurred in the colleges and universities that offer the master's degree as their highest academic award than in any other institutional type" (623; see Mayhew 261). For faculty at public comprehensives that were upgrading their status, specialization represented a really new opportunity.

The crisis that English departments encountered was how to manage the luxury of growth. Before the recession of the early '70s, English departments experienced an expansion—funded by the federal government in some sectors, by private philanthropy in others —that they had never encountered before or, in some cases, since. Part of that expansion lay in students' choice of liberal arts majors such as English and mathematics. Finnegan's case study research at two comprehensives, the public Regional State, and a private institution, Merger University, documents this growth in terms of enrollments, hiring, and institutional mission. Before the fiscal crisis of the early 1970s, both schools were dedicated to providing open access to their state's populations, both espoused a teaching mission, and both still offered professorial positions to M.A.s (677). In the '60s, Regional State's enrollment increased by 5,000, a 60 percent rise in FTEs. In the English and mathematics departments at Regional State in the early '90s, when Finnegan did her research, 61 percent of the faculty had been hired between 1962 and 1971 (626).

The sudden drop in composition courses may have also occurred not only because weaker students were going elsewhere, but also because English departments now had an opportunity to define their mission almost exclusively in terms of literary study. New professors were hired at Regional and Merger not only because of rising enrollments, but because of rising enrollments in the liberal arts. With more choices made to major in English, departments could increase their elective offerings and decrease their offerings in first-year writing courses. Departments with abundant enrollments had more clout—and with more clout, they could (temporarily, as it turned out) abandon their composition courses in favor of more specialized literary study.

To gain college-wide support, many departments apparently promised that they would fold composition into literature courses. This is the trend that Kitzhaber noticed in 1962, and he felt "cynical" about the rationale for these blended courses: "the sort of reconstituted freshman composition course that I have been describing is likely to be at least in part a rationalization, window-dressing for the benefit of the general faculty who years ago voted to grant the English department a fourth or a fifth of every student's freshman schedule to improve his command of the mother tongue. The mention of required writing [within literature courses] minimizes the risk of losing this block of time and putting the course on the same elective footing as other courses in the humanities" (480).

Remediation and the English Department, 1960–70

The specific fate of composition at City College in these boom years illustrates the more general argument that the number of composition courses declined as a result not only of new or better students, but also as a consequence of broader shifts in mission, enrollment, and curriculum. In other words, the number of courses and remediation's role within a program serve political needs as much as students' needs. In 1964, the Department of Language and Literature made moves to "reconstitute" its freshman enterprise in the manner that Kitzhaber predicted. In that year, the Department formed an ad hoc planning committee to develop a proposal for dropping the two-semester composition requirement and replacing it with a one-semester literature and composition course, which would precede a two-semester literature requirement. The 1964 proposal was revised and accepted unanimously in 1965, and the next year, it was offered in the college bulletin under a newly christened Department of English.

This new proposal details how a faculty can shift its orientation toward composition when the political context is ripe for it. First, the proposal argued that English faculty could reduce their teaching loads by abolishing the two-semester writing requirement. Composition could be folded into a literature course; writing requirements could be increased in the required two-course literature sequence; the exit exam in the new course could be stiffened; and extra remediation could be secreted in an hour attached to the new mixed course (the remedial English course was left untouched). There is no mention in any of the planning documents of students needing more or less writing instruction. Yet, as I noted in my opening paragraph to this chapter, the same faculty had announced in 1963 that a quarter of its students were too "backward" for regular composition and would have to enroll in its remedial course. This is strong local evidence for the more general argument that, in institutions of this type, the needs of students changed less than the opportunity of the faculty during these expansive years to redefine their goals within an institution.

The primary rationale of the plan that was accepted in 1965 was a reduction of the teaching load for English faculty and the creation of a new English major, which would involve a more advanced cluster of specialized electives. This major reorientation was the culmination of almost sixty years of transformation that I think was representative of English departments in midlevel public comprehensives that had never had a research mission—that is to say, most public institutions. Between 1901 and 1938, the City College Department of Language and Literature offered an array of courses taught by full-time faculty that were devoted to the study of language in a nonliterary context. Along with eight required terms of public speech, and numerous clubs "devoted to the cultivation of the arts of composition, oratory, and debate," City College boys could elect courses in the history and structure of the language, and in advanced rhetoric and composition. By 1940–41, when English 5 was called Remedial English for the first time, the department also reordered its priorities, announcing that its first obligation was "the study of the English language as literature, as philology, and as composition" (49). More literature electives displaced the courses in language, writing, and rhetoric, so that, while in 1927 it offered fifteen courses devoted to nonliterary study, by the 1940s this department offered only seven such courses. By the mid-1960s, when the department shed the "language" of its former name, the idea of an English major dominated the department for the first time, as it offered more "courses for intensive study by advanced English majors." By the '80s, the study of language or writing in a nonliterary context vanished, leaving only the three basic writing courses that Mina Shaughnessy helped to establish.[5]

This story of one department encapsulates a broader story of the politics of writing instruction that I think is typical for the public comprehensive college, an institutional type that embraced a research mission gradually throughout the '60s. I will discuss the professionalization of composition studies during this period in chapter 3, but here I want to stress that the reduction of writing requirements and a new approach to remediation fulfilled a department's response to the crisis of the 1960s—to growing electives, the increasing pressure to publish, and an emergent sense that English studies was a specialized discipline, one intimately connected to research and to graduate school. In the '60s, public comprehensives were beginning to consider research as a condition for hiring, tenure, and promotion, requirements that, at Finnegan's case study schools, were phased in by their trustees in the next decade.

In 1964 at City College, English professors had a four-course teaching load and a five-day schedule, because City had always been defined as a teaching, not a research, institution. Faculty who met to discuss the new proposal for a blended writing and literature course at City College did not discuss a curricular philosophy and, rarely, students' needs. Rather, the surviving documents testify to faculty's overriding concern with renegotiating their workload in a changing era. In a meeting of the 1964 fall semester, the chair of the ad hoc planning committee "moved the adoption of the attached proposal, reducing the teaching load for members of the English Department to three courses each and creating a new three-credit course, tentatively titled English 1.1, to substitute for the current required composition courses, English 1 and 2" (*Department of English Minutes*, 3 October 1964). The proposed syllabus for Introduction to Composition and Literature was accepted unanimously with the caution on the part of a "few" professors that a new, "more rigorous final examination in composition" be phased in "to insure that no student be graduated from City College who cannot write correctly." At the next meeting, the chairman of the composition committee explained that the department would have to increase its writing requirements within the required literature courses, which would follow the new proposed course, "in order to win administration support for the proposed new English 1 course" (5 November 1964). The Chair then reported that the Dean would support the new course provided that

English faculty stay on campus for whole days and that they conference with students intensively in the new course. During the same
meeting, a professor "spoke of the popularity of our electives
courses. He said that even though we are offering more electives this
spring than in many years, we still have not been able to meet student demand—a demand that will be intensified when the shorter
required sequence will speed their progress toward elective status.
He added that we are urging students going on to graduate school to
take a diversified program" (5 November 1964). To manage rising
enrollments and to realize a new emphasis upon research, the
department "diversified" its offerings and oriented itself toward
graduate study. To persuade the administration to accept this reorientation, it argued what Kitzhaber suspected many others argued: it
promised to incorporate writing instruction—along with ad hoc
remediation—within required literature courses.

However, because deficient students are always with us, "A Preliminary Syllabus for English 1.1" suggested that "a programmed
text, such as *English 3200*" could address mechanical problems (attachment to *Minutes*, 3 October 1964). In the revised syllabus approved in the spring of 1965, the committee wrote:

> *The study of grammar and syntax, puntuation [sic], mechanics
> and spelling* will be primarily the responsibility of the student.
> He will be expected to become proficient in these areas by
> using *English 3200* (a programmed text). Normally the in-
> structor will not discuss these areas in class unless special dif-
> ficulties prompt him to do so. . . . The instructor should in-
> form his students that the fourth credit hour has been allotted
> to English 1 to provide them with time for independent study
> of grammar and related matters and for regular attendance at
> required conferences.
>
> (*A Proposed Syllabus for English 1*, attachment to *Minutes*, 4
> March 1965, emphasis in original)

The proposal went on to explain that, if students failed the final examination given at the end of this course, the instructor could give
them an incomplete and assign them to English 5, the remedial

course, before attempting the exam again. The new course was phased in during the 1966–67 academic year, along with dozens of new elective courses for "intensive study for advanced English majors." Meanwhile, the remedial course remained the safety valve it always had been, supplemented now with an "independent" hour attached to the freshman course for students' self-study of "grammar and related matters."

Within one year, the City College English department had moved from declaring to the *Times* that a quarter of its freshmen were incompetent writers to abolishing its composition requirement and adding an hour of remedial self-study to a "reconstituted" literature course. This move could be accomplished less because of a dramatic shift in students' writing abilities and more because of thriving enrollments—the number of English majors had never been so high. A department made powerful through rising enrollments could sell its package to the administration by promising to embed writing in literature courses, create stiffer exit exams, and offer ad hoc remediation.

The Politics of Writing Instruction, 1970s

The common story of composition's evolution is nested within the broader narrative of the creation of the modern university. In that story, told definitively by Laurence Veysey and cited by virtually every historian of writing instruction, the old college changed after the Civil War when New World scholars imported the German ideal of the research university into the American context. While there is no doubt that this shift occurred, with enduring consequences for all segments of higher education, not all institutions could or even wished to embrace that ideal. Today, the research university represents only one small slice of American higher education. For these reasons, histories of writing instruction need also to be told within the context of the differentiation of higher education into distinct tiers, particularly since, as I have been arguing, writing instruction has played an important role in helping institutions to define their particular niches in terms of mission, curriculum, funding, and admissions standards.

The split between research and teaching, as that is defined con-
cretely through workload, first became visible in the 1920s, when a
top tier of institutions was beginning to emerge (Clark 1987). For
public comprehensives like City College, which lacked a large endowment, offered a prescribed curriculum, and prepared midlevel
professionals (e.g., engineers and teachers), the aspiration to become
a research institution wasn't realized until the '60s, when so many
normal colleges became state colleges, and the latter state universities. The age of diversifying coursework and of preparing undergraduates for graduate study did not arrive at these types of institutions
until the second half of the twentieth century.

Since these institutions form the majority of all public higher education, the story of composition instruction should include an emphasis upon the division of institutions into sectors or, to use Burton
Clark's (1987) apt phrasing, into small, different academic worlds.
From this perspective, composition's fortunes reflect institutional
needs as much as a response to the often-touted needs of always-
new students.

Nowhere does this story become clearer than in the 1970s, when
the institutional need for composition as a crisis management strategy took yet another dramatic turn. The days of expansion after 1964
would come to an abrupt end in the first half of the next decade, as
English departments—and the liberal arts generally—suffered a
severe decline, though this was experienced variously in different
sectors of higher education, and thus would have affected writing instruction's status unevenly across tiers. In Finnegan's case institutions, almost no hiring was done in English or mathematics between
1972 and 1978, while their trustees considerably stiffened requirements for faculty recruitment and advancement during the same
period, even for those faculty who had been hired with the M.A. degree (634–35). I will consider the conflict between teaching and research that resulted from these changes in chapter 3 but here emphasize that this sharp end to expansion affected the politics of
writing instruction because of the need for enrollments in departments whose usefulness and large size were being widely questioned
in times of fiscal chaos. Between 1969 and 1975, majors in the social
sciences and humanities declined by 50 percent, while the same

years saw a national shift in enrollments from 38 percent in the liberal arts to 58 percent in the burgeoning professional schools (Kerr 145; xi). In 1971, institutions awarded 65,000 B.A.s in English, a number that plummeted to 33,200 by the early '80s (Finnegan 633).

So many English departments felt the crisis acutely, for it was not inevitable that, less than a century after they had established their dominance in the humanities, they should continue to exercise clout on campuses in the throes of fiscal crisis, structural shift, and student rebellion. In an autobiographical essay, Charles Moran recalls how the English department at the University of Massachusetts–Amherst suffered "a radical change" in this period (173). Under political pressure, in 1969–70 the department dropped its lucrative Masterpieces of Western Literature requirement. It also abolished its two-semester freshman writing course "and its guaranteed supply of students":

> By 1971 we were therefore a department of 107 with a scandalously low enrollment, an obvious target for retrenchment. Seeing this situation beginning to develop, the department sought enrollment wherever it might be found.
>
> In this new context Walker Gibson was, [in the chair's] eyes, potentially the Department's salvation. (173)

Gibson's various English projects with the school of education and other outreach efforts provided work for English professors. By the fall of 1972, "The English Department's need for enrollment had driven us to this: we opened up our Advanced Expository Writing course and invited the university in" (175). Reinstatement of a writing requirement in this case had less to do with students' immediate needs than with the needs of English departments that could no longer depend on the attractiveness of western literature to satisfy students. For those departments on the brink of retrenchment, a new writing course, alluring to students in an age of downsizing and vocationalism, would bolster sagging enrollments (see Berlin 1987, 182–83).

Finally, increased enrollments in new equal opportunity or affirmative action programs also similarly served to bolster enrollments, either for the institution as a whole or for English more particularly.

In her history of the Educational Assistance Program (EAP) at the University of Illinois–Chicago, Carol Severino shows that EAP, founded in 1968 and abolished in 1993, experienced an influx of both students and program resources in the mid-1970s. EAP's size increased because in these troubled years the university "temporarily needed more student bodies and tuition for survival and to generate Full Time Equivalents" (46). By the late '70s, however, Illinois at Chicago's enrollments stabilized, and it began actively recruiting a nationally renowned faculty to fulfill a newly declared research mission. The institution raised admissions standards, established an honors program, and downsized EAP, cutting it to a third of its original size (47–48). Critics of "special" programs assume that these programs are a "gift" to students, but specific institutional histories suggest that these programs may also help institutions to manage their growth during periods of crisis and change.

The Origins of Basic Writing, 1970

Equal opportunity programs blossomed throughout the '70s and '80s, while the majority of English departments reinstated their writing requirements. In the flush of a dramatic literacy crisis in the '70s, of course, it surely appeared to many, then as now, that the decline in basic skills had as its source the open access movements of the '60s. Popular culture, permissiveness, progressive education, student rebellion, affirmative action, and a host of related reasons could explain the need for basic skills programs. For this reason, the rising number of basic skills courses could be seen solely as a response to the "needs" of a new generation of students. The City University of New York's open admissions policy, adopted in 1969, figured centrally in national debates about higher education and the scandal of declining literacies, while at the same time, the mainstream press reported drops in the most elite institutions, such as Yale, Michigan, and Harvard (Lunsford 1977; Gere, 1991).

Despite the well-publicized literacy crisis at the most elite institutions, by the late 1980s, the decline in literacy skills and the consequent need for remedial writing instruction would become attached to students of color. As has been often pointed out, most students in the first open admissions cohort at City College in 1970 were white, not black or Puerto Rican, though this would change by the mid-1970s as the stratification of higher education by student body and prestige intensified. Consequently, the myth of transience that has always characterized writing instruction and sustained its anomalous status resurfaced in the '80s and '90s to justify institutional stratification and to perpetuate a belief that the doors were opening wide and the working classes were flooding in. It is now often assumed that the shift from bonehead English to basic writing was a direct response to a decade of astounding demographic shift.

The demographic changes of the '60s were large, as enrollments increased at a heretofore unknown rate. But these changes did not necessarily include a shift in the social class backgrounds of students; at the four-year level, they may not have included a significant shift in race. Clark Kerr, a prominent architect of stratification, acknowledges that "progress in increasing attendance from low-income groups has been meager" (150). While more minority students attended college between 1960 and 1980 than ever before, of those, both women and minorities came from middle and upper-income families (150). By 1986, over half of all families earning $50,000 a year would enroll one of their children aged 18 to 24 in a college; about a third of families earning between $20,000 and $29,000 would do so; and less than 15 percent of families earning less than $10,000 per year would send one of their children to college (373). What was true in the 1920s, then, is arguably true today. While ethnicity among whites has changed, the typical student at a four-year college remains a white and middle-class son or daughter of one or more college-educated parents.

The relationship between at-risk students and remediation is a complex one that I'll consider in chapter 4. But it does not now, and never has, involved simple correlations, let alone clear cause and effect relationships. Thus, we must challenge the rhetoric of needs that assumes remediation is a "special" need of nontraditional students. Sharon Crowley argues that the rhetoric "invokes composition's traditional service ethic. It goes like this: 'Our students need what we teach.' Sometimes this claim is buttressed by a second one: 'at-risk students particularly need what we teach'" (256). Since the late

1970s, this rhetoric has helped to place the responsibility for open access policies on programs that are often poorly funded, staffed by a mobile, part-time teaching population, and sustained by a baroque panoply of tests and rules.

Writing courses in general, and especially remedial courses or practices, are widely used today to address enrollment problems involving high school preparation, transfers, the lack of formal writing instruction in content courses, and commitments to affirmative action. To repeat, I am not arguing that particular programs aren't successful or useful in helping underprepared students. But remediation has too often been used to negotiate management crises that are presented as singular crises in student preparation. Remediation often functions to manage the institutional conflicts I have been describing: to boost enrollments while espousing standards; to move students into professional schools without surrendering more credits to an English department; to establish a course of elective literary study while maintaining a compulsory writing program; or to fulfill certain commitments to access for historically underrepresented groups. In these cases, it's not only student need that defines remediation's presence, but also the political needs of institutions.

My overview here also supports the view that remediation in sentence-level concerns persists across institutions and throughout the years because formal errors are connected to errors in understanding the course content. An alternative to skills instruction would be to provide remediation beyond an English department's composition program. This was the opinion that Margaret Ringnalda expressed in 1938, when, like P. G. Perrin and J. D. Clark before her, Ringnalda doubted the wisdom of separating skills teaching from the liberal arts. In "One More Opinion," she described her experiences as a teacher of subfreshman English at UCLA, where she thought that probably fewer than 5 percent of the students enrolled in her courses wrote more poorly than students enrolled in the regular first-year class. After dutifully cataloguing their errors, she wondered whether such a course was really necessary, not because students didn't write or read poorly, but because instruction might be better received throughout the curriculum: "shall we never look outside our classes to the students' actual writing in other courses?" (681). Ringnalda opined that remediation could somehow be embedded within courses outside the English department, for "I have always held that a consultation and advisory course in English should be carried through the whole college program of many students" (681).

Ringnalda's "opinion" challenges how remediation has been institutionalized for a century. Embodied most fully today in writing across the curriculum programs, the longitudinal or vertical view is also crucial for remedial students. The dominant traditions within remedial postsecondary English are formalist and/or based upon process pedagogy. A more robust tradition would draw heavily upon writing-to-learn research, and upon the work of Mike Rose (1983), David Bartholomae and Anthony Petrosky, and Marilyn Sternglass, to develop programs that join the formal study of language and process pedagogies with specific themes and disciplinary contents. Another possibility would be to connect remedial and/or first-year writing courses with liberal arts courses. This was done briefly at City College in the '70s and again in 2000 through "learning communities," where students in one English course enroll together in liberal arts classes whose teachers meet with one another.

As an administrator at City in the late '60s and early '70s, first of the Pre-Baccalaureate Program, and then of the remedial sequence she called Basic Writing, Mina Shaughnessy actively contested the split between remedial English and the academic disciplines. In so doing, she awarded herself and others a "pioneer" status. In his history of basic writing's "birth," Bruce Horner usefully critiques that status, which pervaded both Shaughnessy's work and the discourse surrounding open admissions. Pioneer imagery helps to sustain the belief that only a certain group of students needs to be introduced to standards upon which we have always all agreed. As Horner comments, "The divorce of Basic Writing from the history of 'remedial' writing instruction effected by its claims to 'newness' has prevented teachers from arguing for the historical centrality of their teaching of writing" (18). To repeat, we historicize remediation to understand its always-newness.

But, to fully historicize the shift from remedial English to basic writing, we have also to analyze it within the larger context of the institutional stratification that defined growth in the '60s and '70s. Shaughnessy understood remediation's mediatory role, and she resisted basic writing's alignment with the bottom tiers of higher education. Therefore, an alternative legacy for her emerges within the context of an institutional response to various external pressures that I have explored in this chapter. In chapter 3, I will continue to examine remedial English as a crisis management tool. This time, I will focus upon Shaughnessy's administrative labors in an era of spectacular change for public higher education generally, and for the City University and remedial English more particularly.

3

Looking for Mina: Reforming Basic Writing, 1966–1980

▶ IN 1967, MINA SHAUGHNESSY BEGAN TEACHING as a lecturer in the Pre-Baccalaureate program at City College; three years later, she had earned an assistant professorship and was supervising the Basic Writing program. Over the next few years, she achieved a full professorship and a deanship, wrote a landmark text, and cofounded various publications, including the *Journal of Basic Writing*. Meanwhile, between 1965 and 1970, the Pre-Bac project grew from a bridge program serving 113 black and Puerto Rican students to a nationally renowned academic program serving 1,036 culturally diverse students.

The subject of a biography, symposia, and memorial essays, few writing teachers have generated as much interest as Mina Shaughnessy.[1] Since 1980, the nature of her legacy has also been the focal point of considerable controversy.[2] Shaughnessy's status arouses so much debate because her work illustrates the conflicts that exist within composition—and perhaps in the academy more generally—over defining what we mean by "politics." Shaughnessy's work highlights the difference between the politics of representation and the politics of basic skills as these play out in institutions; in particular, her administrative legacy helps to illuminate the differences between disciplinary and institutional politics.

My goal here is to historicize Shaughnessy's legacy by discussing her institutional work in the context of what was at stake in the struggles waged around remediation thirty years ago. I describe her administrative labors and trace her program's fate not only through archival sources, but also through the history of higher education, revisionist histories of composition studies, and the municipal and state politics that shaped the trajectory of open admissions. My focus on these broad contexts may appear to take readers away from the classroom per se, but in another sense, it returns us to it with a richer sense of how our teaching is mediated through political struggles that have resulted in the strangely anomalous case of writing instruction. Furthermore, as remedial programs are transformed in the new century, our sense of what we can do, what we should have done, or why it is happening may be illuminated by historicizing the politics of basic skills.

A decade ago, that task was begun afresh by composition scholars who focused upon Shaughnessy's legacy and that of the open access period. Especially in their critique of Shaughnessy, scholars tended to depict the conflict over remediation primarily as a discursive wrangle over versions of curriculum. This is so partly because the politics of representation were dominant in the 1990s; it was also so because the focus fell exclusively on Shaughnessy's published work. But when sorting through the surviving documents of her institutional life, one is immediately struck by the sheer amount of time Shaughnessy spent in daily bureaucratic struggle. For that reason, I read her published work alongside her more mundane administrative efforts. I offer an alternative legacy for Shaughnessy that does not ignore the critiques of her formalist approach, which are valuable, but that grounds her work in an era where the politics of access were dominant. In so doing, I also critique scholarship that assumes that reform is exclusively centered in curriculum. While curricular reform remains central to thinking about remediation—to any composition program, as I discuss in chapter 5—it is not necessarily equivalent to the institutionalization of writing programs.

The critique of Shaughnessy's formalism is necessary and correct in many ways, since it makes sense that an enlarged view of English studies would also intellectually enlarge what in 1973 Thomas Wilcox called its neglected but "essential . . . enterprise" (88). However, as I argued in chapter 2, English is not only curriculum, but also a discipline organized institutionally at different historical moments. And though remediation is always with us, it is never present in quite the same ways; it is organized differently to mediate the political needs of institutions at specific moments and places. More directly responsive to changing historical circumstance than any other aspect of English departments, precollege writing instruction is therefore more nakedly reflective of the material and ideological struggles over access to the B.A. than any other aspect of English studies. This is largely so because remediation helps to mark the historically shifting boundaries between institutions—one hundred years ago, between colleges and secondary schools; in the twenty-first century, between comprehensive and elite liberal arts schools, and between four-year and two-year schools.

Selectivity is a fairly recent phenomenon in higher education, less than half a century old; and, as I will elaborate in chapter 4, not since the late '80s has remediation become a conflicted yardstick for judging institutional exclusivity. My exploration of the "legacy" of the open access period therefore focuses as much upon who taught whom, and where, as upon what was taught. I draw this distinction because I assume that the struggle over ideas is materially based, especially when a conflict over ideas occurs within institutions. Here and in chapter 4, I try to flesh out more precisely than I think other scholars have done the connections between remediation and those material goods and territory that the ideological conflicts over remediation have symbolized.

It's important to describe institutional change and struggle because by so doing we identify what we mean by reform. Reform also reflects our sense of agency as teachers and scholars: what we deem worthy of reforming involves imagining the possible within institutions. In basic writing—indeed, in English studies more generally—the most significant and challenging versions of pedagogical reform could be said, at the most abstract level, to involve a critique of, and resistance to, essentialist attitudes toward language. Yet resistance must include not only fresh representations of students, not only a critique of curriculum, but also a challenge to academic selectivity—which was at the heart of the '60s open access movements.

Mina Shaughnessy was concerned with the reform of academic

selectivity, and so she focused on altering structures for learning and working within her institution. Her goal was to integrate working-class students into an institution that is selective not because of its endowment, physical plant, or even its faculty—the case with elite four-year schools—but because of its ability to introduce an upwardly mobile, urban working class to the cultural traditions and professional knowledge—the cultural capital—that characterize the educated middle class. The distinction is obvious but, in light of critiques that don't sufficiently historicize her work, it needs to be restated. Shaughnessy's concern was to promote access to the liberal arts and to contest the barriers between remediation and traditional study.

As a program administrator at City College, Shaughnessy didn't contest the high status of academic language or, as has often been pointed out, even develop a cogent theory of language. Her legacy lies elsewhere, in the politics of basic skills. In that arena, she contested the low status in the academic community of her program, its students and teachers. Through her bureaucratic practice, she challenged academic hierarchy in the most fundamental ways. While her theory of the relationship between skills and content was inconsistent, in practice she consistently contested the institutional split between the teaching of writing and the content disciplines. Shaughnessy's struggle to integrate her program into a traditional liberal arts curriculum challenged the anomalous status of remedial education that has been its lot for a century.

In the 1990s, a burst of rich theoretical activity surrounding basic writing examined students' relationship to traditional academic language (see chapter 5 for an overview). Poststructuralist writing, in particular, offers a powerful critique of the formalism that often restricts the intellectual flexibility of "skills" courses and helps to justify their marginal status within an institution. Partly through the examination of Shaughnessy's legacy, this critique has also asked basic writing teachers to historicize their work, a challenge I answer in this book. But this critique has not politicized the course's gatekeeping function; it has not examined basic writing's relation to liberal arts courses and faculty or to four-year and community colleges.

Nor has this critique explored how a contingent labor force gains access to new professional knowledge. Though it is concerned with linguistic change, it has not asked how such change is assessed or institutionalized over the years through discrete blocks of time. These are the different kinds of questions that I pose here and in chapter 4.

Traditional Education for Nontraditional Students

These questions stem from a particular view of what constitutes "success" in education, a view that's shaped by where we locate access and how we theorize it. In chapter 5, I will describe access to academic knowledge as a process of crosscultural translation, but here I want to describe it from a sociological point of view. City University sociologists David Lavin and David Hyllegard measure the "success" of open admissions policies longitudinally. They see success as the creation of an educated urban class that finds meaningful salaried employment and is able to pass along its cultural and economic benefits to its children. In their studies of the fate of two open access cohorts enrolled in 1970 and 1980, remediation plays a far less singular role than it does in work that focuses on curricular reform. Lavin and Hyllegard conclude, "Overall, there were few benefits from the remedial effort, in the sense that the academic outcomes of students who needed remediation but did not take any remedial courses were hardly distinguishable from the outcomes of those who did take remediation" (203, n5).

For progressives of the '60s, success meant offering working-class students direct access to a four-year college—it meant their aggressive integration into selective institutions. At the City University in the late '60s, minority students were already enrolled in the two-year schools in growing numbers. The only existing alternative to open admissions, widely discussed in New York at the time, was to create a tiered public system similar to the Master Plan adopted in California in 1960. In Nathan Glazer's view, the plan was already unofficially in place: "New York City was in 1968 already equipped with a California-style system of higher education which offered college-level instruction to everyone" (1973, 85).

I noted in chapter 2 that the '60s saw an unprecedented differentiation of higher education. Clark Kerr points out that between 1960 and 1980, public higher education was characterized by its tiering into more specific sectors and by the coordination of those tiers through master plans and governing boards in 40 states. This was the decade that saw the emergence of the public comprehensive, the gradual transformation of junior colleges with a transfer function into two-year colleges with a terminal vocational function, the segregation of the top tiers in terms of federal and corporate sponsorship for research, and the growing phenomenon of selectivity. The uniqueness of the City University model, adopted in the summer of 1969, was that it attempted to stem the flow of working-class students into two-year colleges by contesting the "cooling-out" function of nonselective, vocational institutions that were being aggressively marketed as an alternative to a liberal arts education.[3]

Recent critiques in composition studies do not recognize the sheer radical potential of open admissions in terms of its resistance to the tiered systems that enabled institutions to manage the crisis of growth in this period. In his otherwise excellent history of the "birth" of basic writing, Bruce Horner portrays CUNY's open admissions policy as an attempt to accommodate, and thus to contain, class and ethnic conflict. Commenting on the Board of Higher Education's resolution of 9 July 1969, which established open admissions, Horner writes, "Arguments for open admissions claimed to resolve . . . opposed goals by accommodating all" (10). The Board's language marginalized remedial education: it satisfied competing groups by allowing students to be part of, yet not part of, the university. Consequently, "the change was to be enacted on neither the definition of the university's integrity as it had existed in the past nor on society but on the new students" (11). As I argued in chapter 2, such language may very well sustain the traditional use of remedial traditions as internal admissions mechanisms.

But in some significant ways, the 1969 policy represents a distinct break with those traditions I described in chapter 2. Though Horner faults Shaughnessy for assuming the status of a "pioneer"— a critique that Joseph Harris also advances—the policy *was* unique because it attempted to institutionalize remedial education systematically rather than as a set of ad hoc practices. More important, the policy attempted to change students rather than the university—the focus of much critique of the policy and of Shaughnessy—because the original aim was to provide a traditional education for nontraditional students. The alternative available at the time—and really the only alternative available now—was to create nontraditional colleges or vocational centers for first-generation college students. In November 1968, the students who seized the City College campus gave the administration a petition, signed by 1,600 students and endorsed by several clubs and the Student Government. This petition contained a study that criticized the city's plans to establish by 1975 a California-style master plan, "a three-tiered system of senior colleges, community colleges, and educational-skills centers" that would "perpetuate a tracking process that discouraged nonwhites from pursuing academic diplomas first in high school and then in college" (Hamalian and Hatch 17). Two decades later, plans to retier CUNY resurfaced again, more successfully this time, as I will discuss in chapter 4.

Remediation's anomalous status was not a result of the board's resolution or of the original conception of open admissions—that status was firmly in place when Shaughnessy began teaching in the Pre-Bac program in 1966. Therefore, I view Basic Writing's "birth" as a radical challenge to institutional differentiation, a challenge that dissipated by 1974 in the wake of the worst national recession since the 1930s and the city's consequent devastating fiscal crisis. It's important to recall that in the mid-1960s, as institutions confronted unprecedented growth, they began to differentiate. By the early 1970s, the federal government and private corporations supported this differentiation by funding the occupational education movement. It was widely expected that a bottom level would protect the selectivity of the upper tiers and stabilize a job market that could not be flooded with college graduates in a period of recession (see Shor 1986). Institutions use this strategy to resolve a fundamental paradox in American society: how to fulfill students' aspirations—and demands—for class mobility through postsecondary education without relinquishing the academy's traditional selective functions.

The policy that Horner describes, and that City College students reacted against, was a revised version of a proposed tiered plan. In 1966, the Board of Higher Education and CUNY Chancellor Albert Bowker proposed a three-tiered system modeled after the famous California Plan; the senior colleges would occupy the top tier, two-year colleges the midlevel tier, and "educational skills centers" the vocational bottom. As labor historian Joshua Freeman argues, in a decade that saw the heyday of organized working-class power in New York City (some of it crossing race lines), the resistance to the original three-tiered plan, while complicated by the interests of competing groups, ultimately resulted in a policy that resisted tiering and sought "a radical democratization of the municipal college system" (228). When viewed in the context of tiering, the policy—to sustain academic excellence while also offering access—pioneered a new model in the urban context. It offered first-generation college students a liberal arts, not a vocational, skills, or transfer, education. Open admissions was a product of organized agitation in the city for the democratization not only of education, but also of health care and affordable housing. "Though not without faults," Freeman concludes, "open admissions represented a significant advance toward equal opportunity and the ideal of liberal education for all. It was one of the great triumphs of working-class New York" (233).

Open admissions grew out of a historical moment that saw greater gains for working-class New Yorkers than at any time in the city's history. Though open admissions would ultimately fail, it did not, in its inception, represent an accommodation to conflict. It's my view that the policy constituted a radical challenge to the standardized means of managing the crises of growth and the demand for more access in the '60s. To my knowledge, the City University's challenge to higher education has never been repeated.

This bold challenge to American higher education—the direct integration of a working-class population into a liberal arts college —was an important influence upon Shaughnessy's writing program and should be more fully considered as the backdrop for her legacy. In what follows, I'll situate Shaughnessy's emphasis upon students' acculturation into the liberal arts within this sociopolitical context. I'll begin by examining *Errors and Expectations* through the various critiques of Shaughnessy's work, especially from the influential poststructuralist viewpoint. I'll then move to describe Shaugh-nessy's efforts to contest the anomalous institutional status of her program, both in her published work and in her more mundane, bureaucratic tasks.

Critical Discourse and Errors and Expectations

Over the last two decades, the most substantial discussions of her legacy involve Shaughnessy's status as a theorist of language.[4] Bruce Horner and Min-Zhan Lu have repeatedly noted that Shaughnessy's self-assumed role as a "pioneer" prevented her from drawing upon traditions for language teaching that were being developed in the 1960s. Similarly, in his assessment of Shaughnessy's work, Joseph Harris points to a progressive tradition of dissent in the public schools, linguistic debates during the 1970s in composition (*Students' Right to Their Own Language*), and to Geneva Smitherman's early work (*Talkin and Testifyin* appeared in 1977, as did Shaughnessy's book).

Located outside this intellectual ferment, Harris argues, *Errors and Expectations* is really a conservative "primer on teaching for cor-rectness, pure and simple" (78). It successfully "argues for a new sort of student but not a new sort of intellectual practice. It says that basic writers can also do the kind of work that mainstream students have long been expected to do; it doesn't suggest this work be changed in any significant ways" (79). Citing among other things her lack of in-terest in revision, Harris concludes "that Shaughnessy's failure to at-tend in any sustained way to issues beyond the sentence is what now makes her work, less than twenty years after its appearance, seem of merely historical interest rather than of practical use" (84–85).

Shaughnessy's work is more complex than this critique suggests, however. I showed in chapter 2 that, on the college level, there was little sustained theoretical work in the teaching of remedial writing to which anyone in 1966 could have readily turned. Moreover, Shaughnessy's work with sentence structure did depart from past formalisms by drawing from existing professional knowledge in composition studies that was in turn based on the new sociolinguis-tics. In 1976, she and Alice Trillin presented a videotape at the 4Cs in

Philadelphia that dramatized the use of sentence-combining techniques, then at the cutting edge of professional practice. During the summer of the same year, Frank O'Hare wrote a letter in support of the videotape, which he said "has convinced me that this technique is the most exciting breakthrough in the teaching of writing in the past twenty years." O'Hare praised the videotape because it "approaches the teaching of writing from a positive viewpoint and does not depend on the customary error-oriented esoterica of traditional composition programs"; instead, he thought that, in its emphasis on "constantly re-working prose," it "is a visual demonstration of the infinite manipulability of the English language."

At the same time, Shaughnessy's theoretical approaches were inconsistent. For her almost obsessive attention to grammar also shares space—sometimes in the same text—with examples or expressions of uncertainty about the relationship between form and meaning, so that even as she exhaustively catalogues syntactic constructions, she also sometimes suggests that form can't be taught directly. Patricia Harkin's assessment of John Rouse's 1979 critique of *Errors and Expectations* shows that these contradictions occur because Shaughnessy's work isn't disciplinary. Instead, in Harkin's view, Shaughnessy's work is an exemplar of what Stephen North identifies as practitioner knowledge, or composition's lore. "Lore," Harkin writes, "is nondisciplinary: it is actually defined by its inattention to disciplinary procedures" (125). Lore is flexible, fluid, and "frequently contradictory" (125). Because, in North's phrasing, "its structure is frequently experiential," lore's "social function" helps to bind practitioners together (126).

I will return to the "social functions" of Shaughnessy's work as a program administrator but here would observe that from the perspective of lore, it's more accurate to say that Shaughnessy—lacking a Ph.D. and status in the eyes of the literary establishment—didn't ignore disciplinary work in favor of aligning herself "with mainstream literary studies," as Harris argues, but freely drew ideas from different places (79). For instance, her consistent assumption about the logic of error—from Labov, widely discussed by teachers she worked with—shares room with current-traditional assumptions about teaching writing that were embedded in the program she inherited at City College.

Harkin goes on to say that the critique of lore can occur on two grounds, the disciplinary and the ethical. Rouse's "The Politics of Composition" takes Shaughnessy to task on these grounds: first, for violating the warrants of the discipline of linguistics, and secondly, for exercising undue authority over students' rights to their own language. I will show below that these grounds are essentially the basis for later poststructuralist critiques of her work. But the problem with Rouse's account of Shaughnessy, Harkin points out, is that "Shaughnessy doesn't ask how language works in society; rather, she asks where these errors come from and what we can do about them. Her question is decidedly, consciously, not a disciplinary one. Her answers are 'situated knowledge'" (131). It's precisely this "situated knowledge" that I wish to elaborate upon here: Shaughnessy's institutional location provides an alternative framework for assessing her legacy. It's Shaughnessy's argument "for a new sort of student" that, as Harris rightly notes, motivates her work. However, her argument is not of "merely historical interest" but one that can provide an alternative legacy at a moment when the commitment toward creating an educated, urban working class is far less compelling, both to the public and perhaps also to the profession.

There is a tendency within contemporary composition to equate the politics of basic skills in an *institution* to the politics of language use in the *discipline*. When the two are conflated, formalist teaching is sometimes equated with apolitical views, and more sophisticated responses to language with a transgressive politics. Jeanne Gunner (1998b) has analyzed the decade-long debate to define Shaughnessy's legacy, waged in published work and on listservs, in just this way. Gunner describes a conflict between two essential discourses in the field that signals "a paradigm shift in its disciplinary formation" (25). The first, "iconic discourse," which invokes Shaughnessy, CUNY, and open admissions, is eminently practical, casts the teacher in a heroic role, and evades political controversy. The second, "critical discourse," flows from oppositional figures like Bruce Horner who, writing outside the original community, offer an

abstract discourse that "constructs no heroes. And it is highly theoretical and political, in its relations within the academy as well as in
its curricular and intellectual agenda" (36). Min-Zhan Lu's work,
Gunner writes, is "intolerably transgressive" for scholars like Patricia Laurence, who defend and reproduce the iconic discourse by
rejecting any critique of Shaughnessy, its central ur-figure (37).

Gunner's dichotomy is quite useful in describing the historical
trajectory of disciplinary arguments, but it also assumes that, because critical discourse is professionally transgressive, it is institutionally resistant.[5] I want to negotiate between these polarized debates by distinguishing between, and thus revealing the special
power of, the two kinds of politics that Gunner's dichotomy fuses
together. To do this, I will examine Shaughnessy's work in the context of the most influential and impressive critiques of her legacy,
Min-Zhan Lu's essays, first published in the early 1990s and then
reprinted in a book coauthored with Bruce Horner (1999). Since
their publication, these essays have shaped debates about the politics of language and, consequently, about what constitutes reform in
basic writing. Because they are also regularly cited in writing about
multiculturalism (e.g., see essays in Severino et al.), Lu's critique of
formalism has also influenced composition studies more generally.

In "Redefining the Legacy of Mina Shaughnessy," Lu offers a
"critique" of "an essentialist assumption about language dominant
in the teaching of basic writing" (1999, 105). Her critique is "motivated by my alignment with various Marxist and poststructuralist
theories of language," which we learn in a note includes theorists as
diverse as Althusser and Derrida, Foucault and Raymond Williams.
The "essentialist assumption" that governs basic writing, Lu explains,

> holds that the essence of meaning precedes and is independent
> of language, which serves merely as a vehicle to communicate
> that essence. According to this assumption, differences in dis-
> course conventions have no effect on the essential meaning
> communicated. Using Mina Shaughnessy's *Errors and Expec-*
> *tations* as an example, I examine the ways in which such an as-

sumption leads to pedagogies which promote what I call a politics of linguistic innocence: that is, a politics which pre-empts teachers' attention from the political dimensions of the linguistic choices students make in their writing. (105)

To support this argument, Lu performs a skillful close reading of Shaughnessy's book. In one instance, Lu reexamines sentences that, in her last chapter, Shaughnessy offers as evidence of a change in basic writers' style over the course of a semester. In two passages that Lu selects, the subject is childhood: the first, awkwardly written example speculates on racism in Harlem, while the second, more smoothly written one describes children playing in a decaying neighborhood without reference to racism (110–11). Lu comments, "In the first passage, the writer approaches the 'people' through their racial and economic differences and the subject of childhood through racial rift and contention," while in the second, "the almost lyrical celebration of the children's ability to 'continue to play' 'in the midst of decay' seems a much more 'literary' and evasive form of confronting the world of 'decay'" (111). For this reason, Lu argues, a stylistic change reflects a sociopolitical one: "these two passages also indicate that the change in the length and style of the student's writing can be accompanied by a change in thinking—in the way one perceives the world around one and relates to it" (111). Though Shaughnessy recognized that students have a "choice" to make between styles, she did not make the effects of the choice explicit to students because for her, that choice appeared to be a formal one.

This is a powerful and useful critique, especially if we assume that most students' writing changes within a particular course, and that such change can be measured through a course or sequence of courses. Shaughnessy is equally concerned, though, with those students whose writing doesn't reflect immediate stylistic change. That problem is a crucial one for basic writing administration, and it was central to Shaughnessy's thinking, because basic writing programs are so often institutionalized to determine whether a student can proceed—into freshman writing or general education courses. After providing these passages, Shaughnessy expresses concern with the unequal progress of students, which is important to her because the institution uses the basic writing sequence as a foundation from which to determine a student's continued access in the liberal arts. How is access beyond the first course sequence institutionalized?

Shaughnessy goes on to say that development sometimes occurs in attitudes toward learning that, over time in other courses, could affect a student's academic performance. In raising this issue, she is questioning the limits of basic writing in transforming students' language use. "Leveled for the purposes of placement and group instruction," she writes, "they assert their individualities in a variety of ways—in their styles of learning, their paces and patterns of development, even in the features of their writing that resist or give way to instruction" (280).

To illustrate, Shaughnessy then juxtaposes a passage written by a student at the beginning of the basic writing sequence with one written in another content course three years later. At the end of the basic writing sequence, Shaughnessy comments, "the most marked change in her as a writer was not yet apparent on the page but was reflected rather in a shift in her attitude toward writing, and more broadly, toward achievement in academia" (280). Basic writing, Shaughnessy suggests, may assume other, more flexible institutional roles to play beyond the initiatory functions assigned to it (and to freshman composition as well).

Shaughnessy's concern grew out of her administrative work in overseeing a three-course sequence at City College. In her midterm *Report on the Basic Writing Program* (1971), intended for teachers and administrators, she speculated at some length upon the initiatory role that the sequence played in terms of providing access in content courses. The three-course sequence (Basic Writing 1 and 2, which were remedial, and Basic Writing 3, the freshman course) reflects the old tradition of ability grouping I described in chapter 2. After describing the percentages of students placed into each course, she notes that "Once the students begin to move within the sequence, however, the boundaries of the courses get blurred," in part because students placed at the third level may begin with stronger skills than the student who was placed in the first course but then progressed through the sequence (16).

Shaughnessy devotes a chunk of the report to mulling over the problem of using a writing program as the yardstick by which to measure the academic success not only of individuals, but also of open admissions. For instance, what happens to a student who passes each course but still doesn't write as well as the student who was placed into the third course from the beginning? "Can we, in short," she wondered, "penalize the student who has kept his end of the bargain and who has succeeded in terms of his own base line?" Which "base line" should be used, the teacher's and the student's or a more abstract standard established by the institution? "The answer to this question," she went on to say, "depends on what we expect remediation to do or be. If remediation is a program, rather than a process, then English 3 is the end of the line and the student who cannot deliver a sample of writing that meets the old standards is out. But if remediation is a process that continues far beyond the Basic Writing sequence and *beyond the subject of writing and reading,* then there is some justification in allowing a student to proceed in the curriculum, knowing that, with sweat, the gap between the absolute standard and his performance will narrow and finally close" (17, my emphasis). Shaughnessy's question is crucial because she is asking whether remediation's influence can be extended beyond a single course or program. By suggesting that remediation may not "end" after a course is completed, she is also touching on the thorniest gatekeeping function of these programs and raising one of the most difficult theoretical and practical problems in teaching basic writing—which is to decide when remediation ends.

Shaughnessy also believes that "there is some justification" in allowing students who don't "measure up" to continue into the liberal arts core because she does not consistently assume that skills learning precedes meaning. That split may be an institutional one rooted in the conventional status of writing courses. Her experience with individual students suggests otherwise, as she describes in an example she offers in "Some New Approaches toward Teaching" (1970/1994):

> The term "basic writing" implies that there is a place to begin learning to write, a foundation from which the many special

forms and styles of writing rise, and that a college student
must control certain skills that are common to all writing *before* he takes on the special demands of a biology or literature
or engineering class. *I am not certain this is so.* Some students
learn to write in strange ways. I recall one student who knew
something about hospitals because she had worked as a
nurse's aide. She decided, long before her sentences were
under control, to do a paper on female diseases. In some way
this led her to the history of medicine and then to Egypt,
where she ended up reading about embalming—which became the subject of a long paper she entitled "Post-mortem
Care in Ancient Egypt." The paper may not have satisfied a
professor of medical history, but it produced more improvement in the student's writing than any assignments I could
have devised. (103, my emphasis)

Invoking lore, Shaughnessy questions the widespread academic
practice of institutionalizing skills in one place and content learning
in another. Reasoning anecdotally, she describes how a basic writing
student—"long before her sentences were under control"—successfully pursued an independent research project. Typically, Shaughnessy doesn't use the example to develop a theory of meaning but to
question the bureaucratic use of basic writing as a foundation for
content courses—as a means of access to the liberal arts.

This is the context for *Errors and Expectations*, where Shaughnessy considers change within an institutional framework and remediation as a longitudinal process. For after providing the passages that
Lu discusses, Shaughnessy juxtaposes two passages from the same
student to illustrate how development occurs within institutional
contexts. As with the passages that Lu considers, these also reveal
stylistic shifts that encompass shifts in attitude. The sample from the
placement essay offers a description of George Washington in the
clichéd terms drawn from a high school history textbook:

George Washington has contributed much; in making of
American History. A general in the army during the American Revolution. He commened many victories; that lead the

thirteen colonies to an independent United States. Later
became the First President of the United States. . . . Mr Washington was an outdoorsman in the very sence of the word. He
loved horse back riding and hunting. It has been said, "he cut
down a cherry tree." Making his home in Virginia with his
wife Martha.

In the sample written three years later, the same student wrote
another paper about American history. This time, the subject is
Puerto Rico's economic status:

Many Americans believe that Puerto Rico is fortunate to be
exempted from paying taxes. What most Americans do not
know is that the tax exemption is not for Puerto Ricans, but
for the American investors. The Industrial Incentives Act of
1947, continued even after commonwealth came into being. It
authorized and incouraged private firms (Americans) to in-
vest in Puerto Rico. This Act was enacted to supply jobs and
hopefully raise the Island's economy. At first the idea was
good; however, as time passed the Puerto Ricans received the
short end of the stick. (280)

Ironically given Lu's reading of the previous samples, in the
Washington passage, the "home" or "community" discourse does
not feature the strife that Lu privileges but awards Washington an
uncomplicated historical status. By contrast, in the Puerto Rico
passage, which displays more academic competence, the student
considers history as the site of "rift and contention." Possibly, then,
academic discourse here enables the student to reason more criti-
cally about historical facts—which was indeed Shaughnessy's belief.
  The first passage suffers from an unrelated list of facts and folk
lore gleaned from high school or the culture at large. The second,
however, leans heavily for its coherence and assurance upon the fact
that the Industrial Incentives Act of 1947 created certain economic
conditions. From learning about the act and what it entailed, the student can interpret what happened as a result. On the one hand,
Shaughnessy clearly means to show how language and meaning go

hand in hand. As important, though, this example underscores that language itself doesn't generate specific arguments because writers also require access to the content offered by other teachers in the liberal arts.

The Politics of Access versus the Politics of Representation

The passages also suggest that not all aspects of learning to write depend upon learning to use language because not all learning is discursive. This is why Shaughnessy repeatedly called for longitudinal research, as she thought that time itself and exposure to different readers and contents also affected a student's writing. She often emphasized this point in reports but gradually began to see it as a major research question. In her bibliographical essay "Basic Writing" (1976), she noted that "writing is a slow-developing skill that should be measured over longer periods than a semester, but no system for collecting longitudinal data on writing performance exists to my knowledge in any program" (Maher 160).

Such a study wouldn't be completed until 1997, by Marilyn Sternglass in *Time to Know Them*. These case studies (which I'll discuss in chapter 4) emphasize the minimal role that a basic writing course plays within the overall journey toward the B.A. and maximize the role that mass testing, tuition hikes, technology, mass transit, affordable apartments, and child care all play in sustaining access. A longitudinal perspective also argues for the close relationship between language and meaning, in part because it reveals the influential role that other content courses play in developing a student's writing ability (see Zamel). However, at the same time, this perspective suggests that not all learning, nor all success in college, depends upon language use.

For Lu, the political goal of a basic writing course is to create self-consciousness about students' choices between "low" and "high" languages. It is a reform, I would argue, that centers on individual change as that is effected through curricular change: what goes on within the classroom is more important than what goes on outside. This reform may be central for individual teachers and their students, as I'll document in chapter 5 when I consider the writing of

City College students. But a teacher's challenge to the high status of academic language doesn't necessarily contest the institutional politics of basic skills as Shaughnessy describes them in her midterm report, in part because struggles within an institution aren't always concerned with, or driven by, ideas. In "Conflict and Struggle: The Enemies of Basic Writing," Lu concludes by asking us to "re-read" Shaughnessy's work (and that of other CUNY pioneers) "in the context of current debates on the nature of language, individual consciousness, and the politics of basic skills" (1999, 55). In making this recommendation, Lu assumes that these three areas are vitally linked: if our *ideas* about language change and individual consciousness shift, then the *politics* of basic skills are also altered. One assumption here is that ideas drive the bureaucratic machinery of institutions.

Lu doesn't detail the exact links between the nature of language, the individual self, and the politics of basic skills in part because she is more concerned with the first two areas of debate. She is less concerned with how students gain access to the classroom or exit from it than she is with teachers' allegiance to traditional curriculum. Her version of "reform" stems from the two assumptions she foregrounds in the beginning of this essay: "first, that learning a new discourse has an effect on the re-forming of individual consciousness; and second, that individual consciousness is necessarily heterogeneous, contradictory, and in process" (31–32). Therefore, what needs to be reformed is traditional "values," which are embodied in curriculum: "Ultimately, as I have argued, the teaching of both Shaughnessy and Kriegel [another 'pioneer'] might prove to be more successful in preserving the traditions of 'English language and literature' than in helping students reach a self-conscious choice on their position toward conflicting cultural values and forces" (51). I don't mean to suggest that curriculum reform wasn't or shouldn't be central to preserving open access policies. Nor, as I detail in chapters 4 and 5, do I undervalue either the conflict between cultural identities that students experience or the power of the politics of representation. But the politics of language teaching aren't always equivalent to how institutions use remediation to mediate their growth. The critique of educational models that Lu offers in this essay centers reform in the unfolding drama between students' "individual consciousness" and their encounters with "a new discourse." The "enemy" of this reform would be anyone who ignores the friction that results in the process of encountering a new language: the "enemy" is an attitude toward language teaching that we adopt.

Yet to engage with this particular enemy, teachers must not only have access to new professional knowledge, they must also be able to translate that knowledge into a particular bureaucratic context. Rebecca Greenberg Taylor illustrates a conflict between curricular aims and institutional roles through the teaching journal she kept when she taught a basic writing course at Ohio State University. Taylor found that institutional pressures profoundly shaped students' attitudes toward her, progressive pedagogy, and the course. As she and Jacqueline Jones Royster conclude, "Looming large among these issues [for further research] is how writing professionals at all levels might productively critique the 'gatekeeping' roles of first year writing that seem to be built automatically into the very fiber of our academic system" (44). Given its foundational role within most institutions, the political aim of a remedial program is to prepare students to enter content courses, often as a way to resolve the conflicts over enrollment or institutional mission that I described in chapter 2.

What Gunner identifies as critical or iconic discourses may instead be distinguished as two kinds of goals that have not been separately defined, let alone reconciled: for students to achieve self-consciousness about their individual language use, and for students to pass through a sequence and into the content disciplines. Neither is more transgressive than the other because the first is focused on transforming professional knowledge, while the second is focused on transforming students' access to the disciplines. Lu's influential critique of Shaughnessy focuses on a teaching philosophy rather than on a politics of access. In part, Lu's lack of interest in access to the university reflects a broader shift in the academic perspective from questions of access to identity politics, which Paul Lauter locates in the 1980s. Identity politics—whose importance I do not underestimate—have occupied center stage in the last fifteen years, while the politics of access that characterized the '60s have assumed far less attention, at least in English studies.

But as Shaughnessy was well aware, remedial courses can pose complex and troubling points of access because, for working-class students, access is a process of struggle often waged over several years. For instance, remedial English and other first-year writing courses sometimes function to span the gap between the two-year and the four-year college. Therefore, it's Shaughnessy's attitude toward enhancing access to traditional knowledge, rather than her attitude toward that knowledge itself, that motivates her focus upon the formal structures of language. To call attention to the limits of this focus is necessary, especially when it neglects the intimate relationships between reading and writing or between style and cultural allegiance. But it is problematic to assume that if we change our attitudes about language, we will change how teaching is institutionalized. If we conflate a critique of curriculum change with institutional reform, we might also assume that students' educational success or failure is attributable solely to linguistic change. Such an assumption, as I'll document in chapter 4, can have devastating consequences in public debates about funding for public higher education.

Shaughnessy as Intellectual-Bureaucrat

Jeanne Gunner notes that the Writing Program Administrator (WPA) often supports practices that are at odds with a theory that critiques assimilationist models of language learning (1998a). For Shaughnessy, however, resistance was located in that daily bureaucratic work that affects the material experience of both teachers and students. She was less concerned with what is being taught or how it's being taught than with who is being taught and where. The "where" is especially significant. I've already indicated that the alternative to housing large remedial programs in four-year schools was to shift them to two-year schools, as illustrated most markedly by the 1960 California Master Plan, or to educational skills centers, as envisioned in the original 1966 plan for open admissions in New York. By 2000, the boundaries between schools would be redrawn at the City University—for example, through a nonacademic tier that includes language institutes and special summer programs staffed exclusively by a temporary labor pool and often managed by nonacademic personnel. But in the late '60s, it seemed possible to infiltrate selective schools rather than build a tiered, and racially segregated, system. Shaughnessy focused on integrating an unselective student body into a traditional liberal arts school.

Shaughnessy's notion of reform, and her oppositional practices, were more bureaucratic than disciplinary. She can be labeled an "accommodator"—a view that's easier to sustain if we focus on educational reform as a process of changing ideas about language learning. But such a label tends to decontextualize reform, as if the reform of programs were a matter of changing our ideas, rather than of changing material practices within institutions. This is a time-honored attitude that academics hold of reform, according to Richard Miller's analysis of several reform projects in higher education over the past two centuries. In *As if Learning Mattered*, Miller draws on Larry Cuban and David Tyack's historical work on school reform to pose an alternative vision of resistance where the true "agent of change" only "tinkers toward utopia." Tinkering within the institution, the true change-agent assumes a tricky "hybrid persona of the intellectual-bureaucrat" in the attempt "to harness the energy of the critical impulse to engage effectively with the bureaucratic realities that govern what can occur in the classroom" (41). This hybrid figure improvises "educational possibilities out of the restricted materials available" as she engages directly in "the impure business of building a functioning alternative to current educational practice" (43). An institutional performer, this person skillfully works "with and against the waves of internal and external resistance to change" (43).

Changing reading lists and critiquing how we represent students are critical endeavors, as I describe in chapter 5. But these reforms do not necessarily affect how we institutionalize students' access to four-year schools, or teachers' access to a profession. Thus, chief among the intellectual-bureaucrat's goals is her desire "to exercise a *material influence* . . . on which individuals are given a chance to become students and on whether the academy can be made to function as a responsive, hospitable environment for all who work within its confines" (46, my emphasis). Miller's academic performer works within institutions where change occurs incrementally—not the case with Shaughnessy, laboring as she did at a moment of seismic shift. Nevertheless, Miller's analysis of reformers in various academic contexts illuminates how "change" within institutions is itself a mixed bag, not only a matter of ideas but also of material practices, involving at one moment a clash of ideologies, at another, a clash between personalities. From this perspective, educational reform is halting, inconsistent, and difficult, encompassing issues of representation, as well as quotidian practices that affect access policies and conditions for work.

Shaughnessy's work with the prebaccalaureate program in the late '60s illustrates the daily struggle she waged to integrate her program within the confines of a large, influential department that, as I indicated in chapter 2, was in the throes of change characteristic of midlevel comprehensives during this period. Shaughnessy's struggle to argue for the "new" students is often painted solely as a conflict between those in favor, and those opposing, the "new" students. But some of this conflict also originated in larger shifts that, as Dorothy Finnegan documents, were typical of those public comprehensive colleges and universities that emerged in this period. Chief among these was between a research and a teaching mission, a conflict I'll consider in more detail below. When open admissions began, so too did an effort to upgrade the status of the public comprehensive, which effectively institutionalized an alignment between a teaching mission and remedial education.

In the early days of open admissions, administrators tried to desegregate the remedial program. David Buckley, chair of the English department at City College, informed the faculty that in 1971, the English department had successfully argued for the creation of a new M.A. program focusing on pedagogy and linguistics. The Basic Writing program had also assigned at least one writing course to "every member of the professorial staff instead of only to Lecturers, Instructors and nontenured Assistant Professors," while a literature course had been assigned to members of the Basic Writing program (3). Institutional documents reveal that this move to create "mixed programs" was widely debated—and acted upon—between 1970 and 1973.[6] While Buckley thought this was only fair, he also argued that "it is important that all of us encounter [Open Admissions] students and work with them early in their college careers. And if the City College is, in fact, committed to Open Admissions . . . then incoming students should not be set apart and assigned to some special remedial staff" (3).

Even before the advent of open admissions, Shaughnessy's goal was to link the remedial program with the traditional work of the department. In one report she wrote to her chair, Edmund Volpe, in the fall of 1967, Shaughnessy commented: "I have persuaded most of the Pre-bac teachers to attend the English Department faculty meetings, but they clearly feel unwanted and uncomfortable. I hope something can be done this year to reduce that feeling. Unfortunately, Professor ———omitted me from your agenda at the orientation meeting. He did give my name and then added, with the smile of a professional mourner, that everyone wished me well." Though they attended these meetings, the prebac staff ignored several other luncheons, meetings, and lectures, which prompted Chair Volpe to write a long memo detailing their absence from various functions. "I have been conscious of the strong feelings expressed last year by the prebac instructors concerning their sense of isolation," he concluded, "and I had hoped to remedy the problem this year" (1967). Throughout this period, faculty members would continue to debate the weird status of prebac teachers in their department.

Shaughnessy spent the years from 1967 to 1973 trying to "remedy the problem" of writing teachers' uneasy status that institutionally separated their work from mainstream academic life. In *Errors and Expectations*, she dubbed this split the "anteroom" model, which she thought cleaved language from meaning and forced teachers to work hastily, abandoning the long-term perspective upon development that was consistently a part of her thinking about teaching writing. "We already begin to see," she wrote, "that the remedial model, which isolates the student and the skill from real college contexts, imposes a 'fix-it station' tempo and mentality upon both teachers and students" (293). For her, then, "the politics of basic skills" meant professionalizing writing teachers and enabling them to create an alternative, long-term "tempo" for learning.

To accomplish this, Shaughnessy spent considerable time trying to intellectualize the prebac program. For instance, she and other teachers developed a series of public lectures for students that she publicized to the literature faculty. Students of all sections attended Toni Cade's lectures on "standard problems" like organization and verb tense; Ann Cook's on English, Spanish, and Chinese dialects; or Barbara Christian and Alice Trillin's on poetry. In another semester, students heard Cade lecture on African American literature, while Puerto Rican literature was planned for the spring of 1968. Meanwhile, Shaughnessy wrote to Chair Volpe to request that he invite all English faculty to hear a series of lectures "on some aspect of the English language" that she had arranged for three literature professors to give to prebac students (1967; 1968).

The original proposal that she wrote for *Errors and Expectations*, addressed to the Carnegie Foundation, reveals Shaughnessy's broader administrative views of reform (1972). In this draft, Shaughnessy included several chapters that would have focused on the role of course sequencing, placement, and relationship to content courses. Six chapters were to focus on formal issues, including the writing process, but chapters 7 through 10 were to focus on institutional relationships: how to train teachers (chapter 7), how to establish a writing lab (chapter 8), and the politics of remediation (chapter 9), which was to cover "Observations on the tensions, conflicts, and confusions that can be created by the introduction of remedial programs into the senior college." Chapter 10 was to report on "Future Directions," in the form of "interdisciplinary and linked courses," the use of technology, and creating learning centers rather than skills courses.

The book proposal sketched out a framework reflecting almost seven years' worth of bureaucratic struggle to extend remediation and writing instruction beyond the English department. With administrators, she helped to sketch out a plan for college-wide remediation that included a collaborative role for the director of the Search for Education, Excellence, and Knowledge program (SEEK), which was not housed in an academic department (Gross 1973). In reports and memos, Shaughnessy described several experiments with linked courses, many of which involved SEEK or other departments (1973). One experiment involved a summer session featuring

three linked courses sharing the same content but taught by literature, speech, and SEEK teachers. Another involved creating special
Q sections, where a basic writing course was linked to courses in political science, history, or sociology (Fiellin 1972). In an appendix to
her midterm report of 1971, Shaughnessy described a proposal to
create what in the '90s educators called "learning communities,"
block program schedules for freshmen in which the same group enrolls in a group of classes. One block featured sociological perspectives upon writing, literature, and art, for example. Shaughnessy justified the block program on the basis of the relationship between
language and meaning: "the departments which make up our liberal
arts college represent, not simply content, but distinct ways of pro-
cessing content."

Shaughnessy also tried to reform mundane bureaucratic structures to legitimize basic writing's status. One plan was to create a
program bulletin that described each section of a writing course. As
James Slevin points out, institutions regularly adopt one official
course description that "covers" dozens of sections, which is noteworthy because this practice promotes an official vision of English
studies that no longer exists within most institutions: a department
devoted exclusively to literary teaching and scholarship. Slevin cites
MLA statistics, which reveal that about 70 percent of most courses
offered in most English departments are composition courses; however, most of them, nationwide, are not taught by full-time English
faculty. Yet officially, first-year writing courses are never "authored"
by a diverse array of teachers, except, as Slevin observes, on registration printouts and gradesheets (5).

To assert her program's institutional presence, Shaughnessy
spent several years developing a "teacher-course inventory." In a
memo to teachers dated 18 October 1971, she reported that a "crew"
of seven veterans would meet with each teacher to gather information about his or her course. The inventory was to "serve as a guide
to students so that those who know that they learn best in a certain
type of course can be more certain of getting into a section that is
congenial to them." Each inventory would highlight teachers'
"goals" and classroom "style," usual "topics" and "types of writing

and reading assignments." The teacher-course inventory would describe a program parallel to the one in literature, where each course is individually described, its course topics, books, and key questions listed. It would establish a higher status for writing courses through the most mundane of material practices, the department course bulletin and students' registration.

Shaughnessy also sought to upgrade the status of writing teachers, at that period usually full-time instructors holding an M.A., many of them gifted creative writers and critical theorists. Shaughnessy spoke publicly for their right to have a vote in their department; gained course remissions for writing teachers to conduct research, write reports, and develop proposals for new courses; lobbied for a reduction in teaching load for those teachers involved with Q sections; worked for the creation of the M.A. program and the Writing Center; and, through reports, conversations, and memos, asked chairs to provide "mixed programs" to writing teachers so that they wouldn't be assigned three writing courses, while full-time faculty taught only the literature courses. Throughout this period, these issues were regularly discussed by faculty, some of whom supported Shaughnessy's views.[7] As debates unfolded, Shaughnessy continued to foster collaboration between teachers—pairing veterans with inexperienced teachers; collecting portfolios and publishing anthologies of student writing; creating orientation sessions and various ongoing staff meetings and subcommittees to consider issues of placement, standards, and course content.[8]

Teachers' involvement in placement remained a key issue in Shaughnessy's mind as she considered the problems of sequencing writing courses. In 1967, she developed a midterm report system that asked teachers to describe the progress of each student and to make any recommendations for placement. Shaughnessy bound all the midterm reports together for each semester, and in one thick book that has survived, all teachers for fall 1970 turned in midterm reports for each student in every class. Shaughnessy then apparently read each one and checkmarked each name when the teacher described a possible change in placement; sometimes she scribbled notes like "skip" in the margins.

Serving a "social function" of "binding practitioners together" (Harkin), hundreds of reports offer a rich glimpse into teachers' daily work and reflect the kind of program that Shaughnessy worked to institutionalize. About M. H., a teacher writes:

SEND HIM TO ENGLISH 40 (a writing class for science majors). He belongs there now—or beyond, and I'm conducting a tutorial with him rather than waste his time in English 1. It's my fault that I did not read his first-day diagnostic piece in time to get him to English 40 officially. I'm atoning for it by assuring him a first-rate training program in using the library. Atonement for whoever read his placement exam should be two weeks in Philadelphia—or maybe a month, even; that's how far off the mark it was to send him to English 1.

Addressing Shaughnessy's concern with the power of a sequence to determine students' progress, these reports also allowed teachers to reflect upon how placement affects what they and students do. R. H. writes of L. H.:

God knows why —— is in Eng 1. I gave her a B last spring in Eng 21 (an ESL course). She is often a bit lazy in class, but why shouldn't she be? She doesn't need the course. She does fine when she wants to. She says she got screwed during registration. Who knows? At any rate, she will certainly pass the course.

As James Berlin notes, "subjective rhetorics" were dominant in the late 1960s, and this is reflected in teachers' descriptions of their pedagogy. In particular, the conference or tutorial method appears to have been central to their work, as teachers encourage students to read and produce the kind of writing that is personally meaningful to them:

Miss V—— is a misplaced student. Her work is above average. She turned in a report on *The Power Elite* which was certainly regular Freshman work, and her only difficulty is minor spelling errors. She participates in class discussions and is now doing another outside assignment, an analysis of *Doctor Zhivago*. I will advance her to English 3.

Teachers use the reports as an occasion to imagine students writing in other contexts, beyond the basic writing course:

> He is bright and capable, was placed in 1 by mistake. I think he finds a lot of the class discussions below his level, and he has been cutting rather heavily. I've arranged to work with him on independent writing projects but so far haven't seen anything His prose is awkward, with tangled syntax and too much word repetition. Will jump 2 & 3, may be asked to take 40.

In the margin, Shaughnessy scribbled "misplaced" in pencil, and then in pen, skip 2 3. She wrote skip to 40 in the margin next to another student that the same teacher described:

> An engineering major, this boy lives for cars and sports. In September he could not possibly conceive of enjoying writing or sitting through an English class, and I'm afraid I haven't changed his mind. His papers are as short as he can get away with and very sloppy (punctuation, spelling, descriptive detail). There are also verb agreement and tense problems, though not severe. I can't see torturing him with another two semesters of remedial English, and since the Engineering school requires 40, I may pass him to that.

Crammed with stories about students' lives, observations about language learning, and descriptions of coursework, these midterm reports reveal a flexible attitude toward the course's most institutionally political aspect, its gatekeeping function. There was no exit exam during this period; students were required to take a proficiency exam, a prerequisite for graduating rather than for continuing into the liberal arts. Through the reports, Shaughnessy asked teachers to reflect professionally on their work and to evaluate students' performance in terms of what they might do later on, in other courses. The reports indicate that, for the most progressive teachers, remediation was valued as an ongoing, longitudinal process that could—

should—spill beyond the borders of the official program. As important, they reflect Shaughnessy's efforts not only to intellectualize the
problem of assessment at different levels—a key concern, I've
argued, in the last chapter of *Errors and Expectations*—but she
sought to develop an alternative material practice to cope with the
theoretical problem.

This attitude toward remediation as a collegewide responsibility,
rather than a program situated exclusively within English and mathematics, was characteristic of the early years of open admissions.
Though much has been made of the hostility that professors felt toward the new students, there was also genuine support of open admissions, as reflected, for instance, in the faculty council's vote in
April 1968 to censure a speech professor who had made negative
public comments about the prebac project.[9] From 1970 to 1972, before the city's fiscal crisis paralyzed both the city and its municipal
university system, faculty from several disciplines developed innovative approaches to remediation. For instance, the Chemistry department, soon followed by Physics, developed what educators
today call a "stretch" course, where a two-course sequence is extended into three semesters (Marshak 28). The History department
developed the largest tutoring program outside English (28); the
Puerto Rican Studies and Black Studies departments developed a
cotaught remedial course (45). Ten departments—ranging from
mathematics to psychology, and from biology to sociology—offered
tutoring programs outside English for their first-year coursework
(27–28).

As one result of this ferment, Shaughnessy was no stranger to
curriculums that critiqued traditional knowledge or that made social
conflict—especially ethnic struggle—a centerpiece of reading, writing, and discussion. Curriculum reform was central to open admissions. Between 1970 and 1972, four new departments of ethnic studies were created; along with a new women's studies program,
courses across the disciplines politicized their curriculum and oriented their coursework toward open admissions students. The Institute for Social History, which proposed to train students to become
social historians of their own working-class and ethnic communi-

ties, developed an "oral history" project that made students' experiences the subject of academic inquiry and writing (Marshak 54). Similarly, the reading lists for Basic Writing that English teachers developed, and that Shaughnessy appended to her reports, reflect an intense awareness of cultural difference, and an effort to make that difference a subject for reading and writing. One textbook used in several writing classes in 1970 was titled *The Rhetoric of No*, an anthology containing essays ranging from Nietzsche to Stokely Carmichael, and from Jonathan Swift to Rachel Carson; topics vary from black separatism and civil disobedience to imperialism and environmentalism. This "collection," the editors tell the reader in their preface, "speaks to [today's] student by concentrating on a dominant characteristic of our contemporary dialogue—that of dissent" (Fabrizio et al., v).

Students responded positively to basic writing courses during these early years. Susan D'Raimo, who completed a nursing degree in the '70s and then returned to City College in the '90s as a doctoral candidate, English teacher, and social activist, completed Basic Writing 2 and 3 (along with a remedial reading course) in 1971. She doesn't recall studying grammar; what she remembers is reading other students' work and the shock she felt when she read an essay by D. H. Lawrence, "Sex and Loveliness," and heard liberal attitudes toward sexuality expressed by her peers during discussion. She remembers focusing on introductions and organization of essays, and an emphasis upon analysis in both reading and writing. "I liked the courses so much I took more in English," she said.

Surviving copies of the City College Student Government's surveys show that most students enrolled in Basic Writing 1, 2, and 3 agreed with D'Raimo. In their *Course and Teacher Evaluation Handbook* for 1972, the Student Senate expanded the numerical ratings of specific classes by printing the written comments of students on the surveys that the Student Senate asked teachers to give to their classes. In the fall semester, sets of comments for thirty-two sections of Basic Writing 1, 2, and 3 were published; students spoke glowingly of their experiences in these classes. Repeatedly they spoke of their teachers' commitment to them: "She is open minded and shows a

great deal of concern for her pupils" (Archer 65); "I never expected
to get such a good teacher for such an early class" (D'Eloia 66); "The
instructor was open-minded and created an atmosphere of true
learning" (Fone 66); "She's a beautiful teacher and always willing to
help a student" (Gray 67); and so on. The few substantive criticisms
the students made included advice to teach more grammar and encourage discussion, and to slow down the pace of the classes.

Outside of the writing center, which relied heavily on skill-and-
drill methods, progressive teachers experimented with those tools
that were available in the early '70s: with "happenings" and an emphasis upon autobiographical and creative writing, the reading of
ethnic literatures and sociolinguistics, and discussion of current
events that were rocking the city and the nation. In a large, vibrant
program that drew teachers with widely varying backgrounds (as
well as widely varying opinions as to its success), Shaughnessy tried
to institutionalize a sequence of courses surrounded by support
structures that maximized students' access to the liberal arts and le-
gitimized teachers' intellectual status. Basic writing teachers were
full-time instructors, and they were eligible to be promoted to the
professorial levels when they earned the Ph.D. In these years of academic plenty, Shaughnessy—mistakenly, as it turned out—believed
that writing instructors could gain a foothold in the academy, as she
had done with an M.A., and assert a lasting intellectual presence by
developing and experimenting with the writing curriculum.

By turns oppositional, accommodating, improvisational—
Miller's hybrid reformer—Shaughnessy contested the low status of
the new students through patient lobbying and the building of al-
liances across programs and departments. She skillfully practiced
an influential "politics of basic skills" that suggested that nontraditional students could achieve a traditional B.A. if they, their teachers, and their programs were adequately supported. In so doing,
Shaughnessy contested remedial writing's ambivalent status—in
but not of the traditional liberal arts—that was then, and probably
still is, a feature of much college writing instruction in American
higher education.

Shaughnessy's Legacy in the Post–Open Admissions Era

I framed my discussion of Shaughnessy's *Errors and Expectations* with debates that attempt to define her legacy. In her description of these debates, Jeanne Gunner identifies two discourses, the transgressive "critical" discourse associated with Min-Zhan Lu and Bruce Horner, and the "iconic" discourse associated with Shaughnessy, Karen Greenberg, and some other City University faculty. The result of transgressive critiques, Gunner speculates, is that iconic discourse may be losing its authority altogether, and so she asks: "can there be a poststructural Shaughnessy?" (27). I would like to conclude by suggesting that this question rests, again, on the conflation of two kinds of politics—those of the discipline, and those of institutions. If we emphasize the latter kind, then another, equally potent question arises: can there be a post–open admissions Shaughnessy?

Addressing her institution, Shaughnessy ended her midterm report for 1971 with a melancholy reflection on basic writing's long-term status:

> Too many are waiting for someone else to do the "dirty work" of remediation so that they can go on doing what they have always done. The curriculum still reinforces these prejudices, with the result that too many students are learning the same lesson here that they learned in high school—namely, that bad luck is cumulative.
>
> This remains the long-term problem with Open Admissions, and it is difficult to know what to do about it. (18)

The difficulty that Shaughnessy foresaw in 1971 was, as I've been arguing, institutionalizing remediation beyond a sequence of precollege or freshman courses. And also as I've been arguing, she worked to challenge the split between skills and content that is not exclusively a curricular matter, but a matter of the conditions that foster growth and innovation. Most important, these are the conditions that enable a program director to hire full-time, experienced college teachers.

The problem for Shaughnessy and her successors, then, was not, as Horner describes it in his history, exclusively a duel between those who espoused different educational models, or even a conflict between those who cherished the "old" students and those who welcomed the new. Despite the (genuine) hostility that Shaughnessy experienced, both personally and toward her program, this opposition coexisted with support for, and good will toward, the new policy. What eroded support for open admissions and fueled much of the anger was the unwillingness of the city and state to fund it properly. To complicate that lack of funding, moreover, was the movement to upgrade teaching colleges that began in earnest in the 1960s. Therefore, the key conflict for Shaughnessy and those who would succeed her was the changing nature of the American academy—its increasing differentiation and the consequent fierce competition for funding between tiers. The process of stratification and the battles over resources that resulted from it were not kind to Shaughnessy's program, nor to other remedial programs in midlevel comprehensives facing similar conflicts.

I indicated in chapter 2 that a teaching professorate like the English faculty at City College was beginning to feel external pressures to publish and to develop a more specialized program, one oriented less toward general education and more toward graduate study and research. This conflict between teaching and research—which memoirs like Theodore Gross's *Academic Turmoil* describe in some detail—began to develop for the public comprehensive at the very historical moment when more minorities and working-class students were being admitted to four-year schools. Nathan Glazer comments in his reading of institutional documents, "Ironically, while the undergraduate student body became less selective academically, the new president undertook steps to strengthen the City College academically. President Marshak—for the first time in City College history, as far as anyone knows—enlisted academically distinguished alumni to assist in evaluating departments and strengthening faculties" (1973, 95). In his *Chairman's Report for 1972–73*, David Buckley noted to the English faculty that the Board of Higher Education had decided to upgrade the standards for tenure and promotion throughout the City University, requiring for the first time letters from outside referees, while "book-length publications are being stressed with unaccustomed vigor"(5). This same process occurred in Dorothy Finnegan's case study institutions, which I described in chapter 2. She shows that the process of upgrading helped to create a divided and embittered liberal arts faculty. At Regional University, the trustees redefined the standards for promotion in terms of scholarship in order to "'upgrade' the existing faculty. From 1972 to 1982, the university substantially raised the criteria for both recruitment and retention. The consequential effects were enormous and long-term for both the existing faculty and the newly recruited faculty" (635).

At the case study colleges, Finnegan shows how one consequence was to institutionalize a split between research and teaching, not only in hiring and promotion, but also in attitudes toward students and curriculum. At City College, David Buckley thought that the "problem" with the new standards for hiring and advancement is that they were being raised

> at precisely the same time that they are lowering admissions standards for students and are, in effect, requiring—because of these lowered standards—that teachers in a department with a large number of remedial courses spend an enormous amount of time and energy in the classroom and in conferences if they are to give the students the assistance they need. But the time and energy devoted to this extremely important task cannot also be devoted to literary criticism and scholarship. . . . To raise one set of standards while another set is being lowered seems to me a serious mistake; it seems, at times, schizophrenic. (5–6)

This institutionalization of the conflict between missions affected the fortunes of remediation, of course. Just as composition studies was professionalizing in many schools, its primary labor force was being deprofessionalized, a contradiction that has never been resolved and that affects the quality of remedial programs more than any other factor.

At the City University and elsewhere, a part-time, mobile labor force would be hired to solve the crisis created by a budget shortfall,

a radical drop in hiring full-time liberal arts faculty, and declining yet
still considerable freshman enrollments. By the mid-1980s at City
College, nearly two-thirds of writing courses, taught exclusively by
full-time teachers in 1971, would be taught by a peripheral labor
force, a trend that would intensify in the early 1990s to reach a high
point of 90 percent. When Shaughnessy wrote her midterm report
for 1971, she described six administrative positions, three of them
held by full-time faculty receiving course remissions, not including
lesser administrative roles in the writing center. Of the eighty-one
instructors teaching basic writing, thirty-five were of full-time professorial rank; the others were full-time lecturers and instructors.
Class size hovered between eighteen and twenty-three; tutors were
available to teachers who wanted them; and well over half of all students enrolled passed the proficiency exam. By contrast, in her reports for fall 1975 and spring 1976, Blanche Skurnick noted that
twenty-seven adjunct, part-time teachers were hired in the fall, and
sixteen in the spring; the average class size in the second remedial
course was now twenty-seven, and failure rates on the exam had increased to 47 percent. To cope with the budget crisis, the college created large lecture sections of one hundred students and hired teachers from other departments to work temporarily in English (7).

Ten years later, Nathaniel Norment gloomily noted in his *Report
of the Basic Writing Program, 1985–86* that he supervised a program
that was only a shadow of its former self. While the Basic Writing
program still offered roughly one hundred courses per semester as it
had during the previous decade, up to 75 percent of these were now
taught by part-time adjuncts, and "we now have less than half the administrative staff and released time assigned to the supervision of
the program as we did in the past ten years" (2). Moreover, Norment
asserted that, again unlike the early '70s, there now was no orientation program, no regular means of training a new corps of teachers
or of formally studying the program, and little relationship to either
SEEK or the writing center. Significantly, an entrance test developed by the City University now determined a student's ability to
pass through the sequence; Norment noted that its use within a
program had never been fully studied.

Material changes like these fueled much hostile response to open admissions students, as the detractors of the policy often missed the crucial point that, in times of crisis, institutions, not just students, need remediation. Books like Louis Heller's *The Death of the American University* or Geoffrey Wagner's *The End of Education* are usually read as denunciations of the "new" students and nontraditional curriculums (e.g., Lu 1999). But these memoirs also document the angrily misplaced responses of humanities professors to the diminished status of their disciplines, a change that had immediate consequences upon teaching loads, rules for hiring and advancement, and the composition not only of the student body, but also of the faculty. Since even Wagner stresses that he opposed open admissions because there was no clear way to pay for it, another way to read such books is to locate them within the structural, not just the cultural, changes that the '70s ushered in. Clark Kerr lists eighteen books having titles similar to Heller's or Wagner's that were published by disaffected academics between 1968 and 1973 (164). One overlooked point is that humanists published these books in an era when both prestige and funding shifted toward the sciences and professional schools in the top tiers, while federal attention and some corporate largess began to focus on occupational education in the bottom tiers. At the same time, the majority of all states coordinated separate colleges into centralized, more sharply tiered, systems with consequences for both curriculum and faculty governance.

Unhappy professors like Heller or Wagner made the serious mistake of aligning open admissions with these changes, for they equated a change in standards with changes in the status of the humanities—symbolized by the numerical dominance of writing courses in most English departments by the mid-1970s. At City College, as I showed in chapter 2 and as Finnegan found in her case study research, by the 1970s English departments in struggling midlevel tiers had to redefine their mission to sustain enrollments. The downsizing of the English major and the subsequent emphasis upon basic skills programs and composition studies were institutional strategies for survival in a period of economic and cultural shift. Of course those shifts have received less attention than demographic ones, which serves to perpetuate the belief that students, not institutions, need writing courses.

Therefore, as we reassess Shaughnessy's legacy in the new century, we do well to consider her work within the broader context of institutional politics and structural change that I've been describing. She did not politicize language use; but she did politicize the use of remedial courses as the means of access to the liberal arts, and she problematized the notion of remediation as the primary means of access to traditional study. She understood that remediation is often used to solve institutional crisis and to manage conflicts between enrollment, mission, and curriculum. Her practical emphasis upon administering programs remains important because without it, we tend to locate reform of basic writing too exclusively within the individual classroom, and within curriculum. Shaughnessy, however, saw clearly that what also needed to be reformed were the conditions for teaching and learning that, if supported and enlarged, could in turn generate experiments with curriculum that might transform teachers and the institution, not just the students.

The long-term problem of open admissions, as Shaughnessy saw it, was to spread remediation through the curriculum rather than contain it within one threshold course. Such a policy, Shaughnessy suggested to an interviewer in October 1977, narrowed the responsibility for open access to "a cheap course" (Maher 211). "The institutions that want it both ways finally can't have it both ways; they either have to decide that they can [educate the students fully] or they can't," Shaughnessy flatly stated (211). In 1972, Shaughnessy wrote a twenty-five page memo to the City College administration that explains what she meant by trying to have it both ways, and it is well worth quoting at length:

> This concern for what came to be called "maintaining standards" pressed most directly on the remedial teachers of the college, who were charged with the task of transforming within a semester or two their "disadvantaged" students into students who behaved, in academic situations at least, like "advantaged" students. This, of course, was impossible. More seriously, it started things off in the wrong direction: *it narrowed the base of responsibility for Open Admissions students to the remedial programs,* giving "regular" departments an illu-

sion of immunity from change; it channeled most of the Open
Admissions money into remedial programs and into counseling that was aimed at helping sudents adjust to the college
world; but it provided no support for research into the learning problems of the new students (significantly, the only research so far to emerge from Open Admissions has been sta-
tistical reports on grades and drop-out rates); and it
encouraged remedial teachers, under pressure to produce im-
itations of the model "bright" students as quickly as possible,
to go on doing what writing teachers have too often done before—work prescriptively rather than inductively, removing
mistakes without trying to understand them. (Maher 121; my
emphasis)

If remediation was not institutionalized as a program equal in
status to others within an English department, then its role would
always be a purely initiatory one, unable to extend into and throughout the regular academic life of the college.

After the city's fiscal crisis of 1974, Shaughnessy's program and
other innovative programs like it dwindled in significance and were
never revived in their original form. A historical paradox arose at the
City University between the early 1980s and mid-1990s: as remediation became the symbolic point of struggle over open access, in
actuality it began to lose the institutional importance it had obtained
in the late 1960s. In chapter 4, I'll document more fully how remediation accumulated symbolic capital while it was losing institutional
clout. As one consequence of this emerging role, remediation
became widely viewed as "the" sole avenue into the liberal arts for
what are usually seen as "at-risk" minority students.

Shaughnessy was aware of this aspect of the politics of basic
skills, of how the burden for supporting open admissions could be
centered, unfairly, upon the shoulders of writing teachers. Much of
her work sought to complicate that responsibility, and to shift it
beyond the three-course sequence. When Alice Walker went looking
for Zora Neale Hurston, she found the powerful roots for identifying a tradition of black American women's writing. When I went to
look for Mina Shaughnessy, I found strong roots for identifying a

tradition of educational reform for working-class students. Shaughnessy's legacy calls attention to reforming basic writing's institutional role, and our own roles in maintaining the status quo. Her practice suggests that we must examine how in our roles as specialists who sometimes act as institutional agents, or as scholars who study institutional relationships, we use whatever authority and knowledge we have to contest the use of composition to sustain traditional selective functions. Shaughnessy's administrative legacy suggests to us now that reform does not consist exclusively of a critique of curriculum but of a struggle to improve the conditions for teaching and learning that shape the everyday experiences of both teachers and students. Her bureaucratic labors tell us that composition programs cannot be "reformed" without a better institutional understanding both of the complex, long-term role writing instruction plays in providing access to the university and of the ways in which outside forces determine the kinds of curriculums we can institutionalize.

4 | Representing Remediation: The Politics of Agency, 1985–2000

▶ IN CHAPTER 3, I NOTED THAT, SINCE THE LATE '80S, the politics of meaning have assumed center stage in composition studies. At the same time, by the end of the Reagan years, the politics of access were being debated in state legislatures, on governing boards, and in the mainstream press. In 1987, Joseph Trimmer wrote, "Each new issue of the *Chronicle for Higher Education* contains another story of the dismantling of developmental education. The debate focuses on the claims of excellence and access. Legislators argue that we must reform our educational system to produce a more competitive work force. But many express 'disdain for remedial programs at the college level, calling them wasteful and ineffective'" (4). As Trimmer surmised, debates about remediation reflected the central institutional crisis of the post–1960s era: managing the competing claims of access and excellence. To manage this institutional need, advocates of downsizing developed cultural arguments about remedial education, its students, and teachers. Another version of the discourse of student need justified the institutional need to restratify higher education.

One of these cultural arguments, the social collision between working-class remedial students and the traditional academy, explained why programs did not succeed. By shifting debates toward the cultural realm, advocates of downsizing focused attention on curriculum and standards. In composition studies, curriculum also became an important focus for reform as scholars examined how cultural conflict shaped writers' responses to traditional knowledge. When students' needs become central to explaining educational problems, social class difference can become synonymous with cultural difference. I make this distinction because class difference may point us to structural or material explanations for educational problems, while an emphasis upon the cultural, as I argued in chapter 3, is more appropriate for an analysis of individual students, teachers, or classrooms.

Outside the academy, critics of remediation waved the red flag of declining standards and literacy crisis to justify the need to downsize, privatize, and effectively restratify higher education. By blaming remedial programs for a constellation of educational woes, from budget crisis to low retention rates and falling standards, the critics of remediation practiced an effective politics of agency. They attributed problems that public higher education faced throughout the decade to students—in New York, to their inability to assimilate to mainstream cultures—and to the "expensive" programs designed to meet their "special" needs.

To resolve the friction between access and excellence in the post–'60s era institutions began to restratify, and in the process remediation became one yardstick for measuring the boundaries between tiers. In 1987, Burton Clark offered data to illustrate the stratification of disciplines with institutional mission. He argued that there are "'upward-tilting' and 'downward-tilting' fields in the professional matrix—areas of professorial and student commitment that weigh heavily in research universities at one extreme and in lesser four-year colleges and, especially, community colleges at the other" (44). For instance, biology, an upward-tilting field, constituted about 7 percent of all academics in 1984, but 12 percent of faculty in research universities. English, however, was a downward-tilting discipline, comprising 8 percent of all academics but only 3 percent in research universities, 12 percent in less selective four-year colleges, and 14 percent in the two-year sector (44). A downward-tilting discipline, English continued to perform its durable function as a "key subject" in distinguishing between various educational sectors (see chapter 2).

Below, I will present evidence that institutions began to restratify in the late '80s, and I will argue that the consequence of this trend was to align poorer students with vocational missions and down-ward-tilting disciplines. The process involved a variety of institutional strategies, ranging from restricting transfers between two-year and four-year schools to tightening admissions standards at public comprehensives. At the City University, which offers a specific case of this more global pattern, strategies included privatizing the costs of attending college and abolishing remediation at the four-year level.

Because the public does not always embrace the move to restrict access to public higher education, a literacy crisis—which of course depends on the discourse of student need—can help to justify the institutional decision to stratify by admissions, curriculum, and mission. Scholars show how attacks on the illiteracy of "American boys" in the 1890s or on Johnny's ability to write in the 1970s were not firmly based on empirical measurements of students' literacy.[1] Instead, these scholars view literacy crises as expressive of broader socioeconomic and cultural change. The literacy crisis of the late nineteenth century, for instance, expressed middle-class unease over the fluidity of educational boundaries. In the case of the Harvard Reports, the Overseers' virulent attacks on students' writing probably had less to do with the quality of students' prose and more with their wish to distinguish the proper subject matters for high school and college teachers. Similarly, Ira Shor argues that the literacy panic of the 1970s helped to depress the aspirations of working-class students and to regulate their entry into four-year schools (1986). One strategy to regulate class aspiration in the era of mass higher education is to differentiate more sharply between tiers, in this case between the four-year and the two-year colleges, and between public comprehensives and elite universities.

Unsurprisingly, in the struggle to gain the consent of different interest groups to restratify the City University in the 1990s, a conservative/neoliberal coalition of intellectuals, politicians, and journalists created a literacy crisis in New York City. This crisis, which spanned the years 1993 to 2000, was the chief ideological justification for the retiering of the nation's largest public urban system.

Though the events at the City University are probably unique in many respects, the use of literacy crisis to justify stratification reflects a broader historical tendency in American higher education. If, as John Trimbur argues, literacy crisis expresses class identity, then it makes sense that it also works to forge class coalitions, often between groups having different political interests. In New York, the literacy crisis strengthened the relationship between intellectuals of the university's past and conservative intellectuals of the present who are bent on downsizing the public sphere. In the process, as I will discuss again in chapter 5, the literacy crisis weakened a coalition between the organic intellectuals of the university's future and those of the past, mostly working-class Jewish intellectuals.

Barbara Ehrenreich shows that class struggle in the American cultural domain begins when middle-class opinionmakers who have access to the national media—journalists, pundits, public intellectuals, academics, politicians—"discover" that the "poor" are among us after all. Here I read James Traub's *City on a Hill* as a case in point. Traub's personally "shocking" discovery of remedial students at City College reflects the neoliberal intellectual's personal struggle to define his class identity in relation to "the other." Traub's book is essentially an argument to retier the open access system, but to make that argument, he focuses almost exclusively on the cultural deprivation of minorities who cannot assimilate to the system.

At the heart of the literacy crisis and Traub's book are cultural arguments that assign blame to students for the failure of both remedial programs and open access policies. This is a dangerous tendency in representations of students that threads through even progressive composition scholarship concerned to reform a basic skills curriculum. For in some scholarship as in Traub's book—though, of course, with sharply divergent political intentions—cultural explanations shift analysis away from institutional needs and tend to downplay those material factors that affect students' ability to stay in school over the long term. In the composition scholarship that I examine, agency is not ascribed to structural causes but to cultural ones. In part this happens when intellectuals assume that *working class* is synonymous with *underclass*, a category for analysis that tends to fuse the economic with the cultural and to highlight student need rather than the institutional need to manage the conflicting aims of access and excellence.

What often emerged in writing about remediation in the 1990s was the figure of the culturally shocked student who is trapped in a chaotic urban world. A particular kind of underclass experience becomes equivalent to social class difference in these representations, which says more about an intellectual's distance from the city of today than it does about a student's ability to "cope with" an alien academic culture. Rather than turn to the kind of structural analysis that I offer at the beginning of the chapter—the privatization and retiering of institutions—this cultural analysis tends to portray social class as a set of academically dysfunctional behaviors that cannot really coexist with those habits of mind necessary to succeed in college. To counter these representations, I analyze long-term studies that emphasize the role that material and institutional factors play in the ability of working-class students to stay in school and earn their B.A. degrees.

What is at stake in the struggle to represent remediation is a broader effort to imagine the middle-class sense of responsibility toward the "other" classes through the institution that now most defines a middle-class identity. In this regard, some writing about remediation produced over the last decade probably reflects how aging intellectuals are also redefining their relationship to the Great Society programs of the '60s. The politics of remediation involve working out our responsibility to public institutions and the constituencies they serve. Professionally, these politics matter because they affect our sense of agency as educators—what we decide constitutes a worthy focus of reform. I will conclude by describing the kinds of research that may help us to redefine agency, leaving curriculum reform—how nontraditional students assimilate traditional knowledge—for the last chapter.

Curricular and Economic Stratification, 1980–2000

Over the past two decades, remediation's changing status accompanied broader institutional and socioeconomic shifts within higher education. Before I examine how remediation is represented, I want to spend time discussing those national efforts to restratify higher education that will align certain student bodies with certain kinds of curriculum, mission, and admissions policies. Using CUNY as a local case of these national trends, my goal is to link a stratification management strategy that alters the material conditions for learning to remediation's cultural status in the university.

One clear sign of retiering on the national level was the transinstitutional move to reassess the worth of remedial education in four-year systems. In the '80s and '90s, several systems moved basic skills—at least *officially*—out of their top tiers and into the midlevel or lowest rungs of the institutional ladder. By the mid-1990s, the status of remediation in four-year institutions was debated from coast to coast, prompting fresh surveys of remediation, for example Linda Knopp's for the American Council on Education (1995) or the Institute for Higher Education Policy's report, *College Remediation* (1998). In most accounts, researchers cited declining standards, poor retention rates, and the expense of special programs as the crises that incited institutions to adopt various strategies of differentiation.

Overall, institutional strategies aimed to demarcate and close the borders between programs within an institution or between institutions serving different populations. For instance, along with proposals to toughen admissions standards in selected tiers in Alabama, Louisiana, and Missouri's systems, new top tiers, usually in the form of "honors colleges," have been proposed for CUNY and the University of Massachusetts at Amherst. Between 1990 and 2000, there were proposals to shift remedial courses from four-year to two-year colleges in New York, California, Illinois, Virginia, Texas, and Arkansas. (California had by 1991 shifted remediation out of its top tier to its middle levels.) There were plans to move remediation to adjunct tiers, such as summer programs, or to "outsource" it in Mississippi, Arizona, and New York; and to establish time constraints or attach fiscal penalties to remediation in Florida, New Jersey, and Massachusetts.[2]

Throughout this period, administrators and trustees frequently announced their desire to abolish remedial education in liberal arts schools, usually by shifting it toward two-year colleges. In 1993, the

Boston Globe reported that Chancellor Stanley Z. Koplik wanted to reduce remedial courses in the University of Massachusetts system; these students "would do far better to get their feet planted at a community college" first (Dembner 1993b, 1:24). Two years later, Marian Bagdasarian, a trustee for the California State University, told the *San Francisco Chronicle* that remedial classes "belong in the community colleges" (Wildavsky 1995a, A:11). Trustee Pesqueira, much like his counterpart Herman Badillo on the CUNY Board of Trustees, "advocates sending many of the growing number of freshmen who need remedial instruction to community colleges until they can show that they are ready to do college-level work" (Lively 1995, A:1).

Especially in research institutions, remediation is often offered under the auspices of writing centers or equal opportunity programs. In this case, the abolition of affirmative action in some states has also included the abolition of remediation—and the stratification of large systems by race as well as by curriculum and mission. California enacted Proposition 209 in 1995, and Washington State passed Initiative I-200 three years later, which abolished affirmative action policies in these tiered systems. Evidence is now emerging to suggest that the loss of these programs results in the tiering of state systems by race as well as by curriculum. I will discuss Washington later on, but here note that since 1995, a steady stream of reports has warned that in California, black and Latino students are enrolling in larger numbers in the less prestigious tiers of the system, which still offer remedial courses, while whites and Asian Americans cluster in the UC schools, where remediation was abolished in 1991. Writing soon after the California proposition was passed by popular vote, Tom Hayden and Connie Rice argued, "The new policy threatens to create a two-tier segregated campus system" (264). In his scrutiny of the data two years later, Terry Jones concluded, "the more selective the institution, the more dramatic the decline in minority enrollments" (25). And in 1999 the *L.A. Times* reported that "Statewide, blacks are less than half as likely as whites to transfer from a community college to a UC campus, and less than one-fifth as likely as Asians"; while 7,300 whites and Asians moved from two-year to four-year colleges in 1998, only 293 black community college students did so.[3]

In the '90s, the role that remediation played in stratifying systems was complex because increasingly it was aligned with, but never exclusively connected to, class and race difference, and to institutional status. Statistics about the amount of remediation offered are conflicting, owing in part to methodological problems (see note 5). Knopp's analysis of all undergraduates who said they took a remedial course in 1992–1993 reveals two possible trends. The first is that the majority of students who took remedial courses in this cohort were white, and the majority enrolled in remedial mathematics. Nevertheless, the student most likely to take at least one remedial course—again, the majority in mathematics—attends a public two-year college and is a low-income student of color or student born outside the U.S. Some students at most institutions need remediation, but particular groups who are clustering in low-status public institutions are most likely to be required to enroll first in math, writing, and reading courses that are *officially* designated remedial. And since 82 percent of all minority students attended public institutions in the '90s, 47 percent of them at two-year colleges that almost universally offer remediation (Walters), remedial education may be aligned with minorities enrolled in the vocationally oriented sector.

The tiering of higher education through "downward-tilting disciplines" reveals that the backlash on remediation that began to gain force in the late '80s doesn't culminate in its abolition, but in its increasing alignment with low-status tiers in systems that are more densely differentiated than ever before. As that shift occurs, institutions in the middle that shed their remedial programs may also tighten their admissions standards. A struggle over admissions in a state like Missouri, "observers say," reflects "a national trend of public colleges and universities toughening their standards, bringing them closer to those of private institutions" (Thomson 1992a).

This shifting is especially significant because the last two decades may also have seen a trend in aligning working-class and lower–middle class student bodies with the bottom and midlevel tiers. The well-known widening of the gap between rich and poor affected higher education, and through the Reagan-Bush years, it intensified the class stratification between institutions in terms of the groups of students that they serve. Equally important is that these trends didn't reverse themselves during the Clinton administration, when New Democrats frequently joined with conservatives to denounce "social promotion" and to propose increased testing to regulate the mobility between tiers. I will discuss the neoliberal attitude toward open access in further detail below, when I consider James Traub's critique of remediation.

In chapter 2, I cited Clark Kerr to the effect that the social class background of students didn't change dramatically between 1960 and 1980. From the late '80s and into the 1990s, there was further evidence that the pattern Kerr identified will only intensify. There are trends in postsecondary funding that in the twenty-first century may move substantial numbers of lower–middle class and working-class students toward the two-year college or out of higher education all together. Since in the '90s the international student population increased by 45 percent in all institutions and in half of all four-year schools, it appears that our classrooms are becoming more culturally diverse (Washington 41). However, this linguistic or geographical diversity does not include a diversity in students' social class background, for while the numbers of middle- and upper-income college students have increased, and continue to grow dramatically according to some estimates since the 1970s, the number of low-income students (about 35 percent of the whole) actually decreased in the 1990s (*The Condition of Education*; also see Roy).

In the new century, a college or university degree will become increasingly difficult for even middle-class students to attain. It is this material anxiety, I believe, that partly fuels the attack on remediation as middle class intellectuals feel the need to freshly assert the cultural value of a college degree. If, after all, remediation is viewed as one barometer of institutional exclusivity, then those middle-class parents who send their students to midlevel institutions—which is to say, most parents—want an exchange value for the degree they are going increasingly into debt to finance.

There is strong evidence that, between the late '80s and 1995, these parents did struggle to finance their children's education. Patrick Callan notes that the 1980s saw a steep decline in the federal commitment toward the funding of higher education, for example in the shift away from grants toward student loans. "[T]he 1980s were a lost decade for federal leadership for institutional progress in equal opportunity at all levels of education" because in those years the states assumed the burden of funding expensive social programs (9). Between 1981 and 1986, federal aid to public universities declined 14 percent in constant dollars, while in the early 1990s, thirty states cut their higher education budgets, affecting two-thirds of all public institutions (Benjamin, 54; Nazario).

To cope with cuts as their states managed competing responsibilities such as health care and "corrections," public institutions as well as private ones shifted the burden to students, so that a substantial part of the costs for higher education was privatized. Along with budget cuts, skyrocketing tuition characterized the 1980s and early to mid-1990s. In 1994, the average tuition rate at four-year public institutions rose 6 percent, or twice the rate of inflation (Graham). When compared to state appropriations for public higher education, the rate of increase in tuition increased by 30 percent between 1980 and 1987 (Callan 12). During the early '90s, the tuition rates rose in forty states at a rate faster than personal income, so that where a family used to spend about 12.1 percent of its median income for education, in 1995, it could expect to spend 15.9 percent for public education, and a staggering 39.9 percent for private education (Lauter 76). To restate the case, "with current trends," a student who attends a public university may expect to pay up to $75,000 for a degree, while one attending an elite private school can expect to pay up to $200,000 (Rubin).

Privatizing the costs of higher education may play a role in differentiating it along class and race lines for the new century. While the number of minorities in two-year colleges increased 13.4 percent in 1990–91, there was an unequal 5.9 percent increase in their presence in four-year schools during the same years (Rubin). Along with rising tuitions, there was also a trend toward eroding need-based aid for middle-class and low-income students at the nation's most elite private schools. Student protests in the early 1990s at Brown, Wesleyan, Smith, and Columbia involved their universities' quiet move away from providing need-based aid. These schools were breaking a "long-taboo policy of considering a potential student's wealth when choosing its freshman class" (Jordan). Because of "an increasing flight of middle-class students" from expensive private institutions, "the nation's elite schools appear to be returning to their earlier 20th century days as bastions of the rich" (Jordan; and see "Ability to Pay"). A UCLA study of enrollment at twenty-five of the nation's most selective schools showed that between 1989 and 1992, the percentage of students from families earning $100,000 rose from 31 percent to 37 percent—this is 37 percent of 5 percent of families in the U.S. Since 1988, students from families earning $150,000 rose from 17 percent to 22 percent at schools such as Harvard, Princeton, Tufts, Brown, Cornell, Duke, and Georgetown. At the same time, students from families earning less than $30,000 declined from 13 to 12.4 percent at these schools (Jordan).

In sum, these trends indicate that, as schools raise tuition, tighten admissions, downsize or abolish remediation and equal opportunity programs, they also solidify or even change their missions. According to Dale Parnell, president of the American Association of Community and Junior Colleges in 1989, two-thirds of community college students were on academic tracks twenty-five years ago, and one-third on vocational tracks. "Today, the figures have reversed" (Vobejda A16:1). As *Washington Post* reporter Barbara Vobejda concludes, a "highly stratified" system of higher education is emerging, "[a]nd the dividing lines may be sharpening." No wonder that the Council for Aid to Education argued in January 1995 that "The United States must overhaul its system of funding higher education or face growing stratification along class lines and expanding emphasis on remedial work." Its report for that year warned "continuation of these trends will lead to intensified clustering of rich students in more expensive institutions and poor students in vocational and community colleges" (Dembner 1995a).

Stratification is a strategic management tool that institutions use to respond to crises in growth. Strategies include privatizing the costs of education, tightening admissions, and downsizing selected tiers. Remediation's shifting attachment to various segments plays one powerful role in this complex process. The downward movement of remedial education reflects a parallel movement of students by class, ethnic, and racial background. In this way, stratification through curriculum resolves the clash between democratic access and selective excellence that has been a defining feature of the post–'60s era in higher education.

Restratifying Urban Education, 1990–2000

The specific fate of remediation at the City University of New York between 1990 and 2000 powerfully illustrates the general argument that the architects of stratification can use remediation as a potent symbol of the need to downsize systems by restricting access to specific tiers. In New York, defenders of access to the municipal system focused on its privatization and defunding, while its critics successfully turned the debate toward the size and expense of its remedial efforts. The crisis over access and excellence gradually centered on curriculum, standards, and students' cultural distance from the academy. To justify downsizing, critics practiced a politics of agency: remedial programs were the source of CUNY's woes, not economic or structural shifts.

Unsurprisingly, the politics of agency served to highlight student need and in so doing glossed over the privatization of the university. Yet this shift in funding has drastically curtailed the quality and autonomy of remedial programs more than any other factor in the post–Shaughnessy era of writing programs (see chapter 3). On one level, privatization involves shifting the burden for funding a public college from the taxpayers to students and their families. The City University Faculty Senate, drawing upon data compiled by the RAND Corporation and PricewaterhouseCoopers, noted that the university's tuition increased 93 percent between 1988 and 1997. Meanwhile, New York State's appropriation for the university in constant dollars has decreased 40 percent since 1980, while in 1997, the city's contribution decreased from 19 percent to 6 percent (*CUNY Affirmed* 4).

To compensate for this shortfall, the university has consistently been forced to raise tuition, increase class size, cut electives and specialized programs, and rely more heavily upon adjunct faculty to teach general education courses. The latter practice enables full-time faculty to cultivate the research that will distinguish the top tiers and attract federal and corporate funding. As I noted in chapter 3, the conflict that arose in the early '70s between research and teaching has not been resolved for public comprehensives. This conflict constitutes a dilemma for basic skills programs that demand intensive labor but which do not attract selective funding, let alone the commitment of a full-time faculty that receives rewards for research.

The privatization that affects students' ability to stay in school over the long term takes other forms as well. When the university began charging tuition in 1974, the state of New York created the Tuition Assistance Program (TAP) and the Supplemental Tuition Assistance Program (STAP), which could be used to pay for required remedial coursework. In 1995, the state legislature abolished STAP and later expanded the definition of remediation to include courses in English as a Second Language. STAP and TAP play a crucial role in students' ability to stay in school because the federal government's assistance to working-class students has steadily declined, even as the cost of living in New York City has spiraled upwards during the years of the bull market on Wall Street. The federal shift away from grants and toward loans along with its cutbacks in direct aid to public higher education began in the mid-1970s. As *New York Times* columnist Frank Rich commented, "Ask G.O.P. leaders how universities will replace Federal funding, and the mantra-like answer is 'privatization.'"

Despite this drastic defunding of the largest urban public university in the country, in 1999 the struggle over remediation assumed center stage in public discourse. For example, the mayor of New York City wished to "outsource" remedial courses by shifting them to private institutions or educational companies. To gain support for his position, in 1998 the mayor created an Advisory Task Force on CUNY chaired by Benno Schmidt, president of the Edison Project, which—perhaps not coincidentally—operates for-profit schools that in 2001 sought contracts in the city's low-income neighborhoods. In June 1999, this task force published *CUNY: An Institution Adrift*, a 109-page report with lengthy, separate appendices, two of which I referred to above (RAND and PricewaterhouseCoopers), and one on remediation that I described in chapter 1. Rather than analyze the data contained in its own appendices, however, the mayor's task force focused in its main report upon remediation as the source of CUNY's allegedly low graduation rates and declining standards.

Listing remediation as the first cause of the university's overall decline, the task force assumed that access is synonymous with remediation. The CUNY Faculty Senate noted that "the report focuses on remediation to the exclusion of all other academic programs and activities of CUNY" (*CUNY Affirmed* 5). As the Schmidt Report melodramatically put its case: "the Task Force has been shocked by both the scale and the depth of CUNY students' remediation needs" (21). Not unexpectedly, the task force recommended privatizing remediation at CUNY and radically altering admissions standards to create a tiered system resembling California's.

Tying open access to remediation in this way, the task force could argue that CUNY's budget problems are less important than the failure of its remedial programs. CUNY should view budget cuts as an "opportunity" to abolish remediation, according to the *New York Post*: "As things stand, CUNY is failing—and not because it doesn't have enough funds or top-flight faculty members or first-rate facilities. The problem turns on the readiness of CUNY's administrators to accept the bizarre notion that lack of preparation for college-level work shouldn't deter students from enrolling in the City University's senior colleges or even from receiving a CUNY degree. Thus, a huge proportion of the university budget is devoted not to college-level teaching but to remediation" ("CUNY's Opportunity"). CUNY devoted roughly 2.5 percent of its budget to remediation, and remediation never occupied more than 10 percent of its whole curriculum. And, of course, these courses have prepared thousands of students to take college-level courses in freshman composition and advanced algebra. But data do not always matter in ideological debate. Even Nathan Glazer—who believes that "the huge remedial enterprise . . . engrosses much of "City College's "resources"— noted that the task force coolly ignored the data produced by the independent accounting bodies it commissioned (1994, 38; and 1999). Since 1970, remediation has increasingly assumed the symbolic burden for sustaining access to the university, with the result that CUNY's severe financial deprivation since the mid-1970s cannot assume an equal ideological clout in public debate.

The Schmidt Report also paved the way for a new master plan that will retier the system. Adopted by CUNY's Board of Trustees in spring 2000 and by New York State's Board of Regents the following autumn (e.g., Arenson 2000), the master plan abolished remediation in the senior colleges, created flagship campuses, and established two new tiers. These new tiers are an exclusive, and widely publicized, "honors" college, and a submerged, unacknowledged tier composed of remedial summer programs, adult and continuing education, and language institutes. In the view of the CUNY Faculty Senate, the master plan "furthers the corporatization and privatization agenda of the CUNY Board of Trustees and, additionally, fails to provide a vision for undergraduate liberal arts and sciences education" ("Despite Faculty Protest" 1).

Those who oppose this plan believe that the campuses that serve students with higher incomes will highlight a traditional liberal arts education, while those serving a lower-income population will be designated as technical and/or professional campuses. In the *Chronicle of Higher Education*, Patrick Healy reported that over the last two decades at City College, "humanities and multicultural courses expanded, remediation became a bigger problem, and the college shouldered budget cuts and tuition increases" (A25). CUNY's new chancellor wants to fund professional and technical programs in the 2000s, "reallocating resources and restoring priorities" (A25). It's not unusual that Healy aligns remediation with budget crisis; what's more striking is that he parallels both with the humanities, a linchpin of the traditional liberal arts in elite colleges. The faculty senate reported that after he read the new master plan, CUNY Trustee Michael Crimmins "said at a public meeting that it made him think that CUNY 'was a trade school for the computer age rather than a university'" ("Despite" 4).

Mina Shaughnessy's attitude toward the institutionalization of remedial programs, which I discussed in chapter 3, acquires urgency in this context where remediation is ideologically paired with more vocationally oriented curriculums. To deal with the privatization of the public university—to manage the crisis in growth—administrators and trustees seek to stratify the system. The struggle over access and excellence that has been waged over the past thirty years around remediation, and especially through the downward-tilting discipline of English, will be temporarily resolved. Remediation won't disappear but will reappear in new places, in new guises, and under new management.

The Ideological Functions of Literacy Crisis

To gain consent for their master plan, coalitions in New York aroused anxiety by fomenting a literacy crisis. Generally speaking, one ideological function of American literacy crisis is to justify the educational stratification I have been describing. To persuade the public who gets what kind of education, the authors of crisis also have to blame someone for the decline of skills. For that reason, a literacy crisis will assign agency to particular groups, programs, and institutions, or even to social attitudes. In New York City, stratification was justified by blaming students, the open access policies of the '60s, and remedial programs for the problems of public higher education. Ultimately, a focus on CUNY students' cultural differences as a chief source of problems enabled detractors to avoid discussing the defunding and privatization that have affected so many institutions like CUNY over the last three decades. The literacy crisis involved a struggle over material goods, but critics of CUNY shifted debate from the economic to the cultural realms. This shift always brings an argument neatly back to students' needs. We can therefore predict that, as I argued in chapter 2, critics will also argue that standards don't change, only students' abilities do. Therefore, literacy crisis is always-new.

In part, ideological debate over remediation ensued when middle-class intellectuals reevaluated the conflict surrounding what has become the most prominent means of fostering upward mobility in American society. As Barbara Ehrenreich observes, since the American professional middle classes have no significant capital to bequeath to their children, we can only reproduce ourselves by ensuring the value of a college degree that we prepare our children to compete for and earn. One time-tested means of provoking debate about standards and values in education—and to push for greater differentiation between tiers—is to foment a literacy crisis. Before the literacy crisis of the mid-1970s, the most virulent outbreak occurred in the last decade of the nineteenth century in the wake of the Harvard Reports, a moment when, as I discussed in chapter 2, the American university was struggling to distinguish itself from the public school beneath it.

If the Harvard Reports used literacy as one means to differentiate the college from high school through the curriculums of literature and composition, in the 1970s the literacy crisis widely discussed in the mainstream press served a similar purpose—to distinguish between a more densely tiered system of higher education. As I noted earlier, Ira Shor shows how the culture wars of the 1970s and early 1980s were largely about regulating or "cooling-out" the aspirations for more schooling stoked by the expansive days of the '60s. "The classroom, the workplace, the job market, all became stations for diminished expectations," Shor writes. "Austerity eased itself in through the claims of illiteracy in students and the spectacle of economic exhaustion in society at large" (96). One way to contain those aspirations was to limit entry to the top tiers of liberal arts schools while making the bottom and midlevel tiers more affordable and attractive. Shor shows that federal and corporate largesse directed selectively toward the two-year level, along with an intense media campaign focusing on the virtues of occupational education, helped to make the junior college the focal point of expansion and growth in a decade marked by downsizing in other sectors and national economic recession.

Shor's reading of the '70s crisis is particularly instructive when examining the most recent crisis in the 1990s that surrounded students' literacy at the City University. Though confined to the city, this crisis often spilled into the national press, given New York's role in the media market and the presence of City College alumni who write for the national press. More than any other factor, this crisis prepared the ideological context for the master plan I've just described because it effectively blamed students' cultural deprivation for low retention rates rather than discussing the defunding of the university. For example, several city newspapers had a field day with a scandal surrounding students' failure rates on the university's writ-ing assessment test at Hostos Community College, a bilingual insti-tution (see Gleason). Along with Traub's book, these and other inci-dents concerning students' literacy helped to provoke and sustain the larger crisis over remediation, which culminated in the Schmidt Report, authored by the mayor's advisory task force in 1999 and publicized in virtually every media outlet in the city.[4]

But right-wing intellectuals cannot secure the agreement of their audience without tapping into an anxiety that may already exist—it is the job of ideology to gain a broad consensus. In a thoughtful analysis of the literacy crisis of the mid-1970s, John Trimbur describes how commentators expressed uneasiness less about students' actual writing skills and more about the use of literacy as a marker of dis-tinction: good literacy skills imply a good institution and thus the more powerful exchange value of a college degree. He comments of Merrill Sheils's famous "Why Johnny Can't Write" essay in the mid-1970s, "Lurking just below the surface of Sheils's scenario, however, more powerful because it is not articulated explicitly, is the ongoing crisis of the middle class, the threat of downward mobility to baby boomers and their children as the bubble of postwar prosperity and American global hegemony burst in the 1970s" (278). In the case of New York's literacy crisis, the class consciousness expressed in de-pictions of remedial students reflects a similar crisis of class identity in terms of our responsibility toward the urban poor. Like debates about funding for welfare, the ideological energy spent probably outweighed the actual amounts ever spent on funding the programs. But remediation achieved salience in popular accounts because uni-versal access to higher education does pose a threat to class exclusiv-ity. And since the professional middle class increasingly depends upon education to attain its exclusivity—a phenomenon of the '60s—then we might expect culture wars to swirl around literacy as a marker of that distinction. For this reason, so much ideological debate about remediation involves a critique of the '60s that began to gain adherents from the neoliberal center and that culminated, among other things, in changes to welfare and other Great Society programs.

Predictably, the call to abolish remediation gained strength from the myth of transience—the belief that remediation had never existed before the '60s because it was a creation of a permissive decade that tolerated illiteracy. The literacy crisis is itself always-new, the direct result of expanded access to four-year colleges for minorities. For this reason, it's important to ascertain exactly who needed remediation over the past thirty years. In their empirical studies, David Lavin, Richard Alba, and Richard Silberstein complicate this question, for they remind readers that "the majority of students who attended college [nationally] as a result of expanded access were whites" (230). In the case of CUNY, Lavin et al. further note that substantial numbers of open admissions students were whites. According to one national survey they discuss, 78 percent of all four-year colleges by the mid-1970s offered some type of remediation (230). Again reflecting these national trends, 44 percent of all students at CUNY's senior colleges in 1970 required some form of remediation in writing, reading, or math (234). While "Regular students [at CUNY] were far less likely than open-admissions students to need remediation," even so, 30 percent admitted under pre–open admissions criteria did require remediation in one area (234). That number reflects the "ill-prepared" who, as I described in chapter 2, took remedial courses between 1914 and 1955. "Paradoxically," these researchers conclude, "many of those who were not, formally speaking, beneficiaries of open admissions became eligible for support services that were primarily intended for others" (237).

Minority students at the City University required more remediation than whites, and they benefited from revised admissions standards, but large numbers of white students also required remediation—both those who took advantage of open access and those who were admitted to CUNY under pre–open access standards (which had been quite selective). Indeed, while minority students at the City University in the late '90s required more remediation than whites, a significant 38 percent of white students failed one of the three skills tests all students had to take (Staples). At the California State University, 68 percent of entering freshmen—who graduate with B averages in the top one-third of their high school class—failed at least one of the university's entrance exams in 1998. While 74 percent of the black students and 65 percent of the Latinos required remediation in math, 40 percent of the white students did so as well; 29 percent of the latter failed the test in English composition, compared to more than half of the black and Latino students (Selingo). These are not unusual numbers given the historical struggle over the persistent need for college composition across institutions that I cited in chapter 2. Surveys confirm that, while minorities are the most likely to be required to enroll in remedial courses, students at all types of institutions take them. Estimates on the numbers of institutions that offered remediation in the '90s range from 40 to 81 percent.[5]

I dwell on those white and/or middle-class students who failed basic skills tests in four-year colleges because they are so often absent in a discourse that assumes that remediation is always-new because literacy crises are new. In this argument, the '60s was a watershed decade because this is when open access policies, remediation, and diversity programs were established to placate minorities and to serve their singular needs. Gail Stygall quotes a 1998 article from the *Seattle Times* that describes the origins of the University of Washington's affirmative action program. Marsha King, the journalist, writes: "One afternoon in May 1968, members of the University of Washington's newly formed Black Student Union (BSU) marched into the office of their school's president and demanded, among other things, that the UW admit more minority students. President Charles Odegaard and faculty leaders pledged to address the concerns" (13–14). In a close reading of university documents, Stygall argues that, though Initiative I-200 focused on affirmative action, the university administration and a coalition of community leaders also sought to downsize general education courses, mainly by shifting the first two years of work toward the system's lowest tiers. She concludes that the assault on affirmative action was also an effort to retier the system along curricular lines. In this case, ideological arguments about affirmative action were used to justify stratification of the system.

Journalists similarly foreground the black and Puerto Rican student takeover of the City College of New York when they describe the university's decision to revise admissions standards in 1969. "CUNY's transformation began with a violent student strike in April 1969," announces Heather Mac Donald (11; and 1995). "In the

mid-'60's," syndicated columnist John Leo opines, "CUNY insti-
tuted the nation's first affirmative action program for minority students, but racial disturbances and a violent takeover of one campus
by black and Puerto Rican students upped the ante"(20). "The transformation of City College from the 'Harvard of the poor' into a
place where most students are incapable of doing genuine college-
level work is a consequence of the open-admissions decisions made
under duress in the late 1960s," intones *The New York Post* ("CUNY's
Opportunity").

When journalists from Washington to New York portray open
access as the exclusive result of political "violence," they provide evidence that remediation is always-new—the direct consequence of
affirmative action. Such attacks are consciously orchestrated by specific groups who share the bedrock belief that only the "smartest"
white students "earned" their educations before the "takeovers" of
the late '60s. As Mac Donald puts the case, in the '60s, "It was no
longer enough for a college merely to educate; universities were
called upon to enfranchise minority groups through admissions and
curricular changes. Few universities were as profoundly affected by
this shift in expectations as CUNY" (10). This history awards considerable agency to black students, which of course aligns remediation with students' needs rather than with institutional exigency.
This is not to say that civil rights initiatives and student groups did-
n't apply pressure upon institutions to respond to their constituencies. But these journalists award agency almost exclusively to student takeover without considering what institutions might have
gained in the process. From this perspective, basic skills programs
are a "gift" to minorities.

Institutions didn't develop open access policies exclusively in response to "minority pressures," but to a constellation of pressures
involving how they would manage their growth in the postwar
world that saw the increased value of a college degree, an exploding
birth rate, and heightened differentiation between sectors of higher
education. In his history of the two-year college, Kevin Dougherty
shows how multiple, and sometimes contradictory, coalitions and
constituencies were involved in open access movements at the local,
state, and national levels. The City University's decision to adopt an

open access policy further illustrates how, in times of social change, institutions adopt new standards as a management strategy. In 1973, a group of radical City University professors, the Newt Davis Collective, produced a lengthy monograph that documents how Governor Rockefeller's investment in the fledgling State University of New York system sparked an enormous struggle with New York City's ethnic groups. According to Newt Davis, Rockefeller used free tuition and expanded access at the municipal colleges as a political wedge issue throughout the late '50s and early '60s. The 1969 plan, as I noted in chapter 3, was complicated both by institutional need and by citywide struggles to improve the life chances of its ethnic working classes. Joshua Freeman argues that it was the political pressure from white working-class coalitions that tipped the balance in favor of open access, and that helped to ensure open access took the form that it eventually did.

If we consider what institutions need to survive and grow, we can also see that open access movements don't just involve the "needs" of new students. These movements also concern how institutions mediate broader demographic and economic shifts. In New York, the move toward expanded access was already occurring as a result of demographic changes and the broader use of a college degree within the city. For instance, demography alone would have affected the university's enrollments. The flight of whites to Westchester and New Jersey, the end of quotas for Jewish students at private colleges, the creation of SUNY, and the 1965 Immigration Act, which opened the doors to non-European immigrants, redefined the constituency to which the City University would have to respond if it wished to expand enrollments—or even to survive in a changing urban landscape. Accompanying these demographic changes and political conflicts, of course, was a shift in the postwar urban economy away from manufacturing and toward the financial and service sectors, which gave a college degree a heightened exchange value within the metropolitan area.

By focusing exclusively on students' extraordinary needs, critics deftly tie illiteracy to "new students," glossing over that quarter to a third of "regular" students who might also be similarly classified. In the era of diversity rhetoric, this illiteracy can also be viewed as an expression of minority students' estrangement from mainstream intellectual languages or cultures. Bruce Horner and Min-Zhan Lu have shown, for instance, how discourse in the late '60s and early '70s juxtaposed the apolitical immigrant of the past against the politicized, ill-prepared minority student of the open admissions era. This well-prepared Jewish student is still fondly invoked by some members of the CUNY Board of Trustees (e.g., see Arenson 1997) and by distinguished alumni (Healy). What's significant about these ideological memories is that, as I'll discuss again in chapter 5, they prevent coalition-building between the organic intellectuals of today and those of the past.[6]

The oppositions that Horner and Lu identify focus debates about remediation upon cultural, rather than economic, difference. For a right-wing intellectual like Mac Donald, CUNY students are illiterate representatives of an oppressed urban underclass that emerged as a consequence of the Great Society programs of the '60s. In her discourse, the city's huge working class simply disappears. But the loss of class is problematic because without it, writers can attribute educational success or failure to a student's conflicted relationship to mainstream intellectual cultures. This was the central ideological function of New York City's literacy crisis: to assign agency to students' cultural affiliations and thus to avoid more stringent class and economic analyses. If underclass students are adrift in school, then it is because of cultural, not social class, differences, for in the American dream, college is available and affordable for those who really want it.

The Discourse of Student Need and the Neoliberal Intellectual

We might expect right-wing attacks on urban students' literacy to take virulent forms; but what began shaping up in the late '70s and climaxing with Clinton's first presidency was an emergent neoliberal voice. In the literacy crisis of the '90s no voice was more soothing, and more persuasive, than that of the self-described liberal, James Traub. Warmly received by the mainstream press, Traub's book, *City on a Hill,* was named a New York Times Notable Book of the Year, and its author was accorded the instant status of an "expert" on the City University during these years of literacy crisis (he had just published one chapter about a remedial reading class in the *New Yorker*).

Traub's book is significant for composition scholars to consider because it's an instance of why representation matters: stoking the smoldering fires of a literacy crisis, it provided ideological argument to coalitions bent on downsizing the public sphere. In part, the book's influence, in New York at least, resulted from Traub's ability to articulate for a liberal audience the discontent one segment of the aging post-'60s generation experiences as it reformulates its sense of responsibility toward the urban working classes. *City on a Hill* is a primer for the politics of agency because Traub puts the blame for educational failure squarely upon the shoulders of culturally deprived students.

The basic argument to emerge from Traub's book is that open access doesn't succeed because remediation fails. Remediation fails because it can't hope to erase students' cultural, not just their academic, deficits. As Traub observes remedial and elective courses, he discovers two distinct institutions, "the college of the remedial *Inferno* and the college of . . . [the] *Paradiso*" (303). While remedial courses are often not meaningfully connected to elective courses, Traub finds that this is so because two groups of students populate them. Travelling from the "submarine" depths of remedial courses to the "rarefied" atmosphere of the traditional liberal arts, Traub dramatically discovers that the curriculum reflects an "ethnic hierarchy" created by the students' achievements and cultural attitudes (323; 109). Unsurprisingly, these attitudes correlate roughly with the binary oppositions that Bruce Horner describes. Apolitical, hardworking white students who desire to assimilate into mainstream culture are aligned against remedial black students, a slack work ethic, inner-city culture, ethnic studies courses, and remediation.

Ethnic stratification, Traub argues, naturally restores the meritocratic order that the institution's policies deny. The top of Traub's hierarchy is peopled by the immigrant students, most of whom are foreign-born and/or Asian; the black students who represent "the [top of the] hierarchy of black achievement" are usually Caribbean, and they succeed partly because they are the products of colonial schooling—the "lycée, where students expected to bend beneath the whip" (257; 246). Although the "elite" students bring with them a "solid . . . secondary school education," it is their cultural attitudes that ensure their slots in the hierarchy (13). Unlike their forebears, today's immigrants don't value education for education's sake—sadly, they are vocationally oriented—but they do possess "immigrant drive and first-generation values" (13). They are usually "apolitical," "well dressed, respectful, good natured" (17; 181). Above all, like the Jewish "greenhorns" of the past, the good immigrant student of today accepts the "virtues of acculturation and assimilation . . . almost without question" (84; see 41).

By contrast, the bottom of Traub's ethnic hierarchy is peopled by an inarticulate mass of students, overwhelmingly African American and Latino, marred by poverty and native born. They crowd the remedial writing courses, study skills courses, and Black Studies, where, borrowing a metaphor from a teacher to describe the unhygienic nature of the remedial project, "the shit flowed differently" (166). Rather than bending to the whip of colonial education, these students have been "shaped by the inner-city culture" (91) fostered by the notoriously permissive New York City schools. These students lack motivation—several are, Traub judges, seriously depressed—and are "barely socialized to school" (96). "[V]irtually illiterate" (153), they tend to dress exotically, favoring sculpted hair, Afrocentric robes, or bizarrely painted fingernails.

The new students inhabit the bottom of the hierarchy partly because they bring serious "academic handicaps" to college (207). But crucial as these "cognitive deficits" are to their failure, more important is these students' resistance to assimilation in behavior, style, and thought (136). Many of the Latino students, but especially the African Americans, have internalized the "alienation and hostility" (229) and "an ideology of repudiation and resistance" typical of the "intellectual and cultural isolation of the black community" (230). The Afrocentrist professor (Leonard Jeffries) to whom Traub devotes a long chapter is, he claims, representative of the black remedial student drowning in "the deep currents of anti-intellectualism, and the appetite for consolatory myths, that ran through large parts of the black community" (271). In other words, black students are at the bottom of the ethnic hierarchy because they have produced a culture that keeps them there: "[T]he street world where ancient grievances and suspicions are perpetually revived—the world, that is, that has reared many City College students" (235). Such students can't hope to be "liberated" culturally until they reject the Leonard Jeffries "inside themselves" (271). In sum, the students have so deeply internalized street mythology that it's as inescapable as biology.

An ideologically powerful set of alignments, centered on physical descriptions of students' bodies, emerges from Traub's book. The conventional immigrant students of the '90s resemble the Jewish "greenhorns" of the past—they are aligned with the desire to assimilate, traditional curriculum, rigorous standards, foreign schooling, and neat dress. By contrast, the exotic black/Latino body is aligned with oppositional politics, flamboyant styles, ethnic studies, remediation, soft standards, and the New York City public schools.

Traub uses this hierarchy to establish not only that minority cultures created by inner-city poverty are responsible for the failure of open access; he also argues that the public institutions designed to boost individuals out of poverty perpetuate the cycle of failure, an argument that Diane Ravitch, for instance, frequently espouses in her public remarks about CUNY. For ultimately, discussions about remediation are arguments about middle-class authority and responsibility. As Traub asks early in the book: "Do the limits lie in the college or in the students? And this, in turn, begs one of the threshold questions of modern American liberalism: How powerful are our institutions in the face of the economic and cultural forces that now perpetuate inner-city poverty?" (5). Addressing his middle-class reader, Traub wonders whether "our" institutions can halt these vague "forces" that create poverty. By the book's end, Traub concludes that "we" can't reverse the effects of poverty because poverty generates anti-intellectual minority cultures. "Remedial education," wrote Nathan Glazer in his review of Traub's book, "can only do so much"; now forced to "teach illiterates," CCNY professors can't instruct a chaotic urban underclass. As he puts the case, "New York City's population had changed from a largely stable working class in which fathers worked or looked for work, mothers stayed home, children came home for lunch or took sandwiches from home . . . . accepted the authority of teachers and assumed one had to be smart and work hard to go to college, to something very different" (1994, 41).

Since Traub's most effective criticisms fall upon remedial writing courses, the struggles a few students experience during their first college class become representative of the failure of open admissions more generally. A. M. Rosenthal, former executive editor of the *Times* and a CCNY graduate, thought so: "from a reading of Mr. Traub's book," he wrote, "it is clear that continuing remedial classes would be continuing the basic falsehood of open enrollment at City" (9). In the neoliberal view, the failure of open admissions also becomes representative of other social programs—welfare, affirmative action, bilingual education—that were being reassessed across the country at the turn of the last century.

Unsurprisingly, Traub concludes his book by suggesting that remedial students would be better off in vocational or two-year schools rather than in a liberal arts college. This conclusion was handy when, as I discussed above, the board of trustees, joining a coalition formed by the Republican governor and mayor, the Manhattan Institute and media outlets like *The Post* and *The Daily News*, agreed that open access has failed. Six years later, after much struggle, CUNY's board of trustees voted in a master plan that restratifies the municipal college system, in part by abolishing remedial education at the senior colleges.

The Underclass in Composition Studies

One implication running throughout Traub's book is that college is affordable for everyone, but not obtainable for cultural reasons. Since a neoliberal can't reasonably invoke the bell curve—though Traub frequently refers to students' "cognitive deficits," one of Herrnstein and Murray's favorite catchphrases in their book, also published in 1994—cultural alienation can substitute for it. This theme is a vexed one because, at least since Daniel Patrick Moynihan's pronouncements on the subject, it is part of mainstream liberal discourses. If, the thinking goes, culturally diverse students fail in school, this is not because of their "cognitive deficits," but because of cultural or linguistic ones. Deficit imagery has of course been challenged as a result of research in composition, cultural studies, sociolinguistics, and the anthropology of education. In sophisticated approaches inflected by multiculturalism, students don't fail because they lack culture but because they are forced to choose between historically discordant cultures and the identities that membership in two worlds entails.

In chapter 5, I will explore the liberating aspects of this research in more detail. However, because remedial students' alienation from the mainstream has organized so much writing about them, I want to examine how difference can be ideologically damaging if we assume that cultural attitudes represent class difference. This happens when "underclass" becomes synonymous with "working class," because the former expresses attitudes about urban experience rather than about a specific class experience. Class experience must be rooted in economic and material contexts, not just cultural and linguistic ones, and for this reason, it is particularly difficult to represent.

Class identity is also necessarily relational. When writing about social class difference, we must also unavoidably be writing about class relationships—about our own difference in relation to low or high others. Nowhere is the blurring of underclass with working class more evident than in one of the most venerable texts in composition studies, Adrienne Rich's inspiring essay "Teaching Language in Open Admissions." Along with Shaughnessy's book, Rich's essay, which speaks eloquently to the power of education to change our lives, is probably the most frequently cited text about open admissions. Rich reprinted this 1972 essay in her 1979 collection, *On Lies, Secrets, and Silence*, along with a preface that describes the euphoria of open admissions. After sketching out the collapse of open access, she returns to the present: "And, on the corner of Broadway near where I live, I see young people whose like I knew ten years ago as college students 'hanging-out,' brown-bagging, standing in short skirts and high-heeled boots in doorways waiting for a trick, or being dragged into the car of a plumed and sequined pimp" (52). Since City College students were not in the 1970s prostitutes, why are open admissions students linked in Rich's prose with loitering youth and dangerous doorways, short skirts, high heels, and sequins, pimps and violence?

I think Rich's puzzling comparison reflects her complex attitudes toward New York City, which are as central to her essay as the ostensible subject of teaching language to remedial students. Rich's representation tells us less about working-class students and more about a liberal's conflicted response to demographic, economic, and political upheavals in the 1960s, attitudes that Rich foregrounds early in the essay when she describes how she and her liberal friends reacted to a city on the brink of social chaos. Rich's response to the city's problems was to take the subway uptown to City College, whose physically repellent urban campus she consistently contrasts with the pleasant, bucolic campuses at those private institutions that shaped her own educational history.

Unlike Traub, of course, Rich calls attention to these contrasts as examples of social injustice. Nevertheless, like Traub's, her depictions of noise, crowding, heat, and ugliness also serve to create a particular urban aesthetic that achieves force through a contrast to elite campuses. In this case, I think the underclass student who inhabits the urban college represents an intellectual's conflicted relationship to social change. According to Michael Katz, the underclass is an ill-defined sociological category that emerged in American discourse in the late 1970s. Notable for its lack of agency and its youth, color, joblessness, and urban roots, the underclass appears to exist nonrelationally, beyond the remediation of the middle classes. "The term *underclass*," Katz writes, isn't an empirical category, but instead "offers a convenient metaphor for use in commentaries on inner city crises because it evokes three widely shared perceptions: novelty, complexity, and danger. . . . The idea of an underclass is a metaphor for the social transformation embedded in these perceptions" (3). The metaphor proves useful for the middle-class intellectual who otherwise finds urban changes difficult to explain. And, though class is a relational category, underclass imagery tends to portray the "other" as singularly alienated from mainstream cultures.

Throughout the '90s, much scholarly discourse about basic writing, some written from a left and/or liberal perspective, drew sustenance from the underclass imagery that surfaces in Rich's essay and that Katz describes. In a 1991 essay in *College English*, Barbara Henning evokes the underclass in her critique of formalist approaches to teaching basic writing. Formalist approaches, she writes, are "counterproductive and alienating for those from the underclass, not only ensuring high failure rates at urban colleges, but also sending students straight back into the world of poverty and ignorance" (675).

Though cognizant of her students' economic circumstances, when Henning represents her students' class experiences, she turns to the underclass imagery of "novelty, complexity, and danger," ascribing lack of agency to students and particular power to their middle-class teachers. Henning's essay is replete with students' voices and words, but these writers are "'selfless' and 'voiceless' because their experiences and language do not allow them to construct a recognizable *mainstream* self and voice" (680). In quotation after quotation, Henning's students write of the devastating consequences of poverty, blighted urban neighborhoods, violence, and drugs. There is no affirmative possibility of working-class experience in these texts; the writers' worlds appear to exist beyond the remediating agency of the middle-class observer. Henning glosses this chorus of despair: "Poverty, as depicted in these student texts, is a world with limited paths leading out, where safety is sought behind locked doors and is frequently accompanied by loneliness and abuse" (675).

Like Rich, Henning argues for the power of education to change students' lives, no matter how small the changes are, and she ascribes her students' difficulties in large part to the paltry pedagogy they are served. But in asserting the teacher's agency, Henning is also forced to attribute students' "high failure rates" to a massive cultural collision between them and us. Though well aware of the structural contexts of poverty, Henning nevertheless dismisses social class by focusing upon culture clash as the primary explanation for basic writers' failures and as the foundation for a reformist agenda.

In her award-winning book, *Writing in an Alien World* (1996), Deborah Mutnick similarly focuses on the culture shock her students experience when they come to college. Joe, an African American student, attends South End, the branch campus that "is located half an hour away from the main campus in an inner-city neighborhood that made headline news soon after our interview when a teenager gunned down two of [Joe's] classmates in the corridor of their high school. I have heard similar stories from many students, including Joe, who speak of themselves as lone survivors of childhood friends now dead, on the streets, or in prison" (81). Joe resembles Traub's remedial student, Tammy, whom he dubs "a miraculous survivor" of the South Bronx. Both are lonely "survivors" of the inner city whose educational quests result in a singular cultural disorientation. "For many basic writers," Mutnick concludes, "the university is an 'alien world' like the one Joe depicts in his essay, populated by white professors and dominated by the strange language of academic discourse" (100).

Dedicated teachers who have made important scholarly contributions, Henning and Mutnick offer a useful critique of the formalist approach that historically has dominated basic skills teaching. To argue for their reform, though, these intellectuals tend to depend upon underclass imagery. Underclass imagery tends to turn common economic circumstances into novel ones, and it is this novelty that critics like James Traub powerfully invoke to argue that the struggle to fund a college education is confined to a special urban group. That Long Island University, Brooklyn, students live in crime-ridden neighborhoods and crowded apartments, lack adequate day care, computers, books or tuition money, and must commute long hours are not unusual experiences for millions of New Yorkers. For instance, many City College students and their parents hold full-time jobs as cooks, paraprofessionals in the schools, sales clerks, babysitters, security guards, health care aides, janitors, and receptionists. The fact that they are still poor and cannot afford to go to a liberal arts college challenges the true "consolatory myth" at the heart of a book like Traub's. Benjamin DeMott contends that "the framing of the issue" of failing urban schools "conceals that the troubles of inner city schools are a special, highly publicized symptom of conditions of inequity that extend far beyond ghettos and barrios" (142). The real majority of parents, he argues, are those "whose own experiences of academic" subjects like English or the sciences "were frustrating—conducive mainly to doubt that book learning is con-

nected with the realities of practical life and work" (142). Consequently, "the notion that only for minorities is school an alien culture neatly excises both the fairness problem and the educational
problem from the broader realities of a class society" (142–43).

In addition, if agency is assigned to students' underclass status,
it's difficult to build coalitions between groups who may have shared
economic interests. At CUNY, these groups include the culturally
dominant organic intellectuals of the past, and the city's current, nu-
merically dominant but culturally subordinate working classes. In
Traub's book, City College students' cultural attitudes, especially
their vocationalism and anti-intellectualism, are aligned with their
underclass origins. Yet in an ethnography like Michael Moffatt's
Coming of Age in New Jersey, middle-class students enrolled at Rut-
gers University also express similar attitudes toward the value of a
liberal arts education. But their careerism or resistance to traditional
knowledge doesn't function to mark their class affiliations. The popular press doesn't invoke white alienation as an explanation for the
relatively low retention rates that characterize the midlevel tier of
public higher education (see Blum's statistics).

A more recent ethnography of three Lehman College women,
published by Beth Counihan in the *Journal of Basic Writing* (1999),
provides further "empirical" validation of this cultural alienation,
which she attributes to CUNY students' underclass origins. Like
Traub's informants, Counihan's "freshgirls" are exotically dressed,
anxious and bored by turns, resistant to knowledge, and wary of the
writer's approach. Two of Counihan's "girls," Evone and Kiki, "are
children of the underclass: raised in desperate poverty and neglect"
(101). Their "class" experience "is the factor that does the most in determining their behavior" (100): "For an eighteen-year-old Bronxite
freshgirl, a life in exile is a daunting consequence of 'getting an education.' Home may not be the sweetest place when your shrew of a
grandmother is screaming in Spanish through a locked door, or
when you are raised as a ward of the state, or when your mother
beats you for breaking a plate—but it is that one and only place best
known to you" (101). Many of the students in the ethnography that
Susan Miller conducted with her students at the University of Utah

also exhibit "bad" behavior such as ignoring teachers, talking in class, or not completing homework (Anderson et al.). But the Utah students' "underlife" does not represent their class experience, as it does for the "exiled" freshgirls.

Counihan represents an iconic Bronx etched into American cultural memory via President Carter's visit there in the '70s, which did much to enhance the formation of the underclass in national intellectual discourse. Shifting between reporting events to imagining them, from the third to the first person, a technique that Traub also exploits, Counihan writes:

> Eighteen years earlier, the Bronx burned as Evone, Kiki, and Monique lay snug in their cribs, playing with their toes. The mid 70s saw hundreds of apartment buildings set on fire by landlords looking to collect insurance money, or building strippers in search of valuable copper pipes, or even the tenants themselves, hoping to be relocated from crumbling buildings to brand new public housing. The freshgirls spent their babyhood serenaded by sirens.
>
> Meanwhile, I played Lenne Lenape Indian housewife in my backyard treehouse in semi-rural New Jersey and watched a hard-hatted President Carter on TV as he toured the ruins of the South Bronx. (98)

Like Traub's, Counihan's representation of a representation of the Bronx denies the borough its vital complexities, for she imagines that all Lehman College students inhabit Fort Apache, the Bronx, though many live in my neighborhood, less than ten blocks from Counihan's institution. Students in my classes who have conducted language research projects in the South Bronx or East Harlem project quite different imagery (1997). This is because, unlike Rich, Counihan, or Traub, the students' writing doesn't turn upon antiurban imagery.[7] Patrick Healy reports that Irving Kristol, a prominent neoconservative intellectual, "feels that he's lost his ties to New York and to City [College], and that today's Hispanic, Asian, and black students don't connect him to the largely Jewish student body he remembers. 'It isn't like my old City College. Nothing'" (A26). It's the intellectual's estrangement from the changing city that Kristol unconsciously stresses here, not the contemporary student's estrangement from the college.

The intellectual's alienation also functions as a way to assign the responsibility for failure to the cultural domain. Therefore, again like Traub, Counihan believes that the freshgirls fail because they cannot assimilate into mainstream intellectual culture. Leaving cultural wastelands of "poverty, fear, and instability" (92), the freshgirls have to adopt new allegiances. While these women believe that they can retain an allegiance to both worlds, "In fact, there is no choice: either change or fail" (101). Counihan concludes that the women are "resistant" or sulky, "sabotaging" their grades (101; 99). There is nothing useful that these "girls"—denied the status of their own womanhood—could bring to college. These representations—which I'll read against my students' writing in the next chapter—do not suggest that there could be alternative journeys into intellectual cultures.

Redefining Class Agency

In chapter 5, I will discuss cultural conflicts in more detail, but here I want to stress how they can be used to justify devastating attacks on urban higher education. Implying that students fail because they inhabit a culture that lacks academic values, critics of remediation frequently assign responsibility to the students' cultural loyalties. On the other hand, because they draw from a well-established body of underclass associations circulating within and beyond the academy, such representations effectively negate class as a meaningful category for analysis and thus ultimately for critique or resistance. When this happens, it's not funding for higher education that matters, but the impossible job of reconciling cultural differences.

By invoking the discourse of student need, critics of remediation often focus on students' agency, eluding or downplaying the roles that institutions do or could play in enhancing students' educational progress. Traub and Counihan, for instance, both focus on classes taught by adjunct instructors, and their portraits of these teachers suggest that they are also alienated from their institutions and from their students. Neither writer explores the academy's scandalous reliance upon contingent labor to initiate students into academic life, for to do so would require a fuller structural analysis than either is prepared to develop.

What these representations also gloss over is that an institution like the City University has been successful in transforming the lives of thousands of students. This is the theme of David Lavin and David Hyllegard's longitudinal study of the City University, which followed the progress of two cohorts, the first open admissions group of 1970–71, and then another in 1980, when open access had been considerably curtailed. They conclude that what appears to impact students' progress at the university is a constellation of institutional policies and economic factors. In other words, Lavin and Hyllegard assign agency to broad structural changes based upon their interpretation of empirical, longitudinal data.

After controlling for differences between the two groups, Lavin and Hyllegard conclude that the 1980 cohort "achieved considerably less academic success" (238) than the earlier cohort, and they attribute this difference mainly to "the changed academic context created by policy modifications" (239). Such modifications included charging tuition; requiring students to take a battery of standardized tests and to complete sequences of remedial courses; and tightening policies for withdrawing from courses or for transferring between programs and colleges (210–12). Lavin and Hyllegard emphasize the role that working part- or full-time had on the 1980 cohort as students struggled to pay tuition and for mandatory remediation in a city whose rents were spiraling upwards at a dizzying pace. While socioeconomic background had had a negligible effect upon the 1970 cohort, it became a determining factor in the ability of the 1980 cohort to stay in school.

What Lavin and Hyllegard's study shows is that open access, when supported economically and institutionally, helped thousands of poor, inner-city whites and people of color to find and keep white-collar jobs. Open access succeeded in creating an educated urban class in New York City. From their perspective, providing access to the B.A. represents a realistic commitment that can be realized given the appropriate resources. Similarly, in her longitudinal, fine-grained study of City College students, Marilyn Sternglass concludes that offering access to the B.A. creates new life chances; access to higher education redefined opportunity for many of her case study students.

But in making this claim, Sternglass, again like Lavin and Hyllegard, also critiques the assumption that remediation is the primary agent of open access. First, Sternglass shows how students' progress was affected by their success in mathematics, science, and other liberal arts courses. Second, Sternglass's book sharply underscores how economic and material factors affect the lives of individual students. In so doing, she effectively distinguishes between cultural and social class experiences. While some of Sternglass's students struggled with their initial lack of poor preparation and some had also to learn to negotiate the institution's demands for identity changes, what most negatively affected their academic achievement was outside work and the related stress of commuting and sustaining a meaningful family life.

Consider Delores, a psychology major whose work and commuting schedule changed each semester. In 1991, she lived during the week in the Bronx in order to qualify for in-state tuition but commuted seventy-five minutes each way to New Jersey to work in a restaurant on Fridays, Saturdays, and Sundays; on weeknights, she worked at the library at the City College campus in Manhattan. Chandra, another student who worked two jobs while commuting to City College, told Sternglass, "I could rarely find time to read and write the papers the way I wanted to. I can't cut down on the number of hours I'm working. I may have to take out more loans, so I can finish next year. I want to do quality work, but juggling two jobs and school becomes confusing—what do I do today? My first concern is how to get money to continue next semester. I have to pay off this year's loan and I may need to take another loan for the $500 tuition increase" (105). As Sternglass represents them, Delores and Chandra are not haunting underclass figures because they are well aware of their difficulties, and they know why they didn't complete an assignment. Because they speak across the years—beyond the first semester of college—these women take responsibility for what they haven't been able to do while also analyzing their progress within an economic and urban context. Delores and Chandra don't sulk or sabotage themselves; practiced urban border crossers, they are comfortable in more than one world. The "exile" that Counihan identifies is a common experience for many freshmen and not necessarily tied to social class difference. What may be more expressive of class affiliation is the confusion Chandra encounters when she asks: what do I do today? The periods of detachment from the institution that Sternglass's students experienced were not the result of "discordant pedagogies" but the consequence of their long-term struggles to pay tuition and rent, care for family members, and commute across the city.

In this regard, Sternglass focuses particularly upon the experience of Ricardo, an immigrant and a bilingual, a political and social activist, a struggling writer and a successful student of the sciences. Ricardo's case "encapsulates the feelings and frustrations of many of his classmates. After 2 and one half years in the college, Ricardo felt the oppression of his economic situation weighing on him" (105). In response to Sternglass's question about changes in his "academic commitment," Ricardo replied:

> It's diminishing. It's more and more frustrating to stay in college and survive. I'm very committed to keep my academic standards, but cut backs have depressed me [in college aid, in rising tuition costs]. I could get "Cs" with no effort, because grades don't mean anything to others. But I will try not to diminish the quality of my work. I've been on the honor roll for three years, but if I can't pay the rent and eat, who cares about grades? Twenty to 25% of the students in the Communications program didn't register because they think they won't have the money. The economy is bad, financial aid is worse, tuition is higher, the faculty can't pay attention to so many students—there are 30 students instead of 15 in the production classes. (105)

When analyzing his situation, Ricardo connects it to the privatization of CUNY that, as I described earlier, affected him and his classmates in the late '80s and early '90s. When he dropped courses at one point, it was not because he didn't see the possibility of cultural coexistence—it was because he had increased his working hours outside school. Ricardo persisted and garnered high grades in advanced math and science courses, but, given his financial obligations, his struggles to pass writing assessments, and the exhaustion of his protracted economic conflicts, he finally abandoned his dream of becoming a doctor and instead completed the physician's assistant program. In this case, of course, Ricardo did succeed by earning his degree and completing a first-rate program. But the price he paid was high, and his ultimate dream could not, in this context, be fulfilled.

The Professional Politics of Agency, 2000

In chapter 3, I argued that distinguishing between the politics of representation and access matters because the politics we practice also help to determine the nature of a reformist agenda. The politics of representation shape our sense of professional agency: who is to blame for what is happening to our programs. Within the subfield of basic writing, scholars are struggling to clarify their responsibility in light of the national backlash against remediation that I described at the beginning of this chapter. One response has been to call for "hard" data to justify the worth of our programs, especially in sustaining retention rates (e.g., White; Wiener).

Unfortunately, as I also argued in chapter 1, these calls for hard data don't always account for the politics of remediation and the ideologies developed to support stratification. Referring to an experimental writing course we evaluated at City College in the early 1990s, Barbara Gleason writes, "The empirically verifiable account that we were striving for in this evaluation was fatally compromised by the socio-political forces that had gathered around the issue of remediation" (582). Empirical accounts remain central to arguing for the worth of programs, but evaluation is a political enterprise in many respects, which is merely to say that alone, data won't do the job of ideological justification.

In the wake of downsizing, scholars also apparently feel that some blame must rest on the shoulders of those who have focused on cultural and political issues at the expense of individual students and basic writing programs. Susanmarie Harrington and Linda Adler-Kassner assert: "It seems clear that our collective failure to explore the real political consequences between the broad cultural approaches to basic writing and the cognitive approaches leaves us, our programs, and most importantly our students, vulnerable to legislatively-mandated cuts" (16). They believe we are vulnerable to cuts because we have spent time analyzing cultural issues or attending to the politics of remediation rather than examining the "dilemma that still counts": individual students' errors. "Renewed attention to error," they write, "will help us to better define and understand what basic writing is, who basic writers are, how we can talk about *writers' needs* among ourselves, and how we can represent basic writers and talk about their *needs* with public officials" (20; my emphasis).

Harrington and Adler-Kassner offer a valuable critique of disciplinary perspectives, but in their laudable concern to preserve programs, they invoke the discourse of student need. Though she lavishly documented student need in terms of errors, as Harrington and Adler-Kassner recommend, Mina Shaughnessy's program was radically downsized—despite her unusual moral status (see chapter 3). The discourse of student need may not serve us well in these debates primarily because it depends upon a cluster of assumptions, the chief of which is that only students require remediation, not institutions, coalitions, or interest groups. Never so powerful as when it is attached to urban students of color, remediation becomes an anomalous program centered on providing access to the liberal arts for a culturally distant few. In the hands of commentators like James Traub, remediation functions as "the" symbol of open access policies and thus must bear the burden of blame when some students don't succeed.

Rather than neglect the politics of institutions in favor of the individual student's needs, as Harrington and Adler-Kassner recommend, I would argue that we need more research and specific case studies of the political roles that remediation plays at colleges. Taken together, careful descriptions of the fate of particular programs can suggest that our struggles may be local, but they unfold similarly within global contexts. Histories of stratification (Severino 1996), studies of institutional documents (Roy; Stygall; Crouch and

McNenny), or ethnographic research of institutional conflicts (DiPardo) reveal that the destiny of remedial programs is neither accidental nor isolated. The fate of remediation at the City University that I detail throughout this book is specific in many ways to New York, but in others it illustrates the broader dynamics of institutional growth in American higher education and the political uses of remedial English to manage that growth.

Understanding the relationship between the politics of representation and access is important because it determines to some extent where we locate our reform efforts. For instance, specific studies of attacks on remediation can provide us with models for critique and possible action. Gail Stygall recommends that composition teachers adopt the role of public intellectual and become involved in these debates that will affect what we do in the classroom. Her analysis also suggests that composition scholars become involved in committee work, faculty senates or councils that determine educational policy and often directly engage in dialogue with community coalitions. As my analysis of the City University also shows, we need to document which specific groups or coalitions oppose us, for "public officials" have to be named to be known. Deborah Mutnick (2000) advocates joining coalitions to defend affirmative action or building partnerships with the public schools. In New York City, groups like the CUNY Coalition of Concerned Faculty and Staff, the New Caucus faction of our faculty and staff union, the PSC-CUNY, and the New York Public Interest Research Group (NYPIRG) offer places for faculty to oppose the defunding and retiering of public higher education. By adopting strategies like these, we can also explore how activism can usefully inform scholarship and scholarship can inform activist work.

Finally, in our positions as WPAs, we can use what we know about testing and retention rates to critique specific proposals at our institutions and to offer possible alternatives. In some cases, we can build coalitions on our campuses with faculty in the disciplines who also have a stake in the institution's use of writing courses, remediation, or assessments. Within our departments and WAC programs, we need to continue to develop alternatives to first-year skills instruction. Reflecting upon City College students' educational journeys, Sternglass concludes: "Composition instruction cannot be seen in a vacuum. Perhaps that is the greatest lesson that can be learned from examining student writing over an extended period of time. Composition instruction is an important first step in assisting students to formulate their ideas and learn how to express them clearly. But composition instructors should not believe that they are the final influence, or perhaps even the most important influence, in the development of writing abilities" (141). With Sternglass's caveat in mind, we might approach remediation as a program that most richly supports access to the liberal arts over the long term. For, as Vivian Zamel argues from her case studies, while ESL students do make genuine "progress" in first-year writing courses, "their process of acquisition is just that, an ongoing and incremental process of approximation" (8). Therefore, she concludes that the most effective approach to remediation for ESL students is to spread it across the years and to connect it to teaching in the disciplines wherever possible.

Writing teachers do well to cultivate relationships with faculty in other departments while also developing intellectually substantial courses that are sensitive to cultural issues. Our courses have to perform a delicate balancing act here, remaining mindful of the historically constricting role that skills instruction plays while also responding to a course's gatekeeping function within an institution. I consider this difficult negotiation in the next chapter, where I will shift my focus from institutional access to writers' access to mainstream cultures. In this last chapter, I will explore curriculum in the context of the assimilation of "new" students to academic discourses, a cultural concern that, as I've shown here, has powerfully organized public debates about the institutional status of remedial English.

5 | Writing between Worlds: Access as Translation

▶ AN ENGINEERING MAJOR AT CITY COLLEGE, RUBEN Acosta describes in "Amid America and Latino America" his journey from Puerto Rico to New York City, where he gradually lost Spanish, adopting along the way standard English and some Spanglish.[1] At his father's urging—"Mijo! Se te está olvidando el español. Te tengo que mandar a traer pá ca, que aprendas español de nuevo"—Acosta immersed himself in standard Spanish through newspapers, the Bible, and literature. He now believes that he lives "amid" two cultures: "two languages . . . should lead one to aspire for more knowledge to continue dominating two ways to interpret life and acquiring a bilateral view of the world. . . . I knew that in this land that I once considered strange and mysterious I faced many obstacles, yet I had successfully embarked on an unexpected and enriching two-way journey into both Americas . . . into Las Americas" (6). Like Rosario Ferré and Ruth Behar, two intellectuals whose crosscultural journeys he parallels with his own, Acosta appropriates a conventional form, the familiar or belletristic essay, to theorize a "bilateral view of the world," the state of cultural betweenness. Acosta accents the traditional form with dual languages and experiences to explore questions of assimilation that have been so important to previous generations of American organic intellectuals at City College and elsewhere. Appropriately, Acosta's essay "Amid America and Latino America" foregrounds the subject of this last chapter: how writers portray their access to dominant cultures and to academic life, and why that access is meaningful to composition studies in the twenty-first century.

Throughout this book I have complicated those assumptions that underpin the "discourse of student need." In chapter 4, I argued that the always-new remedial student emerged in public debate to justify the downsizing of public higher education and to manage social class anxieties about the economic worth of a B.A. degree. James Traub's critique of remediation rests partly on his subtle portrayal of students who resist assimilation to academic culture. A book like *City on a Hill* thus gathers cultural strength from what sociologists call "straight-line" immigration theory (Portes and Zhou). Traub's pernicious ethnic hierarchy achieves cultural persuasiveness by suggesting that those City College students who succeeded in the past did so because they assimilated smoothly to the mainstream. Unlike the students he meets today in black studies or remedial courses, those "desperately poor students fifty and sixty years" ago "believed in, and were comfortable with, the kind of abstract endeavor involved" in traditional academic study (296–97).

The status of straight-line theory has long been a subject of debate in composition studies; there is a robust tradition of scholarship crossing several subfields that discusses how students write between worlds.[2] Composition teachers address questions of translation because the collision between language worlds has shaped the discipline of college English studies from the beginning. In his history of the origins of English studies in eighteenth-century Britain, Thomas Miller argues that the teaching of college writing was embroiled in the creation of a colonial identity. He shows how a group of marginalized intellectuals developed a rhetoric for middle-class, upwardly mobile students in the British cultural provinces—Scotland, Ireland, and later, North America. Middle-class colonials and dissenters, these students wanted a rhetoric for everyday life, not only Latin and Greek, the classical education that was the birthright of their elite counterparts at Oxford and Cambridge. At the same time, these students and their teachers were also attracted to the elite cultural capital of their upper-class peers. In these earliest years, composition studies mediated a linguistic conflict waged by upwardly mobile students and their teachers, organic intellectuals who expressed ambivalence to elite centers of learning. The "first professors and students of English . . . shared a dialectical identity as both Britons *and* dissenters, Irish or Scots, and they studied English because they were not accepted as English" (18).

The curriculums that Miller describes were focused on translating elite knowledge into marginal institutions for marginal students. In the process of translation, teachers and students created innovative knowledge. Along with the focus on the experimental method that Oxford or Cambridge eschewed came a new rhetoric with a (short-lived) focus upon writing in the vernacular. Then, as now, a primary question arose out of this competition that reflected the uneasy relationship these intellectuals had to elite classical knowledge. Should the new rhetoric teach students to assimilate to the elite culture or to resist it? Or is it possible to transcreate new knowledge and identities out of a negotiation—possibly a fusion—between different cultures?

These questions have long been salient for those organic intellectuals who have successfully appropriated the cultural capital that is especially embodied by elite institutions of higher learning. When, like Anzia Yerzierska's Sara Smolinsky in *Bread Givers*, they return to their communities as teachers, writers, and intellectuals, they live between cultures and must navigate those thorny questions that are never settled in the teaching of writing, and perhaps especially in remedial courses. To what extent is one obligated to perpetuate standard forms? To what extent is transgressive teaching possible? Is it possible to affirm and critique dominant discourses at the same time?

Though these are the questions that teachers, students, and professional writers often explore, a New York intellectual (and City College graduate) like Alfred Kazin imagines a different process. In a review of Traub's book, Kazin writes: "And page after page, here are so many damaged people, usually fatherless, themselves premature parents struggling with after-school jobs, that it is no wonder many are apathetic even about their chances of survival. In this world, culture doesn't exist in any traditional sense and, even when

projected in the 'World Humanities' course, is not assimilated."
Underclass imagery achieves resonance with middle-class readers
by suggesting that students travel from the social wastelands of their
neighborhoods into the culturally dense worlds of the academy. As I
suggested in chapter 4, the cultural argument serves ideologically to
exclude thoughtful discussions about the affordability of a college
education for working-class students. A focus on remedial students
as representative of a special urban "underclass" neatly shifts debates about funding toward debates about underclass anti-intellectualism.

In what follows, I describe the processes of intercultural contact
and assimilation to new discourses as a far more complex social and
intellectual effort, and I theorize a pedagogy in part from the perspectives of City College students like Ruben Acosta. My purpose is
to engage these young writers with critics of their education like
Kazin or Traub. In the process, however, I will also try to disentangle
curricular reforms from institutional ones, for I will conclude with a
critique of the limits of my practice and of border pedagogy more
generally.

The writers I discuss throughout this chapter, most of them
working-class intellectuals, others born in postcolonial settings,
struggle not with the lack of culture, but with its overabundance. In
quoting from students' narratives, however, I don't assume I have
access to their unmediated experience because that experience is
written (see Lu and Horner 1998). The form I choose to discuss here,
the familiar essay, offers a rich ground for making this distinction
because it underscores how writers represent what happened,
rather than report what happened. Though others are available, I
choose this form for a variety of reasons: traditionally it has been
concerned with crosscultural traveling; it can accommodate and
subvert academic conventions at the same time; and, not least, my
students *like* to read and write familiar essays.

Ideally, translation would provide moments for student writers
to bring different literacies, languages, or cultural experiences together. Juan Flores's concept of "trans-creation," a way of bringing
together, applies here: "It confronts the prevailing ethos by congre-

gating an ethos of its own, not necessarily an outright adversarial but certainly an alternative ethos" (217–18). "'Trans-creation,'" he writes, "understood in this sense of intercultural variability and transferability, is the hallmark of border language practice" (220). In my experience, student writers' attempt to accent traditional forms with their words or purposes occurs when they address general audiences in ethnographic reports, editorial writing, debates, and the familiar or belletristic essay, though more standard forms like the critical essay and research paper could also offer fertile grounds for experimentation. Through forms addressed to general audiences, students have the opportunity to translate between languages, to dramatize their literal roles as translators between their families and the larger world, and to explore the possibility of transcreating new knowledge, self, or belief out of the movement between languages and cultures.

Contrary to James Traub's argument that political beliefs hinder intellectual growth and flexibility, I have found that students who bring a politics to the classroom are more open to critical thinking we associate with the traditional liberal arts. Politically active students from across the disciplines like Ruben Acosta (or Ricardo, the science student from Sternglass's book whose case study interview I quoted from in chapter 4) often experience a growing critical consciousness about different discourses and their interactions in the world. In many cases, this happens when students can present their private literacies to a readership within a broader, more public framework.

What I call translation pedagogy is not unproblematic, of course, and I'll end by exploring those moments that highlight the difficulties of contesting the status of academic writing from within an institution. In part this is so because the politics of language use are not equivalent to, or necessarily aligned with, changes in institutional policies, structures, or materially organized hierarchies. That is to say that translation pedagogies now being developed in composition studies do not, by themselves, challenge academic selectivity. But translation theory and practice can counter prevailing ideologies, especially when they are used to bolster a discourse of student need that remedial and other first-year service courses often perpetuate. As a metaphor for thinking about a practice, translation also offers teachers and students the intellectual pleasures of exploring the intersections between private and public literacies. A pedagogy of translation calls into question, while also at the same time enriching, the traditional institutional goals of a composition course.

"Becoming an American": Appropriating the Familiar Essay

The familiar essay offers one powerful tool for theorizing a writer's access to dominant languages because, according to its most accomplished practitioners, it is a syncretic or hybrid form, capable of mixing registers and conventions (e.g., Klaus). On the one hand, writers of familiar essays take liberties with form and content—where or whether the thesis appears, a nonlinear organization, and the direct quotation of stigmatized dialects or languages. Familiar essays don't depend upon specialized knowledge to achieve their readability, and they are addressed to general audiences. On the other hand, those essays we recognize as well-formed are highly allusive, and they acknowledge, usually in their closing, that individual experience is interesting when it's interpretable. In this way, familiar essays participate in traditional academic work.

Literacy narratives, which are usually familiar essays, aren't interesting if they provide chronological descriptions of "how I learned to write." In composition studies, accounts by various scholars are readable for broad audiences because these intellectuals blend their private literacies into a framework of larger social significance. Mike Rose's autobiography (1989) continues an American tradition of literacy as empowering, which stretches from Benjamin Franklin to Frederick Douglass and Malcolm X. Min-Zhan Lu, Fan Shen, Linda Brodkey, and Keith Gilyard speak to the cultural conflicts that learning new languages arouses. This is a common theme in immigrant literatures, from Anzia Yezierska to Amy Tan, and in postcolonial writing, from Salman Rushdie to Arundhati Roy and Ahdaf Soueif. Nancy Sommers's desire to express her individuality reflects a teacherly skepticism toward the high status of theory and specialized languages that has always been present in the academy, and of course within composition studies more particularly.

A writer's struggle to make local knowledge interpretable also provides a moment of intersection between the familiar and other academic forms, possibly because this friction reflects how writers produce and realize genres across the disciplines. In one case study, Carol Berkenkotter and Thomas Huckin show how a senior research professor in biology revised a manuscript for publication in a scientific journal several times between 1989 and 1990, when it was finally accepted. The editors rejected Dr. Davis's early drafts because she didn't situate her experiment within the readership's history of related experiments; these readers wanted her to reinterpret her findings within an ongoing narrative of communally sanctioned research. Though resistant, Dr. Davis did assimilate to her readers' demands; and while she described her revised introduction as a "phony story," for outside readers, her revisions constituted greater interpretability (54–55). Davis's belief that she had to construct a "phony" story reflects similar conflicts about authenticity that many writers experience when moving between worlds, encountering editors, readers, and other power brokers of discourse along the way. Davis's conflicts highlight a key tension in intercultural narratives as well. Did she tell a phony story when she revised the original narrative and thus betray herself? Or did she transcreate knowledge when she agreed to translate the specific events of the lab into a public narrative of science?

An explicit moment of public recognition distinguishes the familiar essay from journalism and related nonfiction prose. In an essay like "The Hanging," George Orwell narrates an event, but the essay qualifies as familiar rather than as reportage when the narrator pauses two-thirds of the way through the story to reflect explicitly upon the execution's meaning. Phillip Lopate notes in his introduction to *The Anchor Essay Annual*, "the trick is to project one's experience on the page in such an enhanced, objectified way that it acquires, or merges with, a larger significance" (x). As the subgenre is evolving today, the personal experience acquires larger significance not just through what Peter Elbow calls the private "rendering," but through a writer's self-conscious comments on its public meaning. Daniel Mahala and Jody Swilky write that, in composition studies, "Little sanction is given to defining alternative uses of experiential narratives to explore the writer's historical location in relation to others and the world" (369). From this perspective, the familiar essay that Lopate anthologizes shares a common ground with Dr. Davis's scientific article because both achieve generic resonance with readers when a local experience is made interpretable.

Since the late '70s, "initiation" into discourse has provided a root metaphor for teaching basic writers to learn the conventions of academic discourse. Shaughnessy's *Errors and Expectations* or a textbook like Brenda Spatt's *Writing from Sources* reflected teachers' concerns to make dominant genres explicit for nontraditional students whom, it was assumed, have the least knowledge of formal conventions. But Kurt Spellmeyer took initiation models to task by arguing that the Spatt approach equates learning a new discourse with an unreflective assimilation to alien forms. Spellmeyer's specific comments on Charles Bazerman's *The Informed Writer* represent a wider critique that emerged in the late '80s. "The proponents of discourse-specific writing," he asserts, "typically invoke the ethos of 'empowerment'—of breaking down long-standing distinctions between student writers and 'real' writers—but their sense of the term is often synonymous with pragmatic accommodation" (108).

In the 1990s, a wave of scholarship contested teaching nontraditional students to mimic academic forms.[3] To counter the dominance of "discourse community" models, multicultural pedagogies tended to privilege narrative as a means of validating what students already know and of contesting the academic hierarchy of forms. Reading and writing literacy narratives, autobiography, ethnography, and ethnic literatures are central to intercultural practices in progressive composition classrooms, and especially in remedial or summer bridge programs.[4]

Douglas Hesse and David Bartholomae (1995) both note that this professional interest in personal writing springs partly from teachers' suspicions of theory. Bartholomae argues that advocates of personal writing desire to reoccupy an anti-institutional niche where the individual author, so diminished by poststructuralism, can be safely resurrected. He defines creative nonfiction as "a first person, narrative or expressive genre whose goal it is to reproduce the ideology of sentimental realism—where a world is made in the image of a single, authorizing point of view" (69). The essay is a "corrupt, if extraordinarily tempting, genre" (71): tempting because it appears "to celebrate individual vision, the detail of particular worlds" (68), but corrupt because it masks the teacher's role. Yet "to hide the teacher is to hide the traces of power, tradition and authority present at the scene of writing" (63). Advocates of the familiar essay evade discursive struggle and validate a common language uncomplicated by jargon, bias, appropriation, and analysis, hallmarks of critical thought (64).

However, as Susan Miller (1990) notes in a comment on Spellmeyer's work, the essay is a genre or subgenre rooted in "power, tradition, and authority." For instance, while Bartholomae assumes that the familiar essay is dedicated to describing a "true" experience, essayists often fictionalize their experience, as Wendell Harris and others point out (e.g., Harvey). Therefore, even while Annie Dillard announces that "no subject matter is forbidden, no structure is proscribed," Hesse points out that her own work echoes other essayists', for example Virginia Woolf's (137). "This is not to claim that the range of possibilities for the genre—or even for personal agency—are narrowly bounded and fixed," Hesse reasons. "But the genre does cast a trajectory for those who would write in it" (137). Because the familiar essay does cast a long shadow, it's quite difficult to write, which is probably why teachers complain as much about students' personal essays as they do about their research papers.

Paul Heilker shows that the familiar essay mingles common registers of language and experience with more culturally elevated styles. From this Bakhtinian perspective, the genre is compatible with the kind of discursive appropriation that Bartholomae describes. For instance, in "From Outside, In," a widely anthologized literacy narrative, Barbara Mellix analyzes the relationship between self, ethnicity, and writing by weaving different languages into her piece through narrative, analysis, and quotation. She renders conversations with parents, daughter, and relatives in Black English; she displays her awkward attempts to write like a scholar in Basic Writing and other college courses; and she mingles these attempts with the abstract language of Franz Fanon and terms from academic sociolinguistics. Though often celebrated as formless, the essay as Mellix writes it mixes up various registers, balancing, as Thomas Recchio asserts, "Montaigne's personal vision and the authority of a discourse tradition" (280; see Haefner; Chadbourne). The form thus has the potential to "congregate an ethos" by mingling the particular voice with the more collectively established form.

One discourse tradition that shapes the essay is the intercultural encounter. In Spellmeyer's estimation, the essay originates from Montaigne's playful desire to make crosscultural contact (96; and see Hall). Living between worlds is a key concern in the contemporary belletristic essay of Maxine Hong Kingston, Jamaica Kincaid, Chinua Achebe, Margaret Atwood, Alice Walker, Terry Tempest Williams, and many others anthologized in readers for composition classes. Udo, a City College biochemistry major, joined this discursive flow when he explored the North American immigrant's relationship to a dominant culture through familiar essays he wrote like "Beyond the Paper House" and "To My Nigerian." In the latter essay, Udo was clearly influenced by essays about colonialism that we read and discussed extensively in class: George Orwell's "A Hanging" and "Shooting an Elephant," Chinua Achebe's "Named for Victoria, Queen of England," and V. S. Naipaul's "Columbus and Crusoe." [5]

For instance, the first sentences of Udo's beautiful essay imitate Orwell's "A Hanging": "It was the rainy season. The earth smelled rich and dark with moisture. Fresh, green corn stalks and yam tendrils grew out of it. I watched the old men shuffle by. Their worn clothing, white hair and unhurried gait seemed incongruous with this their land in its season of change. My uncles had warned me against them: they were pagans. Yet they possessed an enticing magic I felt was part of me, so I followed them to their place of worship." In the rest of his semifictional essay, Udo dramatizes his rejection of, and disgust toward, the old men's pagan worship, which included animal sacrifice, and his childish attempt to desecrate their place of holiness. Afterwards, during a storm, he realizes the full extent of his Americanization in a moment of Orwellian "clarity":

We destroy ancestral worshipping places every time we deny our identity. What shall we tell our grandparents when we meet them in the corridors of afterlife? That we didn't know they could see us in a foreign land? That we didn't know they could see us ashamed to put on their clothes? That our children wouldn't have the right voice inflections to communicate with their grandparents? Wouldn't they die again? Is it too much to ask to respect our tradition? Didn't those ways protect the delicate helices that dictate who we are?

Becoming an American is a two-edged sword. It is like a river: it gives life but it drowns. To throw away one's identity is to throw away one's face, to lose one's culture is to lose one's character. Identity is the old man's spittle blessing in the palm of my hand, it is the yam and red palm oil that makes teeth yellow, it is who we must remember to be, it is me.

For a writer and a recent immigrant like Udo, "becoming an American" constitutes a process of aggressive appropriation—he strategically uses a traditional Western form to dramatize a conflicted relationship between old and new. Udo uses traditional prose strategies —for instance, careful shifts between I and we—to portray cultural conflicts that a self-aware writer encounters when moving into the mainstream. But Udo invents his own metaphors to describe the "two-edged" process that Achebe similarly explores in "Named for Victoria, Queen of England." Both a sword and river, both creative and destructive, the dual process of Americanization shapes the "helices" of an identity that the Nigerian biochemist trained in the Western tradition views as culturally "dictated." Using a traditional Western form, Udo transcreates his Nigerian identity for his American readers as a spittle blessing, a yam, and red palm oil.

Udo appropriates an established genre to translate his particular experience into a more general representation of cultural estrangement that is resonant for readers in our postcolonial moment. "To My Nigerian" provides an alternative to straight-line theory as that applies to living and writing between worlds. Udo's effort to describe "becoming an American" also offers teachers working in less culturally diverse settings than mine a powerful metaphor for describing the process of assimilation to the norms that Dr. Davis encountered. To navigate this often conflicted process, conventional forms like the familiar essay may provide powerful tools for writers like Udo, who imitates George Orwell's style to draw a conclusion of his own.

"Sneaking Culture": *Private and Public Literacies*

The always-new remedial student that I've discussed throughout this book is often popularly perceived as a minority because these students appear most distant from school languages. But students defined as well-prepared have to surrender what they already know, or at least they believe that they must do so, to assimilate to academic discourses. One consequence is that middle-class students also experience alienation from the university and resist its totalizing discourses that honor public knowledge at the expense of private experience and ways of learning.

In her ethnography of student experience at the University of New Hampshire, Elizabeth Chiseri-Strater followed two students, Anna and Nick, through their composition course and courses in their majors, art history and political science. White and middle-class, Anna and Nick are artistically and verbally talented students who, like those students that Marilyn Sternglass followed at City College, have trouble mastering a discourse that requires them to analyze material in their major courses and then produce essay exams or short critical essays. For instance, Anna's art history professor complained to Chiseri-Strater that most students in her class revealed "an inability to name the general trends and abstract concepts of modern art, offering instead a list of very specific but sometimes unrelated details" on their exams (68). Struggling with his political science papers, Nick commented in his journal, "Critical Analysis may slaughter me, in the end" (132). Both students dropped out of college for a semester before finishing, and while Nick experienced some economic trouble, he and Anna took a break because they were alienated from the institution. "When I reflect on Anna and Nick's experiences at this institution in their chosen majors," Chiseri-Strater concludes, "aside from their commonality as university students, there is no doubt that they felt little affiliation with the university or with other students in their majors" (143).

In part, Anna and Nick were alienated by the specialized discourses of their majors that excluded what Chiseri-Strater calls their "private literacies." Anna and Nick's alternative ways of knowing, such as their highly developed visual sense, were not privileged at the university, which valued propositional discourses. Though Anna had once considered becoming an art history professor, after graduating "she had discarded any notions of being part of academic life" (171). Anna used the metaphor of worlds to describe her distance from the professors she had once thought she would emulate: "[Anna] said that once she had been attracted to intellectuals, explaining that her art history professors all seemed 'to have their own worlds, their own discourse: they are so into it,' but that in the end she realized that they were mainly 'just talking to one another,' and she didn't see the point to it" (171). Numerous studies highlight a similar slippage between private desires and institutional roles for writers: Robert Brooke's of students' underlife at the University of Nebraska; Anne Penrose and Cheryl Geisler's study of Janet, enrolled at a midwestern university; Lucille Parkinson McCarthy's ethnography of Dave, a stranger in strange lands enrolled at a private liberal arts school in the northeast; Geoffrey Chase's study of Kris and Karen, both seniors at Miami University; and Susan Miller's collaborative ethnography with freshmen honors students, who studied courses across the disciplines at the University of Utah (Anderson et al.). These students we identify as mainstream may very well agree with Nick that critical analysis will slaughter them in the end because it is divorced from their personal literacies, values, or goals.

While McCarthy and Penrose and Geisler suggest that we create richer ways to initiate students into academic discourse, Chase, Brooke, and Chiseri-Strater conclude that students actively resisted academic discourses that were distanced from their intellectual ambitions and everyday concerns (or, as Brooke puts it, sense of self). These scholars turn a critical eye upon teaching students to master conventions without questioning their use in sustaining professors' separateness in "their own worlds." All point toward a pedagogy of translation because they are less concerned with inviting students into academic writing than with understanding how their private literacies might more productively intersect with university discourses.

Again, in this respect the familiar essay offers grounds for intersection, especially when students discuss their private language use as a marker of personal and/or subcultural identity. In the latter context, writers can explore their daily use of low-status dialects or languages, and reinterpret the cultural work that such languages perform. François, an engineering major in a remedial writing class, depicts in "Broken English: A Tiny View of a Caribbean Dialect" the cultural dynamics of Cocoi, "a conglomerate of Patois, French, English and some other African language":

> During elementary school, especially during recess, where all the students of my school would gather in the playground with their friends, we communicated with this dialect our grandparents and the people before them created. I remember using the word "pan" a lot, which in standard English means "on." If someone climbed a tree or some sort of erect figure out of the ground (including houses) someone would sometimes say, "look pan tape de. Me hope he don't fall down." In classrooms, this use (or as many teachers saw it, abuse) of the English language almost always made the teacher mad, almost literally driving them up the wall. To teachers, our use of English was abuse. And I guess this is part of the misconception for children, we looked at what the adults said as the absolute truth. Although they—teachers and parents—used the same language as the students, we thought it was wrong because our teachers and parents said it was. Moreover, to defy our parents and other "good" authority, we continued to use Cocoi language anyway. In a way, we were sneaking culture. (2–3)

In this class, we read essays by Judith Ortiz Cofer and Paule Marshall that described how the women in their families used oral stories to pass on and reinforce ethnic subcultures. François used their insights to understand the crossgenerational uses of Cocoi, a language created by "their grandparents and the people before them." Commenting upon his schooldays in broad strokes, François tries on the voice of the organic intellectual who uses the ethnic past as a way to comment on its cultural work. It's this enlargement of self that makes familiar essays readable—the moments when François analyzes the narrative: "to defy parents and other 'good' authority, we continued to use Cocoi language anyway." Translation occurs when a writer like François connects the individual experience to a collective one.

François points out that sneaking culture is a hallmark of resistant discourses. There is an international body of sociolinguistic and ethnographic research that addresses those struggles at every level of schooling between standard English, English dialects, and second languages, and between mainstream and subcultural values and belief systems.[6] Since translation can involve exploring moments of intense ambivalence, discussing that alienation through the familiar essay might provide an occasion of relief for the writer and illumination for teachers who are shocked to discover it (e.g., see Flower).

Responding to familiar essays by Rachel Jones, Amy Tan, and Richard Rodriguez, Keisha wrote "Street Tongue," an often angry exploration of her conflicted relationship to English dialects. Keisha enumerates three kinds of black students she knew in high school: those who spoke like whites and had white friends, those who used a mixed dialect ("standard English intermingled with slang") and had friends of both races, and those who spoke only BEV ("They usually were seen with other minorities that spoke similarly"). She "would identify" herself "with the category of African Americans who are versatile in speaking"—border crossers who code shift between BEV and standard forms.

Keisha recalls how she accommodated herself to a high school English class, which was

> the only class where I would try to improve my English to fit in with the majority of the students. It was not because it was an English class, but it was because it was an Honors English class where street slang, which sounds unsophisticated to society, is inappropriate and would be looked upon as insuffi-

cient. . . . Honestly, I did not feel entirely complacent in the class because it consisted of students that I do not identify with. There were a lot of white standard English speaking people and a few black standard English speaking people in there. This created a language barrier between me and them. I feared if I spoke casual street slang around them they would wonder what I was doing in this "proper" class, therefore, I held my tongue—rarely breaking the barrier. I knew my participation in class must improve because it would affect my grade. Later on I resolved to continue to think what I wanted to think but to translate my thoughts to speak the way the class expected me to speak. My participation in class became a little better but I still felt uncomfortable. I felt like I was being phony to "my tongue." (3)

Keisha uses this essay to explore the cultural bargains she has had to strike in the process of "talking white." Holding her tongue in classes, she translates between the private and the public dialect because she must, but assuming that public self raises questions about authenticity that occurs to varying degrees for all writers engaged in self-aware translations. What is useful for Keisha's teacher and peers to see is that there are no easy answers to a process that is particular to African American experience but which may also serve to illustrate the tensions writers often experience when they move between worlds. What is useful for Keisha to see is that the cultural friction she now openly discusses—one that the students Valerie Balester worked with were reluctant to discuss at all—has been experienced by other black intellectuals who make different choices at different times in their lives.

Speaking publicly about private conflicts is also important because personal literacies might offer writers a rhetorical resource when translating across worlds. Geneva Smitherman developed a rubric for the National Association for Educational Progress to assess how public school students used Black English Vernacular (BEV) discourse. She concludes that the higher the use of BEV discourse (regardless of the use of BEV grammar), the higher the primary trait scoring on the student's essay (1994, 94). Smitherman advises teachers to "capitalize on the strengths of African American cultural discourse; it is a rich reservoir which students can and should tap"; "the narrativizing, dynamic quality of the African American Verbal Tradition will help students produce lively, image-filled, concrete, readable essays, regardless of rhetorical modality" (95).

The familiar essay can allow students from diverse backgrounds to explore the discursive crossover that Smitherman recommends. In my classes, this sort of verbal play surfaces most frequently in the texts of young Latino and African American men who identify with what they call "street talk," in New York a fusion of English with Spanish, Spanglish, and slang. Rap music is the most popular springboard for crossover in my classes, perhaps because this cultural form is emblematic of the identity conflicts that accompany the commercialization of a local ethnic form. As I've discussed elsewhere, rap music provokes lively debate between young men in my classes who have written about it in several genres, including the research paper (1996). In "N.Y. State of Mind" (the title of a rap song), Ivan uses the familiar essay to explore his relationship to the music during the summer of 1990, when he identified so heavily with gangsta rap, he says, he began living a wild life.

Consciously selecting the present tense to tell the story, Ivan wants the reader to understand the role that rap music plays in sustaining a young man's New York State of Mind. Using white space to break the essay into three blocks of time, Ivan structures the first part around his relationship to the music and its culture: "I hear this song (NY State of Mind), and I get hyper and feel extremely indomitable at the moment" (2). The last two parts detail the narrator's rejection of hip-hop as a result of his mother's decision to exile him temporarily to the Dominican Republic. When Ivan returns to New York, his state of mind has changed, for he now identifies more with the traditional Caribbean music of his elders—"The Spanish music lets the virtuous side of me pop out"—and no longer idealizes rap music as the authentic voice of young men from the barrio. He expresses his moment of turning outward through the coordinate cadences of street talk: "rap artists talk the talk, but don't walk the walk, and it is a business like everything else in life" (4).

"NY State of Mind" mingles different language styles together to achieve its readability. Recalling his attachment to the music that summer, Ivan invokes the fancy talk—mixed registers—characteristic of BEV: "Hip hop music is my life and my rap tapes are the golden goodies that provoke the malicious side of me to rise" (1). Spanish reflects the double self he is creating: "At home, my grandmother always asks me, 'donde tu estaba?' My response is 'a fuera.'" Playfully, he piles up metaphors to describe his duplicity: "I am trusted at home. I am also a sweet child that is usually very much at peace. Like margarine, I am slick. Like John Gotti, I have a baby mafia, where we all run together like a wolfpack. Yet to the family, I am the new rising generation with plenty of talent to separate me from the other children. Little does the family know about my undercover personality" (2). The oral rhythms of parallelism, and the occasional neologism of BEV, permeate the essay: "In NY I am invincible, but with my mother I am completely vanquishable" (4). Street language is manifest in the rap song, which he reproduces without comment as a gloss on his "malicious" behavior, but also through his dialogue with his family, or through remarks about his suspicious aunt, who is a schoolteacher: "I hate this aunt, why is she always in my damn business. She keeps sticking her rat tail where it doesn't belong" (3, 4).

Sneaking culture into his essay, Ivan finds an occasion to critique a powerful subcultural discourse, the language of gansta rap that claims to be authentic. Ivan's implicit critique of rap music in this context is that it is a commercialized form of culture that authorizes a tough masculine behavior that the combined efforts of mother and aunt finally "vanquish." He resolves his conflict through the process of what sociologists call "segmented assimilation" (Portes and Zhou). The new generation practices "segmented assimilation" to resolve the competition in many U.S. cities today between ethnic styles associated with two generations—the elders from the home country who are aligned with traditional ethnic heritages, and the "rising generation" that is attracted to American popular cultures (Waters). The former ethnic allegiance is more closely aligned with the school, a fact that Ivan only hints at in his depiction of the tyrannical schoolteacher aunt. But while Ivan now identifies with school life, he still retains connections to both street talk and "virtuous" ethnic music. Assimilating irregularly into dominant culture, Ivan draws skillfully upon the resources of "street talk" to accent the traditional essay with a distinct New York State of Mind.

"Double Identity": Discursive Traditions

Cultural conflicts are popularly associated with oppositional subcultures such as those that Ivan describes in "NY State of Mind." For this reason, if the remedial student is always-new in much public discourse, so too are identity politics. But City College intellectuals from Vivian Gornick to Irving Howe have discussed cultural betweenness as a particular New York state of mind that the immigrant experiences when moving from the neighborhood to the academic institution. Writing about his remedial students in 1968, Leonard Kriegel saw his students' conflicts as a mirror of his own: "I can still remember how desperately I wanted to retain the shrill Jewish street life of Jerome Avenue *and* Keats' sonnets" (273). Yet, he thought, it was impossible to live with both: "Unfortunately, the day comes when one has to choose, and it seems to me a lie to pretend otherwise. You can afford to be nostalgic about a ghetto only when you have left it. The fact that these students, especially the black ones, also had to choose between their militancy and their desire for 'the knowledge you have' accounts for why a goodly number have already dropped out of the program. It is an extremely difficult problem to handle. America is a cruel country; it thrusts choices on us" (273). Acutely aware of cultural conflicts, the assimilated intellectual reads their resolution through his or her own experience, a tendency in writing about cultural difference that I analyzed in chapter 4. But in controversies from Ebonics to the uses of bilingual education, memoirs like Kriegel's have circulated powerfully to sustain a persuasive ideology: the choice to assimilate is especially acute for black or Latino students, and if it isn't made, then they will drop out of school. While I will consider this logic later on, here I want to stress that, as Min-Zhan Lu has argued, a tradition of ambivalence exists within immigrant and ethnic memoirs. In this context, not all Jewish intellectuals have been satisfied that ambivalence could only be solved by making a "cruel" choice between cultural allegiances.

To counter current assumptions given voice most vividly by writers like James Traub, I'd like to spend some time considering Anzia Yezierska's work, produced during the modernist moment that is a precursor to our postmodern concerns with cultural identity. A sweatshop worker and Russian Jew from the Lower East Side, Yezierska earned a degree from Columbia Teachers College and was catapulted to fame in 1920 with her first story collection, which was made into a movie. Yezierska's life and work are significant today because she reflected extensively upon the hazards of translation during the Progressive Era, the time when, in the wake of urbanization and the huge influx of immigrants (and black migrants), the urban public school was self-consciously assuming its cultural role as an agent of Americanization. While Yezierska recognized the "cruel" choice "thrust" upon the educated immigrant, she, like her contemporary Jane Addams, also proposed that educators—and the culture at large—explore different metaphors to deal with the "difficult problem."

As she reflects in her 1950 semiautobiography, *Red Ribbon on a White Horse,* Yezierska's fame rested not only on her fiction, but also on the fact that she illustrated the living embodiment of the fruits of assimilation through hard work, literacy, and education: she was the "Sweatshop Cinderella" come to life. A scriptwriter tells her, "You're the poor girl who struck it rich. The personification of the happy ending that Hollywood has been turning out" (54). A publicist contacts her to say that a college professor wishes to include her story in an anthology of American literature that he is editing "to illustrate the opportunity America offers to every ambitious immigrant" (79). When journalists merchandize it, Hollywood romanticizes it, and the academy canonizes it, straight-line assimilation becomes a dominant plot for self-translation.

During her brief experience in Hollywood, Yezierska encounters several East Side Jews who have successfully translated themselves out of the ghetto and into a glittering world of privilege and ease. While they refuse to discuss what they have left behind, Yezierska is herself plagued by the loss of her connection to the teeming world of the Lower East Side that she despises but that is the source of her creative energy. Yet, as the scriptwriter suggested, Hollywood doesn't turn out plots concerned with cultural confusion. When Yezierska meets Samuel Goldwyn, he asks her what the plot of her next script will be, and she replies that she is working on a double-murder story. Amused and interested, Goldwyn asks for details about her upcoming thriller. "The plot is the expiation of guilt," she explains. When Goldwyn looks slightly alarmed, Yezierska continues: "I had to break away from my mother's cursing and my father's preaching to live my life; but without them I had no life" (72). She concludes, "And now, here I am—lost in chaos, wandering between worlds—" (73). Goldwyn, who expects a tidier plot and can't accept Yezierska's claim that "I never know what I'm trying to write until it's written" (60), simply flees—and Yezierska, caught between conflicting attachments, leaves Hollywood soon afterward, never to return.

Yezierska dreamed of inventing a passage between the Jewish and the Anglo-Saxon worlds that—to paraphrase Addams in *Twenty Years at Hull-House*—entailed a reciprocal way of giving meaning and relation to both. In *Bread-Givers* (1925), she dramatizes the possibility for translation through higher education, as Sara Smolinsky works her way out of the ghetto by attending college and becoming a teacher. Her account of life at college, "Between Two Worlds," portrays Sara's bitter estrangement from the serenely middle-class life of the school, which excludes the working-class student who labors as a laundress to pay the rent and speaks a heavily accented English. Sara has a wealth of experience that the school cannot validate, and her expressive response to new knowledge is embarrassing in the classroom, where professors emphasize rational, objective analysis. She struggles to master the alienating language of psychology ("words about words") until one day the professor asks his students to supply examples from their experience of a time when a strong emotion interfered with their ability to make a decision (222). At this point, Sara declares that she began to understand college discourse because she saw how knowledge could intersect with personal experience. Still, while she celebrates becoming "a person of reason" (223), she never fully trusts an academic discourse that she believes is divorced from "real life."

Throughout her college years, Sara fantasizes about her contact with a young professor that for her idealizes a cultural union between the rational, self-sufficient male and the expressive, other-oriented female. But it is only in private talks with the older professors that she is able to find moments of true translation: "With the older men I could walk and talk as a person. To them, my Hester Street world was a new world. I gave them mine, and they gave me theirs" (231). In such moments when she becomes a fully translated "person," Yezierska invokes the power of education to offer a place where meaningful translation between cultures could occur to the benefit of both worlds. At the end of her novel, the only possible resolution for the restless heroine seems to be her union with an Americanized Jew, a school principal who returns to the ghetto to teach and to learn Hebrew from Sara's tyrannical father. Similarly, at the end of *Salome of the Tenements* (1923), the vital East Side heroine fails to realize a crosscultural romance with her rational Anglo-Saxon millionaire and ends up with an Americanized Jew, a successful Fifth Avenue designer with whom she plans to establish a nonprofit dress store on Grand Street.

In the modern city stratified by class, ethnicity, gender, and race, Yezierska's mobile heroines yearn to find a space where segregated cultures come into meaningful contact; wandering between worlds, they desire to appropriate aspects of more than one cultural experience. One could say that Sonya Vrunsky's ambivalence toward both the East Side and Fifth Avenue is finally resolved through a syncretic passage between tenement and mansion that ends in the dressmaking store on Grand Street.

Restlessly crossing between worlds, Yezierska's heroines dramatize the sheer complication of the choices that are cruel, but not dichotomous. On the one hand, her heroines highlight the alluring pull of mainstream American values—the restrained rationality of the Anglo-Saxon ruling and professional classes. On the other hand, they usually discover that this elite culture, embodied in men, denies bodily expressiveness and a spiritual dimension to life. Even while Yezierska's characters want to return to the ghetto, they are not nostalgic, for they critique what they've left behind. Though it holds out the promise of spiritual meaning, the traditional patriarchal culture represented by Sara's father is oppressively rigid and hypocritical in many respects. It is neither an embrace of the new nor a complete shedding of the old that Yezierska explores, but a critical perspective that results from her travels across the urban landscape organized by competing cultures and languages.

Rather than being forever caught "between worlds," one might explore a double identity to resolve the tension. In their essays, City College students speak frequently to this possibility, and they often highlight language as the means through which to transcreate self. Translation as a literal activity becomes a motif in such stories, especially when student writers describe their own roles as translators for their immigrant parents. In "Double Identity," Sandra Gonzalez describes how, "at some point in my childhood," she rejected her parents' Latin culture and embraced English literature and language. Like Richard Rodriguez, "I decided to isolate and prefer English as the vehicle to express my 'public identity'" (3). At a garage sale, Gonzalez bought a copy of a Howard Phillips Lovecraft novel in Spanish translation. She bought the book because Lovecraft was her favorite author in English, but to her surprise, "As if I were reading him for the first time, his words seemed to have another dimension, a whole new significance. And they were in Spanish" (4). The translated text brought Gonzalez to her "double identity":

> I could no longer face my appreciation of language without realizing how much I had shut out from my life because of my limited awareness of Spanish.... With the energy of a rebirth, I came to realize that learning Spanish could only enhance and broaden my view of the world. I didn't have to compromise my love for the English language, but added Spanish to my vocabulary. I studied it again, wrote it and spoke it as much as possible, and read its best uses in literature.... My "new" old language opened up new ideas that I had closed myself to. My perception of language superiority completely changed. I sought more books in Spanish. I began to understand and appreciate those customs and behaviors I saw in my parents. Slowly things came full circle for me. (5)

Sandra's desire not to "compromise" her allegiance to one language at the expense of another brings her "full circle," back to a "broader" view of the world, her parents, and her past.

Readers who are interested in exploring transgressive forms of writing in the classroom will object that Sandra's essay illustrates the "taming" of multiculturalism, for she writes like "a thoroughly assimilated college student" (Vandenburg 563). However, my purpose is not to encourage students to "resist" academic discourses that can empower them institutionally and intellectually, but to encourage young writers to examine their private experiences in public contexts so that, like Yezierska's heroines, they can develop a critical perspective on the nature of their choices in a readable form. That perspective might involve a critique of Americanization, as Udo experiences it in "To My Nigerian," or of their attachment to an ethnic subculture, as Ivan describes it in "NY State of Mind." Writers like Zora Neale Hurston and Louise Erdrich, who traveled from rural subcultures to elite private universities, did not lose their allegiance to their ethnic worlds as a result of their educations; rather, they write between conflicting cultures, exploring the oppressive aspects of the ethnic as well as of the mainstream cultures. While both incorporate "low" languages into their fiction and essays (Erdrich uses folklore, Hurston BEV), neither abandons her fidelity to established discursive forms or "high" languages.

Because essays like Sandra's are addressed to general audiences, they sometimes assume a life beyond the classroom, and in this way travel beyond conventional rhetorical situations. Since 1996, "Double Identity," which was written for another teacher in a mainstreamed freshman course, has traveled through several writing classes and the writing center. Published in a departmental newsletter—where I first read it—"Double Identity" has been read by dozens of Sandra's peers, who in turn have cited it in their own essays. Students also cite the familiar essays written by their peers that are published in textbooks like Chitra Divakaruni's *We, Too, Sing America*. It's not unusual for my students to address their essays to their parents, and on occasion to give the finished versions to them to read for comments. In their particular rhetorical situations, a writer like Sandra achieves the status of a public student intellectual, one who addresses readers beyond one classroom.

Sandra's essay also provides alternative images of possible translation for those students who do struggle with a keen sense of loss described in memoirs like Richard Rodriguez's *Hunger of Memory* or Eva Hoffman's *Lost in Translation.* For those intellectuals as for many City College students, translation has already occurred, irrevocably, in the past—as Kriegel suggests in his memoir, conflict can be best understood in terms of what one has lost. "To me," writes Palwinder in "One Word at a Time," "English was the language of the rich, famous and knowledgeable. I struggled day and night to forget Urdu, and I did—one word at a time. But what I didn't realize is that I didn't just forget Urdu, instead I deliberately threw away my identity, my character, my roots and my culture" (1). Similarly, in "Who Am I?," Ana describes how "I needed to hide from society my knowledge of Spanish so I could be seen as an equal"; "I tried not to speak Spanish in public and as little as possible at home" (3).

By contrast, essays like Rebecca's "My Parents: The Language of Love" try to reassert, in the present tense, the double identity that Palwinder or Ana hadn't thought possible when they assimilated to American culture and language. "Shalom, na nishma Imma? Hi, what's up Jinji?" is the dual greeting Rebecca gives to her Israeli mother and her American father on the phone. She now will "explain everything twice. I came to enjoy both worlds, Hebrew and English, Israel and America. I realize how these are intermingled in my thoughts and feelings" (4). At the end of "Who Am I?," Ana cites Min-Zhan Lu's "From Silence to Words," Judith Ortiz Cofer's "The Myth of the Latin Woman," and Ruth Behar's "Translated Woman" to explore the tension that, unlike Rebecca or Sandra, she can't fully resolve. Aligning her conflicts with those experienced by published intellectual women, Ana decides that she cannot choose between her desire to be a good American student and a U.S. citizen who is deeply estranged by U.S. involvement in her parents' home country, El Salvador.

Whether a writer finds the possibility of "intermingled" selves like Rebecca, or, like Ana, starts "to ask questions," the point is that the familiar essay provides a discursive tradition concerned with questions of crosscultural identity, allegiance, and authenticity. Through the essay form, a writer like Ana can dramatize rather than resolve the private tension, which is a hallmark of critical thought. She narrates her specific experiences while also aligning her interpretation of them with her reading of sophisticated academic texts like Lu's "From Silence to Words." Yet Ana produces a form that is readable to her parents as well as to her teachers and classroom peers. Writers like Sandra or Ana transcreate self by exploring the possibility of cultural doubleness or conflict in the present, rather than invoking the dominant imagery of loss and desire rooted in the distant ethnic past.

"Two-Faced Language": Contact Languages

Nowhere is the transcreation of culture more evident today than in the quotidian contact languages developed in U.S. cities like Los Angeles and New York. Contact languages like Spanglish or Chinglish are highly stigmatized in the educational world and in ethnic neighborhoods where border languages can represent a break between generations or between the families in the city and those in the home country. These are truly between tongues, which Amy Tan captures in her fiction, where, as she says in "Mother Tongue," she attempted to invent a liminal speech. To write *The Joy Luck Club*, she says, she practiced a creative translation between her mother's Chinese, the English she used to talk with her mother, and "what I imagined to be her translation of her Chinese if she could speak in perfect English, her internal language, and for that I sought to preserve the essence, but neither an English nor a Chinese structure" (130).

The fused speech that characterizes Tan's fiction is a literary rendering of what the linguist Braj Kachru calls "nativization," an alternative to models where one language wholly supplants another in everyday use (1982, 1990). Nativization goes beyond syntactic or rhetorical changes to create "a new ecology for a non native language" (1982, 7). Linguists have identified new ecologies and distinct Englishes in contact zones in Kenya, Nigeria, Singapore, and India (see essays in Kachru 1982). Kachru writes: "A language in contact is two-faced; it has its own face, and the face it acquires from the language with which it has contact" (341). In his study of nativized English in India, Kachru argues that Indian English is, to use a Sanskrit compound *dvija*, "twice-born" (329). In this double-edged process of assimilating English, Indians have transcreated the language: "In terms of acculturation, two processes seem to be at work. One results in the *deculturation* of English, and another in its *acculturation* in the new context" (329).

Within these contexts, English is nativized in daily life—in newspapers, conversations, or literature—as language users in the postcolonial situation appropriate the dominant language for their particular purposes. In other cases, multiple contact languages are created. "This hybridization of English and an indefinite range of languages is the most extensive of its kind ever known," writes Tom McArthur (14). While critics point to the hegemonic impulse of worldwide Englishes, "few have predicted that under certain circumstances English would simply flow into rather than supplant so many tongues—much as, almost a thousand years ago, the blending of Anglo-Saxon and Norman-French produced something new" (14). Specific hybrids may be transitory, but the condition of hybridity, as the history of English itself illustrates, may be a permanent feature of the geopolitical history of languages.

Pidgins, creoles, border languages, and bilingual code-mixing that exist throughout the world offer the most spectacular cases of creative transculturation. For instance, in the Bronx, the contact between Spanish and English has created a street English that infuses bodega conversation, rap music, and Nuyorican poetry (see Zentella). Chicano literature also makes use of Hispanicized English. Gina Valdés's poem "English con Salsa" welcomes us all to "ESL 100, English Surely Latinized/ ingles con chile y cilantro, English as American / as Benito Juarez" (4). Ana Castillo's novel, *So Far from God*, makes extensive use of English Surely Latinized and provides strategies for writing the familiar essay as well, some of which Ivan used in "NY State of Mind." Though English is the dominant language in Castillo's novel, both narrator and characters frequently lace their English with (sometimes untranslated) Spanglish and English words; use various kinds of code switching (i.e., tags, within and between sentences); allude to Mexican proverbs; and employ an English syntax that bears traces of Spanish (e.g., prepositions or adjectives occupy slots in English that they normally would in Spanish). Bearing the marks of betweenness, English reflects its long contact with Southwestern Mexican Spanish, a transcreation of language in everyday use.

Two-faced language is celebrated today by Latino/a intellectuals, for example by Gloria Anzaldúa, but within ethnic communities and schools it is a highly stigmatized form of language use that students are reluctant to discuss or acknowledge. As François pointed out in his essay on Cocoi, the older generation will often admonish children for using a language that they themselves may use, perhaps unconsciously. In some classes, my students have pursued language research projects where they study border talk using ethnographic techniques like note-taking, interviews, and taped conversations (1997). These projects allow students to analyze the social functions of private literacies from an academic perspective; writers in more so-called mainstream classrooms could also develop projects suitable to their own experiences.

The familiar essay, as I noted with Ivan's "NY State of Mind," lets students nativize their private languages within what is usually a new form for them. Nativization in this case might include the direct quotation of other (untranslated) languages or the use of low registers. But the familiar essay also offers a space for students to critique the widespread, debilitating assumption that they use border talk because they don't speak either language well. Like Sara Smolinsky, these students can feel trapped irrevocably between worlds, half-members of each, because they also share the common assumption that language functions primarily to convey information through grammatical structures. Yet even everyday language performs aesthetic as well as social and historical functions, of which signifiying is only the best-known example.

Ivette, a student in a basic writing class, describes in "Spanglish" her own struggle to view her two-faced language use as a possible transcreation of language. Ivette begins by expressing the distress she feels when she mingles nonstandard Spanish with English because this reflects her distance from her parents' generation. She goes on to use her merged speech as a text for analysis:

> For example, if I am over reacting about any incident my sister may respond by saying "cojelo con take it easy." When

"cojelo con" is translated to English it means "take it with."
Similarly I tell my mother "you are tan nice." "Tan" means
"very" when translated to English. When around my relatives, who are usually very fluent in Spanish, I might say
"pasenme el kechu." "Pasenme" is said correctly and means
"pass me" while "kechu" is "ketchup" in English but is correctly said as "salsa de tomate" or "tomato sauce." When I say
such words as "kechu" my relatives may not understand what
I am saying or simply laugh at me for using such combinations of words to express what I want. (3)

To "remedy" her problem, Ivette considers all sorts of possibilities,
even translating the technique of "free-writing" into her speech as
"free-talking" so she could lose her self-consciousness about her
habits. But she finally concludes that the true resolution of her conflict is understanding why people use Spanglish: "Why should I feel
embarrassed about using Spanglish? The answer lies in why I use
Spanglish. I often use Spanglish when I cannot find the appropriate
or correct Spanish word I want to say" (3). While it appears to reflect
a speaker's lack of fluency, Spanglish, Ivette speculates, may be better viewed as reflecting the peculiar cultural situation of betweenness. A "survival tool" for new immigrants who awkwardly straddle
two worlds, "it is the offspring or child of two languages that col-
lided with one another. Spanglish in itself tells the history of my people in the United States." Therefore, "In my search to find a remedy
for my usage of Spanglish or an unnecessary 's' or 'r' I saw myself
differently. It occurred to me that using Spanglish is a true sign of ingenuity. When in doubt of the meaning or pronunciation of a word,
I and many others have combined what we know of Spanish and
English to create a word that fits the moment. Spanglish is sponta-
neous and its use indicates that one can synthesize and apply their
knowledge. Although comical when spoken, Spanglish serves the
speaker a purpose" (5). Creating "a word that fits the moment," the
speaker caught between languages exhibits "a true sign of ingenuity"
by "spontaneously" "synthesizing" two languages. That synthesis is
a product of a historical "collision" that results in playful, possibly
"comical," speech. Frances Aparicio writes, "What prescriptive lin-

guists, editors, and authorities in education deem a deficit—the so-called interference of Spanish in English—a hybrid, Latino-centered approach values as positive, creative contributions to literature" (202). A "hybrid, Latino-centered approach" allows a writer like Ivette to translate border speech to the written page and to comment to her teachers and peers on the cultural contributions it makes. Ivette says she sees herself as Aparicio the intellectual does—"differently," as a speaker who struggles with an abundance of words, and as a writer who can situate the "comical" low style within "the history of my people."

The Crossover We Like

While most embrace it, for some students, my emphasis upon the moment of interpretation is at times tiresome, and it occasionally invites their resistance, for analysis defines most fully the difference between academic and other kinds of writing For many students, analysis smothers individual response, feeling, and experience—interpretation might be said to be, in Sara Smolinsky's phrasing, "words about words." For students who are members of distinct, oppositional subcultures, analytical academic writing also threatens the self-sufficiency of their own modes of interpreting the world. For teachers who inhabit the academic world, of course, the reverse is true. Responding to a student's essay on gay bashing, Richard Miller concludes that "fault lines in the contact zone" may be a permanent feature of classrooms that invite in a diverse array of private, often oppositional, discourses (also see Morgan).

Such fault lines also suggest that some discourses are more amenable to potential crossover than others, and the borders between some worlds remain, I think, closed to travelers. This may be true, Amy Goodburn shows, for students who bring the perspective of fundamentalist Protestant religions to classrooms. The "narrativizing, dynamic quality" of BEV, for instance, is congruent in many respects with the belletristic traditions with which many writing teachers already identify. The oppositional street talk that enlivens essays like Ivan's is far more acceptable to progressive teachers than the oppositional values of fundamentalist religions, even though, as

Goodburn points out, they constitute a critique of, and resistance to-ward, the dominance of mainstream values. Protestant or Islamic discourses insist on their singular dominance as modes of interpret-ing secular experience, and thus their collision with academic styles may be especially acute. Sacred discourse especially highlights the limits of border pedagogy because it calls attention to those institu-tional roles—and the values that sustain such roles—that may be in-escapable.

The familiar essay works so well within a pedagogy of translation because it accommodates—traditionally, even celebrates—the con-flicted mind that's associated with the crosscultural sensibility char-acteristic of Enlightenment thought. This is, of course, a secular frame of mind that opposes the kind of fundamentalism that Good-burn describes. In "My Father's Religion and Me," Sharn describes the "guilt" and conflict she sometimes experiences in "my thoughts . . . for agreeing with the beliefs of Beckett that contradict the belief of my father's [Muslim] religion" (1). To dramatize "my dilemma," Sharn structures her essay around an internal dialogue with her fa-ther. In the two revisions that she gave me, she rewrote the end-ings—in one, she thinks she will give him the essay to read, but in the other she says she will delete the essay from her disk after printing out the final copy for a grade. Using white space, Sharn juxtaposes a string of Islamic images and prayers with a list of questions about women's role in fundamentalist Islamic religion, politics, and daily life. Both the structure and the content of the familiar essay allow Sharn to express a divided mind that has been a feature of the genre since Montaigne's experimental assays. In its tension between two ways of viewing the world—the sacred, her father's Islam, and the secular, embodied by Western writers like Beckett—Sharn's essay is highly readable.

But for students like Yolande, who accept a fundamentalist reli-gion without question, Sharn's "dilemma" cannot usefully structure a form that depends upon some sort of complication to achieve readability. In "An Angel Was Born," Yolande planned to describe how her family gradually came to accept the death of a little girl, Mercedes, through their religion. When Yolande revised this essay, she had difficulty finding a point of interpretation in a story of spiritual transformation that precludes the kind of "dilemma" that Sharn, an English major, can more easily dramatize. Like Dr. Davis, who struggled to narrate the story of her lab experiment and to rerepresent it for the journal editors, Yolande had to translate between her particular story and the dominant values of her readership, for both writers experienced a moment of friction centered on whether to produce a "phony story."

Yet unlike Dr. Davis's, Yolande's translation involved expressing values and beliefs that don't belong in the academic world. To solve the problem—to allow Yolande to tell her story, while also helping her to produce an essay that would be readable in my class—I asked her to defamiliarize the cultural setting within which the spiritual experience took place. Yolande chose to describe Mercedes's death and change into a "guardian angel" as an illustration of how her family has accumulated memories that help them to sustain an ethnic identity. Using Judith Ortiz Cofer's "Silent Dancing" as a model, Yolande focused on a Puerto Rican song (Cofer uses a home movie) as a marker of the family's memories of Mercedes. Songs, like some of the daily household objects Yolande describes, "float around our lives [and] make the memories impossible to bury" (2). By interpreting those aspects of the experience that are secular, Yolande preserves the climactic moment of Mercedes's change into an angel, making an effort to translate the dominant discourse of her life into a school context. Yet such a crossover is difficult to achieve through the use of the familiar form, which has unyielding secular roots; possibly Yolande felt that she compromised herself.

Two-Sided Access: Translation as Mainstream Appropriation

The student writers I've discussed make genuine contributions to translation theory by offering their distinct imagery to supplant deficit or emptiness, and by writing stories that complicate straight-line models. City College students expand a body of translation scholarship that already exists in composition studies, inflecting it with their own particular experiences as urban border crossers. Because many of these and dozens of others I haven't discussed won departmental awards and have been circulated about the campus, these intercultural narratives have also had a strong local impact on other students, who frequently cite each others' literacy narratives when writing their own. When these writers return to their neighborhoods as new professionals or move to the suburban metropolitan area, as others do, they may carry with them alternative images of the conflicted relationships between identity, language, and cultural value.

Over the years, my knowledge of these relationships has been immeasurably enlarged as I continue to read students' intercultural stories and/or research. Translation has occurred for me, as I've questioned the dominance of the critical essay and reconsidered the kinds of reading that I assign in writing, linguistics, or literature courses. In my conferences with Yolande, I experienced discomfort when describing the effect her essay had upon me as a reader; it was difficult to say to her that what she found meaningful sounded like a cliché to me. My experience with Yolande and many students like her illustrates one of the greatest benefits of using translation to think about composition teaching—it heightens our awareness of how profoundly we are, as writers, scholars, and teachers, settled in institutions that serve both to reproduce the dominant culture and to critique that reproduction. I therefore want to end by recontextualizing translation, a linguistic and a cultural process, within the more material, historical, and institutional terms that have framed this book.

Yolande's struggle to appropriate the familiar form to describe her spiritual experience offers one illustration of the fault lines in the contact zone that Miller identifies. But another fault line in the zone may be how mainstream or dominant cultures absorb subcultural difference for social and economic gain. In the U.S., the entrepreneurs of mainstream cultures appropriate oppositional subcultures for profit. In part, the profit is cultural for, as Michael North argues in his revisionist study of literary modernism, white writers do blackface both to transgress middle-class norms and to reinforce the low status of the appropriated cultural style. However, as Ivan noted in "NY State of Mind," syncretism can also be a "business like everything else in life." The blending of private and public literacies that I think can be accomplished through the familiar essay is also akin to the globalization of cultures, a complex and often troubling intertwining of the economic with the sociopolitical that is dramatized in postcolonial fiction like Edwidge Danticat's *The Farming of Bones*.

Cultural fusion has always characterized mainstream American cultures, as Albert Murray pointed out some time ago, but that fusion often works to suppress rather than to liberate subcultural groups. Particularly useful in this regard is Edwin Burrows and Mike Wallace's history of New York City, which provides several examples of the appropriation of subaltern cultures by mainstream entrepreneurs and political groups. The minstrel show's fate in the city stands as an especially racist intermingling of discourses in American popular culture. In one of the most bizarre twists of cultural history, P. T. Barnum, who aggressively appropriated street culture and marketed it for a mass audience, found himself at a loss when, early in his career, one of his white dancers who entertained in blackface became ill. Scouring the slums for a replacement, Barnum found a young black boy whom he dressed up as a white in blackface so that he could perform for a white audience (644). This hybrid crossover did not constitute a change in essential class relationships but in fact obscures a history of economic struggle. Burrows and Wallace explain that before the rise of the minstrel show, the black West Indian entrepreneur, William Henry Brown, owned and operated the African Grove, a theater featuring black talent. Eventually Brown expanded and renamed the Grove the African Theater in the early 1820s. The African Theater was quite popular with both blacks and whites, but when it threatened to compete with the white-owned Park Theater, Brown's days were numbered: repeated attacks upon actors by thugs hired by the Park's manager, a hostile city government, and the beating of Brown himself finally resulted in the venture's demise (487–88).

The abortive and violent history of the African Theater in New York City illustrates that a cultural takeover was also an economic appropriation—whites denied blacks the right to institutionalize their culture, to distribute it themselves for a profit in their own theater that was drawing integrated crowds. Coco Fusco points out

through several historical illustrations that "the mainstream appropriation of subaltern *cultures* in this country has historically served
as a substitute for ceding to those peoples any real political or economic power" (30). The upsurge of Jumping Jim Crow soon after the
African Theater's demise involved a racist fusion of cultural forms
and an economic seizure of a commercially profitable venture.
Again, as Fusco points out, "interracial or intercultural desire,
whether it goes by the name of 'slumming,' border crossing, or appropriation, in and of itself does not disrupt historically entrenched
inequities" (76). Intellectuals should be aware of the distinction, for
otherwise, "we lapse back into the integrationist rhetoric of the
1960s, and conflate hybridity with parity" (76).

If we should be aware of how we "conflate hybridity with parity,"
then it follows that we also must be conscious of how we conflate access to knowledge with access to institutions. Even a more radical
hybridization of forms than I've described here will not contest academic selectivity. An uncritical celebration of border pedagogy can
sometimes be used, as I suggested in chapter 4, to mask material differences. For instance, retention rates, a point of heated debate at the
City University and elsewhere, can be exclusively linked to cultural
rather than to economic struggles, despite intellectuals' differing political intentions. As Danticat painfully reveals in *The Farming of
Bones*, a rhetoric of linguistic difference can serve to cover up the
more essential economic differences that materially organize social
relations, in her case Haiti and the Dominican Republic.

The distinction that a novelist like Danticat makes is crucial because, as with the African Theater's history, cultural intermingling
depends upon or perhaps follows shifts in class relationships. James
Traub insists that the Jewish greenhorns who enrolled at the City
College before the 1960s eagerly assimilated to dominant intellectual cultures. But these students, all men, also didn't pay tuition
when they were the majority. According to Lavin and Hyllegard's
study, the fact that students of color had to pay tuition when they became the majority at City College in the mid-1970s constitutes a material difference that affected their academic performance. As I
showed in chapter 4, a powerful coalition of educational reformers
in New York has successfully argued for the downsizing of the City

University by attacking remediation and invoking a rhetoric of cultural difference that has long had an ambivalent resonance in American society.

A contradiction arose in the late '80s that further illustrates these unequal relationships between kinds of access that I distinguished in chapter 1. While articles in the *Chronicle of Higher Education* questioned the value of open access policies and remedial education, multiculturalism flourished throughout the academy and in composition studies more particularly. In other words, culturally responsive scholarship was being developed while an institution like the City University, which probably enrolls the most diverse student body in the four-year sector, was being steadily privatized and institutional policies were being phased in to curtail nontraditional students' access to traditional knowledge. Similarly, in 1995, Alice Roy showed how at the California State University, the increase of diversity rhetoric in university documents paralleled the downsizing of composition programs that usually support working-class and culturally diverse students in the system. "My informal consultations, by telephone and email, with colleagues in English studies and composition across the country," she notes, "provide information that, although in a very few cases attention to diversity has resulted in an expansion of composition programs and resources, most show significant reductions in response to financial constraints" (190) Drawing from Kenneth Burke, Roy concludes that diversity rhetoric performs therapeutic, rather than resistant, functions, for "the good intentions of documents on inclusion and diversity remain lodged within the social and economic 'scene' which they would improve" (191).

Roy's close reading of university documents, admissions policies, and students' financial backgrounds underscores the gaps between the rhetoric of diversity and the academy's essential selective functions. We need, then, to question whether border pedagogies actually can or do address social class differences. We need to examine our own assumptions about what constitutes reform and resistance, and what role we can play, as WPAs, scholars, or teachers, in contesting selectivity. Mina Shaughnessy's "iconic" status arouses so much passion because her legacy highlights this tension between points of access that aren't equivalent. Her status as a translation theorist remains conflicted, because, though she acknowledged students' intercultural struggles, Shaughnessy did not make them central to either her scholarship or her pedagogy. In chapter 3, I tried to disentangle Shaughnessy's work as a language theorist from her administrative labors—her concern to create and sustain access to a traditional, high-status education for nontraditional, low-status students. While her approach to translation assumed that students must ultimately make "cruel" choices between worlds, her goal was always to enable students to be in the position to make these choices. Border pedagogy can't resolve the tension that Shaughnessy's work embodies, but it can remind basic writing teachers that their programs are often institutionalized to perform the conflicting political goals that I described in chapters 2 and 3.

I am not suggesting that we return to error as a root metaphor for organizing basic writing scholarship, as some scholars are beginning to argue in these troubled times (see chapter 4). On the contrary, my work here argues that the politics of language use should remain central to classroom work. Another way to think about the tension surrounding Shaughnessy's legacy is to critique but not to abandon the initiation model, which assumed from the beginning that cultural estrangement was a feature of learning to write. In her forward to *Academic Discourse and Critical Consciousness*, Patricia Bizzell explores the "ambivalence" inherent in the term "initiation" as she originally used it in the '80s to describe her work as a basic writing teacher. While she later understood how the term functions negatively to evade issues of power and authority, I think its more positive dimensions remain valuable to teachers now. In a "positive sense," Bizzell saw "initiation" as a social ritual marking the journeys that college students everywhere always have to make: "as a process that provides mechanisms of inclusion and empowerment, especially for so-called nontraditional students." Though she later complicated, perhaps even abandoned the term, she recalls that it "foregrounds the personal feelings and culturally constructed, perhaps unconscious prejudices and assumptions in teachers and students that condition the entry process" (19).

I've tried to "foreground" the "constructed prejudices and assumptions" of the academy by stressing in my classes the "culturally constructed" ways in which "personal feelings" are represented. The pedagogy I've implied here attempts to relate "the personal feelings" and voices of students with conventional forms, to enlarge their private concerns by engaging them with public ones. In the classroom, I explicitly teach the contours and histories of forms as a way to make meaning—in the case of personal writing, to shape not what student writers say happened, but how they represent what happened. In this respect, the school's ways with words are expressed through dominant forms whose discursive histories and shapes I think progressive teachers have to consider more explicitly than might currently be the case. The critique of the initiation model was necessary in composition scholarship, but, because writing courses are often institutionally organized to perpetuate that model, we cannot afford to ignore its power, which motivated curricular reform in the '80s. Most of us wouldn't want to abandon a two-faced discourse that reproduces the dominant culture while providing access to its critique. The tension between making "pragmatic accommodations" and fostering "critical consciousness" will never be resolved—but we can openly discuss the tension with students as a struggle that writers often experience when writing meaningfully across worlds.

In the practice I've described here, I invite students to render their experiences through a conventional form that in some ways exceeds academic norms because it depends upon knowledge and experience that writers already bring with them to the classroom. My emphasis upon the interpretation of texts and self-reflection upon experience are hallmarks of traditional critical thought that I hope will be useful for students when they write critical essays in required humanities courses or research papers for electives in several fields. But the familiar essay represents only one among several approaches to crossovers in perspective, discourse, audience, or content. Paul Heilker's hybrid research paper, the ethnographic projects developed by Richard Courage or Eleanor Kutz and her colleagues, and excellent textbooks that are introductions to cultural studies, such as Diana George and John Trimbur's *Reading Culture*, represent other, equally viable possibilities. In such cases, teachers validate students' worlds by giving them access to powerful forms that are two-faced, capable of being nativized by the writer who accents them with his or her voice.

Advocates of border pedagogy must continue to raise those questions with which I began this chapter. As important, they must provide concrete examples with which to illustrate their particular answers (the same, of course, might be said of critics like Peter Vandenburg). Does the acculturating pull of an institution create conflicts for both students and teachers who are interested in exploring more transgressive models than I've done here? Is discursive crossover—especially when the writer controls nonstandard forms—possible only when it's managed self-consciously? What kinds of traditions already exist in American history and culture that will provide continuity for our efforts? I mentioned in chapter 3 the short-lived work of the Institute for Social History at City College, which attempted to teach students to gather data from their own communities to construct social histories. What crossovers are being developed in courses outside English departments? Where else might personal literacies usefully intersect with public ones?

My local answer to these global questions is to emphasize to my students that they can speak, read, and write like a public intellectual. In their responses to Richard Rodriguez, Ruth Behar, and Gloria Anzaldúa, my students frequently talk back, invent their own metaphors, and self-consciously imitate the styles of authors with whom they identify. They can reflect upon, validate, or critique their private languages in broader, more historical or public contexts. They cite each other's essays or those by other students reprinted in textbooks and often give copies to their parents and friends outside of class. In my view, to strive to make such connections between private and public literacies, between specialized and general audiences—to "congregate an ethos"—is one of the most meaningful goals of a liberal arts education.

It is this striving, finally, that characterizes the best translation scholarship and the practices resulting from it. Such scholarship will not resolve the tensions between access and excellence, though it does help us to see the differences between disciplinary and institutional politics, and between the politics of access to institutions and the access to traditional curriculums. Within composition, cultural, and literary studies, and through ethnographic, fictional, and autobiographical accounts, translation theory offers a robust tradition that both sustains and critiques the traditional goals of a composition course. In its own restricted political context, translation theory also counters reactionary representations of students while offering a substantial intellectual practice for the classroom. Translation theory seeks to embrace the struggles that most writers live through and to invent metaphors, styles, and forms through which writers from subcultural groups gain access to dominant languages. If it remains a self-critical theory whose practices are continually revised in response to institutional history, identity, and authority, translation is a root metaphor that can speak powerfully to the cultural moment in which we live now.

Notes

1. A note on terms: I use the phrase "access to the liberal arts" even though traditional liberal arts study may no longer occupy the center of a university education. My reasoning is that most four-year institutions still require students to complete distribution or core course requirements before entering a professional program in architecture, engineering, nursing, business, or prelaw. Following the standard use of scholars of higher education, I also use "vocational" to distinguish between the missions of different segments of private and public higher education. "Vocational" is an especially tricky term—since the turn of the twentieth century, students report in surveys that they enrolled in college less for the sheer love of learning and more for vocational reasons (see Veysey 1965 and Astin 1993 for data). In my view, the salient difference between the vocation of, say, dentistry as opposed to dental hygiene assistant is large enough in economic and status terms to warrant a specific use of the word "vocational." Vocational tracks usually deemphasize impractical curriculums like the humanities and, as Clark (1987) illustrates with data, hard sciences that are devoted to pure research (e.g., physics). Furthermore, as Shor (1986) points out, the emphasis upon vocationalism may also serve to quell political dissent and the critical thinking associated with impractical curriculums in the humanities and some social sciences. Institutional stratification also ensures that students who desire to become dentists, doctors, or lawyers, even teachers or engineers, will find it more statistically unlikely that they will realize that aspiration if they begin a career in the two-year college. As Dougherty (1994) points out, the diversionary role of the two-year college is nevertheless complex; see note 3 in chapter 3 for a summary of research on this question.

2. See Lunsford's dissertation (1977) for historical background. Books that focus on the institutional dynamics of remedial courses include DiPardo's ethnography (1993) and Tom Fox's study of debates about standards (1999). Articles exploring the extrainstitutional and institutional politics of remediation have begun to grow in recent years. One of the first was Jensen's (1988) study of the politics of developmental programs in Georgia; Greenberg discusses the politics of assessment at Hunter College (1993). Severino describes the program

at the University of Illinois at Chicago (1996), Royster-Jones and Taylor at Ohio State University (1997), Stygall at the University of Washington (1999), Collins and Blum at the University of Minnesota's General College (1999), and Crouch and McNenny in the California State University system (2000). Gunner (1993) describes the status of basic writing teachers and Mutnick (2000) the politics of downsizing. Shor (1997, 2000) analyzes remediation and social stratification.

CHAPTER 2

1. Ohmann's collection of essays (1976/1996), including a chapter by Wallace Douglas on composition at Harvard, was the first to analyze composition's status in the academy; he developed this trenchant critique in a later collection (1987). Berlin's important histories (1984, 1987) also introduced Kitzhaber's dissertation (1953/1990), probably the first to chart the decline of rhetoric and the rise of composition in the modern American university. Berlin's work on the emergence of composition studies within particular sociopolitical and historical circumstances was critiqued and/or extended throughout the 1990s, most effectively by Susan Miller (1991), Brereton (1995), and Crowley (1998). Through a string of articles published in the 1980s, Stewart analyzes the departmental politics of literature and composition (see, for starters, 1992), as does Winterowd (1998). Herzberg (1991) ties curriculum to class and institutional stratification. Connors (1996) provides thorough treatment of composition teaching in the nineteenth and the early twentieth centuries. Thomas Miller (1997) focuses on composition teaching in eighteenth-century England, which provides a striking parallel to composition's roles in the American academy.

2. Daniels (1983), Adams (1993), and Trimbur (1991) supply examples of literacy crisis within and beyond the nineteenth and early twentieth-century academy; Ohmann (1987) offers a critique of both the 1890s and 1970s crises. Lunsford (1977, 1987) and Gere (1991) discuss how the mainstream press reported on the literacy crisis of the 1970s, which offers parallels to nineteenth-century panics. General histories like Rudolph's (1977), Wechsler's (1977), or Brubacher and Rudy's (1976/1997) also supply vivid examples of complaints about students' literacy over the last three hundred years.

3. For the history of the curricular subdivision of upper-level writing courses, see Russell (1991), Adams and Adams (1991), and Adams (1993).

4. Gere (1987) gives the best account of how writing groups functioned both on and off the nineteenth-century American college campus.

5. Coursework is described for these years in the annual *Registers* for 1901–2; 1902–3; 1906–7; 1912–13; 1915–16; 1927–28; 1930–31; 1931–32, all in the City College of New York Archives. Coursework for later years can be found in *Bulletins* for 1938–39; 1940–41; 1950–51; 1959–60; 1965–66; 1966–67; 1968–69; 1970–71; 1983–85, all in the City College of New York Archives.

CHAPTER 3

1. See *Remembering Mina Shaughnessy* (1994), which includes reprints of her essays and remarks from friends and luminaries. Lyons (1985) memorialized her; Maher (1997) wrote the biography. Books like Brereton's important anthology (1995) are dedicated to her.

2. Harris (1997) provides a detailed summary (129–131); see note 4, below.

3. Clark (1960a, 1960b) first advanced the cooling-out thesis and since then, leftist scholars have critiqued and extended the argument that the two-year sector exists to protect the upper tiers by containing students' aspirations through what became primarily a terminal mission. Cohen and Brawer (1987) thought that the transfer function of community colleges was on the rise in the 1980s, though they expressed concern about the heavy stress on vocationalism in the schools they studied. Dougherty (1994) argues that the two-year college does provide access to higher education for students who never intend to go beyond a few courses or an associate's degree. However, he also shows that a substantial group of students enters two-year colleges with backgrounds similar to students at four-year colleges—yet this group drops out or does not transfer to the four-year school while the other group completes a B.A. Therefore, he concludes that the two-year college is a contradictory institution, one that provides access while also protecting the upper tiers of higher education. Brint and Karabel (1989) present data to bolster their arguments that two-year schools divert low-income and minority students from the B.A. They refine "cooling-out" by arguing that, up until the 1970s, students and parents resisted the vocational function, while corporate sponsors paid little attention to this sector. They show how, over a half century, sustained lobbying by community college presidents and boosters who formed coalitions with powerful presidents and educators in the four-year sector replaced the transfer mission with a vocational mission. Dougherty confirms this analysis but adds that local and state officials helped considerably to shape the institution for reasons having to do with their own advancement in local politics. Case study research of students' experience in the two-year college such as London's (1978) or Weis's (1985) suggests that teachers, students, and their institutions themselves reinforce the diversionary function. Lavin and Hyllegard (1996) summarize the debate this way: "Our findings, in line with those of others, indicate that both in the 1970s and the 1980s, community colleges had a net negative influence on educational attainment" at CUNY by diverting minorities from the B.A. offered in senior colleges (241). Shor (1980, 1997) first applied Clark's "cooling-out" thesis to college remediation. Two-year faculty in recent collections like Alford and Kroll's (2001) also describe the cooling-out functions of remedial English, even as they seek to develop resistant pedagogies and institutional practices.

4. John Rouse (1979) began the assessment of Shaughnessy's legacy through

a critique of her formalism, which in 1980 provoked a firestorm of response and counterresponse (Allen; Graff; Lawlor; Rouse). Bartholomae (1986) and Hunter (1992) offered less polarized analyses that also highlight Shaughnessy's shaping influence on a generation of composition scholars. Lu's challenge to Shaughnessy's formalism (1991, 1992/1999) sparked a scholarly uproar. This debate was fueled by the *Journal of Basic Writing*'s decision to award its Mina Shaughnessy prize to Lu's essay, and then to award Laurence's rebuttal essay (1993) the same prize in 1994. The debate continued in a lively "Symposium" (1993). Subsequent articles include Gay (1993); Mutnick (1996); Horner (1996/1999); Harris (1997); Gray-Rosendale (1998); and Gunner (1998b). Gunner notes that debates about Shaughnessy's legacy were held in the 1990s through electronic forums as well.

5. Clark (1987) shows in his analysis of faculty attitudes, workload, and governance within the American academy that professors' allegiance to their disciplines is strongest in the top tiers and weakens considerably in the lower tiers. Several of the two-year college faculty in Alford and Kroll's collection (2001) describe and analyze the keen differences they feel on a daily basis between disciplinary and institutional allegiances, and the sometimes sharp divide between disciplinary and institutional resistance.

6. *Department of English, Minutes of the Regular Meeting* 4 November 1971; 18 November 1971; 2 December 1972, in the City College of New York Archives, contain references to mixed programs, as does Skurnick (1972).

7. *Department of English, Minutes of the Regular Meeting* for 8 October 1970; 4 November 1971; 18 November 1971; 2 December 1972; and 7 December 1972 contain vigorous and interesting debates on these issues, as does Gross (1970–71) and the unsigned *Chairman's Report* for 1973–74 (City College of New York Archives).

8. Fiellin (1972); Gross (1972); *Department of English Newsletters* (1971, 1972); Shaughnessy (1970); and Skurnick (1971, 1972).

9. Gallagher (1968); *Department of English, Minutes of the Regular Meeting* for 9 September 1969 (City College of New York Archives). The *Department of English, Minutes of the Regular Meeting* for 28 September 1973 (City College of New York Archives) also record a lengthy censure from a faculty member of Geoffrey Wagner's public remarks about open admissions, which a majority of professors present voted to put on the record. The censure of Wagner takes on added interest because Lu (1992/1999) uses his book to illustrate the pressures that Shaughnessy endured. While I would never minimize the opposition toward Shaughnessy or open admissions, at the same time Wagner's views were probably not typical of the City College faculty but are more usefully located within the "decline of the university" genre that Clark Kerr remarks was typical of the academy's response to severe budget cuts in the early 1970s. Personnel records in the City College of New York Archives indicate that Wagner had a personal axe to grind with his institution that predated open admissions. Material considerations like tenure and promotion, the increase of teaching loads, and unequal

funding for the humanities, all fueled by personal conflict, are more deeply inter-woven with curricular reform or reforms like open admissions than is some-times appreciated or understood.

CHAPTER 4

1. Ohmann (1987) called the 1970s crisis "a hoax" and offered his own data in support of this thesis; he also provides a cogent reading of the 1890s crisis, as does Susan Miller (1991) and Brereton (1995). Trimbur (1991) and Shor (1986) offer excellent analyses of the crisis of the 1970s. See also Sledd (1988), Lunsford (1997, 1987), and Gere (1991).

2. Discussions in the mainstream press on admissions requirements in the context of reducing or shifting remediation can be found for California in Wil-davsky (1995a, 1995b) and Stewart (1995); a scholarly overview appears in Crouch and McNenny (2000). For Florida, see "Majority Need Remedial Help" (1995); for Louisiana, Bacon-Blood (2000); for Massachusetts, Dembner (1993a, 1995b); for Chicago's City Colleges, James (1992, 1993); for Missouri, Brown (1994), and Thomson (1992b); for Mississippi, Applebome (1996). Lively (1993, 1995), Gold (1995), Lauter (1995), Schrag (1999), and Mutnick (2000) touch on several states in national overviews.

3. "Black, Latino Students Lag." For similar and more recent figures, see *Newsweek* ("Berkeley's New Colors," 2000) and O'Brien (2000). The best overview of the long-term consequences of affirmative action is Bowen and Bok (1998); Mutnick (2000) discusses affirmative action and basic writing programs.

4. Solomon with Hussey (1998) and Cooper (1998) offer instructive close readings of the politics of downsizing in New York, for example, by tracing out the network of relationships between politicians, intellectuals, and business groups who have an interest in privatizing public higher education. Significantly, Solomon writes, the bitter attacks on all public higher education in New York State didn't originate in popular demand but were specifically fomented by "a fairly small and closely connected set of groups, who share a broader ideological agenda, institutional affiliations, and deep-pocketed right-wing financial spon-sors" (1). Solomon underscores how attacks on open access, affirmative action, and bilingual education can be orchestrated by a specific network of intellectu-als, politicians, and well-funded think tanks. It's no accident that, in New York, a leader of these attacks, Heather Mac Donald, is affiliated with the Manhattan In-stitute, an influential think tank that has supported intellectuals like Charles Murray or Abigail Thernstrom, who are outspoken critics of remediation, open access policies, multiculturalism, and affirmative action in all public higher edu-cation. This institute supplied educational policy ideas to Republican Governor George Pataki, who led attacks on SUNY's multicultural curriculum, and to Mayor Rudolph Giuliani, who appointed Mac Donald to the Advisory Task Force on CUNY, which produced the Schmidt Report I've described. As Solomon concluded, these attacks did not have as their main goal the improve-

ment of student writing or learning, but the downsizing of the public sphere. Trustees, politicians, and intellectuals having ties to groups like the Manhattan Institute or CHANGE-NY/Empire Foundation, and "almost all graduates of private schools and recipients of corporate largesse," she writes, "they want to do away with government support of—everything" (1).

5. Boylan (1995) notes that in 1991, the National Center for Education Statistics reported that about a third of all entering freshmen took at least one remedial course. The problem with this figure, he argues, is that it focuses only on freshmen and ignores that considerable group of students who receive tutoring over the years in lieu of remedial courses, or who for various reasons don't take remedial courses until well after the first year. Boylan estimates that this group represents about 15 percent of the whole. Along with the 700,000 enrolled in equal opportunity programs, Boylan estimates the total number of students receiving remediation in all institutions to be about 2,909,079. Schrag (1999) cites Clifford Adelman's analysis of transcripts, which puts the figure at 40 percent for students in four-year schools who have taken at least one remedial course. Selingo (2000) reports that 81 percent of all institutions offer at least one remedial course. *College Remediation* estimates that 78 percent of all institutions in the fall of 1995 offered at least one remedial course, or 81 percent of public and 63 percent of private institutions. Both Knopp and *College Remediation* discuss the difficulty of counting remedial courses. Knopp notes that students and institutions supply conflicting numbers, while *College Remediation* offers anecdotes of underreporting, especially at private schools nervous that the presence of a remedial curriculum might damage funding opportunities. As I discussed in chapter 2, much remediation has always been ad hoc, not systematic. The most systematic kind, of course, and thus the most easily countable, is found at the two-year college, which surely increases the official amount of remediation that appears to go on in the two-year sector.

6. This may be why, for instance, articles about CUNY students' illiteracy often appear in policy journals next to essays about Afrocentrism, with City College's Leonard Jeffries occupying a central role. The issues of *City Journal* and *The Public Interest* that featured Mac Donald's lead articles also contained essays attacking Afrocentrism, including one by Nathan Glazer in the latter. Similarly, the longest chapter in Traub's book concerns an Afrocentrist professor whose institutional presence and influence are central only in documents like these. Jeffries's presence is far more monumental when it is represented than in the daily institutional life of students and faculty. Traub's fascination with Afrocentrism helps, of course, to stress that both remediation and the humanities have run amok in an era of declining standards and politicized curriculums.

7. An instructive contrast here is with E. R. Braithwaite's autobiography, *To Sir, with Love* (1959; rpt. 1987, New York: Jove Books), which I often assign in writing courses required for education majors. Braithwaite begins the autobiog-

raphy by juxtaposing the ugly, smelly urban aesthetic of London's bombed-out East End and its disorderly schoolchildren with his pleasant memories of schooldays in British Guiana, characterized by green lawns, orderly rows of desks, and disciplined children. By the book's end, however, Braithwaite's dichotomy breaks down as he begins to see the students' aesthetic as a creative, working-class response to difficult conditions. One reason Braithwaite re-represents the students is that he begins to see them through his own degraded status as a black colonial in postwar Britain who also embarks on a sexually transgressive relationship with a white teacher.

CHAPTER 5

1. All the students I've quoted here generously gave me permission to use their work for educational and/or research purposes. I have changed their names except in Sandra Gonzalez's case, since her literacy narrative was published in a composition program newsletter in 1996.

2. A concern with linguistic and cultural translation preoccupied scholars who first developed basic writing as a field of inquiry. Shaughnessy (1977), Smitherman (1977), Rose (1983), Bizzell (see essays collected in 1992), and Bartholomae and Petrosky (1986) provided a framework that was expanded later by Fox (1990), Horner and Lu (see essays in 1999), Gilyard (1991), Severino (1992), Kutz, Groden, and Zamel (1993), Courage (1993), and more recently, Bizzell (2000). Translation has also been a focus in writing across the curriculum research, especially in those case studies that follow a novice's initiation into new discourses, for example Haas's (1994) longitudinal study of one student's efforts to learn to read and write biology. Translation theory also inflects work concerned with the freshman course: Brooke (1991), Spellmeyer (1993), and Harris (1997).

3. See a lively symposium, "Writing within and against the Academy" (1990), which established the parameters of the debate. Canagarajah (1997) discusses parodic resistance to academic discourse. From her analysis of professional discourse produced by academics in the humanities and social sciences, Susan Mac-Donald (1994) offers a brief but thoughtful critique of the debate by demonstrating the difficulties of defining what we mean by academic discourse.

4. Lu's (1987) and Shen's (1987) literacy narratives were among the first to explore these issues, followed soon after by Rose (1989), Gilyard (1991), and Brodkey (1994). For discussions of pedagogy in multicultural contexts, see Dean (1989), Kutz, Groden, and Zamel (1993), Anokye (1994), Soliday (1994), Sirc (1994), and essays in Severino, Guerra, and Butler (1997).

5. Essays by Orwell, Achebe, and Naipaul can be found in Gilbert Muller and Alan Crooks's 1994 collection, *Major Modern Essayists* (2nd ed. Englewood Cliffs, N.J.: Prentice Hall). Literacy narratives may be found in dozens of collections, which have proliferated since I began teaching the form a decade ago. Bar-

bara Mellix's "From Outside, In," can also be found in Sara Garnes et al (1996) *Writing Lives: Exploring Literacy and Community* (New York: St. Martin's), along with related essays, poems, and stories. Other essays that students read and alluded to in their narratives that I discuss in this chapter include Amy Tan's "Mother Tongue" and Judith Ortiz Cofer's "Silent Dancing," which are reprinted in Robert Atwan (2001), *The Best American Essays* (3rd college ed., Boston: Houghton Mifflin). Paule Marshall's "The Making of a Writer" and Cofer's "Casa: A Partial Remembrance of a Puerto Rican Childhood" can be found in Lynn Bloom's (1998) *The Essay Connection* (5th ed. Boston: Houghton Mifflin), which also contains intercultural narratives written by Bloom's students. Ruth Behar's literacy narrative (1993) can be excerpted from her ethnography, *Translated Woman: Crossing the Border with Esperanza's Story* (Boston: Beacon). The essay that Ruben Acosta used, Rosario Ferré's "On Destiny, Language, and Translation: or, Ophelia Adrift in the C. & O. Canal," can be found in Anuradha Dingwaney and Carol Maier's 1995 collection, *Between Languages and Cultures: Translation and Cross-Cultural Texts* (Pittsburgh: University of Pittsburgh Press). Essays in this collection also provide translation strategies that are transferable to composition classrooms. Rachel Jones's "What's Wrong with Black English" can be found in Richard Holeton's 1992 *Encountering Cultures: Reading and Writing in a Changing World* (Englewood Cliffs, N.J.: Prentice Hall). In addition, Henry Knepler and Myrna Knepler's 1991 *Crossing Cultures: Readings for Composition* (New York: Macmillan) and Chitra Divakaruni's 1998 *We, Too, Sing America* (Boston: Houghton Mifflin), contain intercultural narratives that I used in these courses; Divakaruni includes students' narratives from her college, which were especially helpful to students at mine. The best cultural studies texts I've used are Diana George and John Trimbur's (1999) *Reading Culture: Contexts for Critical Reading and Writing* (3rd ed., Longman) and Joyce Moser and Ann Watters' (1999) *Creating America: Reading and Writing Assignments* (2nd ed., Prentice Hall).

6. Erickson (1987) overviews resistance research. Ogbu (1974) was one of the first to perform ethnographic research on cultural resistance in America, followed by Willis (1977) in Great Britain. Individual studies in American schools include Ballenger (1992), Schultz (1994), and Rumbaut (1996). For Great Britain, see Edwards (1997). In the two-year American college, Weis (1985), using British cultural studies work, for example Willis's, documented these collisions for African American students; London examines the clash between white working-class and academic cultures at a community college (1985). Authors in Zwerling and London's (1992) collection study the struggles of first-generation college students in all sectors of higher education. In the four-year college, see Balester's (1993) and Wallace and Bell's (1999) work with African Americans, and Helen Fox's (1994) with international students at the University of Michigan.

Works Cited

"Ability to Pay Becomes Factor in Admissions." 1990. *New York Times* 6 May: 51: 1.

Adams, Katherine. 1993. *A History of Professional Writing Instruction in American Colleges.* Dallas: Southern Methodist University Press.

Adams, Katherine, and John Adams. 1991. "Advanced Composition: Where Did It Come From? Where Is It Going?" In *Teaching Advanced Composition.* Ed. Katherine Adams and John Adams. Portsmouth, N.H.: Boynton/Cook, 3–15.

Addams, Jane. 1910. Rpt. 1981. *Twenty Years at Hull House.* New York: Signet.

———. 1930. "Widening the Circle of Enlightenment: Hull House and Adult Education." *Journal of Adult Education* 2: 276–79.

Alford, Barry, and Keith Kroll, eds. 2001. *The Politics of Writing in the Two-Year College.* Portsmouth, N.H.: Boynton/Cook

Allen, Michael. 1980. "Writing away from Fear: Mina Shaughnessy and the Uses of Authority." *College English* 41: 857–67.

Anderson, Worth, Cynthia Best, and Alycia Black, et al. 1990. "Cross-Curricular Underlife: A Collaborative Report on Ways with Academic Words." *College Composition and Communication* 41: 11–36.

Anokye, Akua Duku. 1994. "Oral Connections to Literacy: The Narrative." *Journal of Basic Writing* 13: 46–60.

Anzaldúa, Gloria. 1987. *Borderlands/La Frontera: The New Mestiza.* San Francisco: Aunt Lute.

Aparicio, Frances, and Susana Chávez-Silverman. 1997. *Tropicalizations: Transcultural Representations of Latinidad.* Hanover, N.H.: University Press of New England.

Applebome, Peter. 1996. "Mississippi's Latest Equality Issue." *New York Times* 24 April: A14.

Arenson, Karen. 1997. "Why College Isn't for Everyone." *New York Times* 31 August: 4: 1, 10.

———. 2000. "Plan Approved to Invigorate City University." *New York Times* 23 May: B1.

Astin, Alexander. 1993. What Matters in College? *Four Critical Years Revisited.* San Francisco: Jossey-Bass.

Bacon-Blood, Littice. 2000. "Getting in LSU Will Be Tougher; Remediation Classes to End in Fall 2002." *Times-Picayune* 31 July: A01.

Balester, Valerie. 1993. *Cultural Divide: A Study of African-American College-Level Writers.* Portsmouth, N.H.: Boynton/Cook.

Ballenger, Cindy. 1992. "Because You Like Us: The Language of Control." *Harvard Educational Review* 62: 199–208.

Bartholomae, David, and Anthony Petrosky. 1986. *Facts, Artifacts, and Counterfacts: Theory and Method for a Reading and Writing Course.* Upper Montclair, N.J.: Boynton/Cook.

Bartholomae, David. 1986. "Released into Language: Errors, Expectations, and the Legacy of Mina Shaughnessy." In *The Territory of Language: Linguistics, Stylistics, and the Teaching of Composition.* Ed. Donald A. McQuade. Carbondale: Southern Illinois University Press, 65–88.

———. 1995. "Writing with Teachers: A Conversation with Peter Elbow." *College Composition and Communication* 46: 62–71.

Bates, Katherine Lee. 1895. "English at Wellesley College." In *English in American Universities.* Ed. William Morton Payne. Boston: D. C. Heath, 141–48.

Benjamin, Ernst. 1995. "A Faculty Response to the Fiscal Crisis: From Defense to Offense." In *Higher Education under Fire: Politics, Economics, and the Crisis of the Humanities.* Ed. Michael Bérubé and Cary Nelson. New York: Routledge, 52–72.

"Berkeley's New Colors." 2000. *Newsweek* 18 September: 61.

Berkenkotter, Carol, and Thomas Huckin. 1995. *Genre Knowledge in Disciplinary Communication: Cognition/Culture/Power.* Hillsdale, N.J.: Lawrence Erlbaum.

Berlin, James. 1984. *Writing Instruction in Nineteenth Century American Colleges.* Carbondale: Southern Illinois University Press.

———. 1987. *Rhetoric and Reality: Writing Instruction in American Colleges, 1900–1985.* Carbondale: Southern Illinois University Press.

Bizzell, Patricia. 1992. *Academic Discourse and Critical Consciousness.* Pittsburgh: University of Pittsburgh Press.

———. 2000. "Basic Writing and the Issue of Correctness, or, What to Do with 'Mixed' Forms of Academic Discourse." *Journal of Basic Writing* 19: 4–12.

"Black, Latino Students Lag on Transfers to UC Campuses." 1999. *Los Angeles Times* 7 August.
<www.latimes.com/HOME/NEWS/Front/t000070257.html>

Blum, Debra. 1993. "Graduation Rate of Scholarship Athletes Rose after Proposition 48 Was Adopted, NCAA Reports." *Chronicle of Higher Education* 7 July: A1, 44–48.

Bowen, William, and Derek Bok. 1998. *The Shape of the River: Long-Term Consequences of Considering Race in College and University Admissions.* Princeton: Princeton University Press.

Boyer, Ernest. 1987. *College: The Undergraduate Experience in America.* New York: Harper & Row.

Boylan, Hunter R. 1995. "The Scope of Developmental Education: Some Basic Information on the Field." *Research in Developmental Education* 12: 4.

Brereton, John, ed. 1995. *The Origins of Composition Studies in the American College, 1875–1925.* Pittsburgh: University of Pittsburgh Press.

Brint, Steven, and Jerome Karabel. 1989. *The Diverted Dream: Community Colleges and the Promise of Educational Opportunity in America, 1900–1985.* New York: Oxford University Press.

Brooke, Robert. 1991. *Writing and Sense of Self: Identity Negotiation in Writing Workshops.* Urbana: NCTE.

Brown, Susan. 1994. "Students Struggle with State's Stiffer College Standards." *Saint-Louis Post Dispatch* 6 March: D6: 1.

Brubacher, John, and S. Willis Rudy. 1976. Rpt. 1997. *Higher Education in Transition: A History of American Colleges and Universities.* New Brunswick, N.J.: Transaction Publishers.

Buckley, David. 1972–73. *Chairman's Report. The City College of New York Department of English.* City College of New York Archives.

Burrows, Edwin, and Mike Wallace. 1999. *Gotham: A History of New York City to 1898.* New York: Oxford University Press.

Callan, Patrick M. 1993. "Government and Higher Education." In *Higher Learning in America, 1980–2000.* Ed. Arthur Levine. Baltimore: Johns Hopkins University Press, 3–19.

Campbell, Oscar James. 1934. *The Teaching of College English.* New York: D. Appleton-Century.

Canagarajah, A. Suresh. 1997. "Safe Houses in the Contact Zone: Coping Strategies of African-American Students in the Academy." *College Composition and Communication* 48: 173–96.

Castillo, Ana. 1994. *So Far from God.* New York: Plume Books.

Chadbourne, Richard. 1983. "A Puzzling Literary Genre: Comparative Views of the Essay." *Comparative Literature Studies* 20: 133–53.

Chase, Geoffrey. 1988. "Accommodation, Resistance and the Politics of Student Writing." *College Composition and Communication* 39: 13–22.

Chiseri-Strater, Elizabeth. 1991. *Academic Literacies: The Public and Private Discourse of University Students.* Portsmouth, N.H.: Boynton/Cook.

"City College Finds 25% of Freshmen Deficient in English." 1963. *New York Times* 10 December. City College of New York Archives.

Clark, Burton. 1960. *The Open-Door College.* New York: McGraw-Hill.

———. 1960. "The 'Cooling-Out' Function in Higher Education." *American Journal of Sociology* 65: 569–76.

——— 1987. *The Academic Life: Small Worlds, Different Worlds.* Princeton: The Carnegie Foundation.

Clark, J. D. 1935. "A Four-Year Study of Freshman English." *English Journal* 24: 403–10.

Cohen, Arthur, and Florence Brawer. 1987. *The Collegiate Function of Community Colleges: Fostering Higher Learning through Curriculum and Student Transfer.* San Francisco: Jossey-Bass.

College Remediation. 1998. The Institute for Higher Education Policy, Washington, D.C. <www.ihep.com>

Collins, Terence. 1997. "A Response to Ira Shor's 'Our Apartheid: Writing Instruction and Inequality.'" *Journal of Basic Writing* 16: 95–100.

Collins, Terence, and Melissa Blum. 2000. "Meanness and Failure: Sanctioning Basic Writers." *Journal of Basic Writing* 19: 13–21.

Cooper, Sandi. 1998. "Remediation's End." *Academe* July–August: 14–20.

Connors, Robert. 1997. *Composition-Rhetoric: Backgrounds, Theory, and Pedagogy.* Pittsburgh: University of Pittsburgh Press.

Courage, Richard. 1993. "The Interaction of Public and Private Literacies." *College Composition and Communication* 44: 484–96.

Course and Teacher Evaluation Handbook. 1972. Student Senate Committee on Educational Affairs. City College of New York Archives.

Crouch, Mary Kay, and Geraldine McNenny. 2000. "Looking Back, Looking Forward: California Grapples with 'Remediation.'" *Journal of Basic Writing* 19: 44–71.

Crowley, Sharon. 1998. *Composition in the University: Historical and Polemical Essays.* Pittsburgh: University of Pittsburgh Press.

CUNY: An Institution Affirmed: Response to the Report of the Mayor's Task Force. 1999. University Faculty Senate of the City University of New York. <http://www.soc.qc.edu/ufs/response.htm>

"CUNY's Opportunity." 1995. *New York Post* 20 February: 20.

Daniels, Harvey. 1983. *Famous Last Words: The American Literacy Crisis Reconsidered.* Carbondale: Southern Illinois University Press.

Danticat, Edwidge. 1998. *The Farming of Bones.* New York: Soho Press.

Dean, Terry. 1989. "Multicultural Classrooms, Monocultural Teachers." *College Composition and Communication* 40: 23–37.

Dembner, Alice. 1993. "Northeastern to Raise Standards, Cut Budget." *Boston Globe* 24 September: 24: 2.

———. 1993. "Bay State College Admissions Called Lax." *Boston Globe* 17 November 1: 1:24.

———. 1995. "Freshmen Classier at 2 UMass Campuses." *Boston Globe* 1 January: 22: 1.

———. 1995. "Overhaul of College Funding is Urged." *Boston Globe* 6 January: 4.

DeMott, Benjamin. 1990. *The Imperial Middle: Why Americans Can't Think Straight about Class.* New Haven: Yale University Press.

Department of English, Minutes of the Regular Meeting. 3 October 1964, with attachments. City College of New York Archives.

————. 5 November 1964, with attachments. City College of New York Archives.

————. 4 March 1965, with attachments. City College of New York Archives.

Department of English Newsletter. March 1971; January 1972. City College of New York Archives.

"Despite Faculty Protest, Regents Pass Master Plan." 2000. *Senate Digest* 31 October: 1, 3–4.

DiPardo, Anne. 1993. *A Kind of Passport: A Basic Writing Adjunct Program and the Challenge of Student Diversity.* Urbana: NCTE.

D'Raimo, Susan. 2000. Telephone Interview. 25 March.

Dougherty, Kevin. 1994. *The Contradictory College: The Conflicting Origins, Impacts, and Futures of the Community College.* Albany: State University of New York Press.

Douglas, Wallace. 1976. Rpt. 1996. "Rhetoric for the Meritocracy: The Creation of Composition at Harvard." In *English in America: A Radical View of the Profession.* Ed. Richard Ohmann. Hanover, N.H.: Wesleyan University Press, 97–132.

Duffus, R. L. 1936. Democracy Enters College: *A Study of the Rise and Decline of the Academic Lockstep.* New York: Scribner's.

Edwards, Viv. 1997. "Patois and the Politics of Protest: Black English in British Classrooms." In *Sociolinguistics: A Reader.* Ed. Nikolas Coupland and Adam Jaworski. New York: St. Martin's, 408–15.

Ehrenreich, Barbara. 1989. *Fear of Falling: The Inner Life of the Middle Class.* New York: Harper Collins.

Elbow, Peter. 1991. "Reflections on Academic Discourse: How It Relates to Freshmen and Colleagues." *College English* 53: 135–55.

Erickson, Frederick. 1987. "Transformation and School Success: The Politics of Culture and Educational Achievement." *Anthropology and Education Quarterly* 18: 335–60.

Eurich, Alvin C. 1932. "Should Freshman Composition Be Abolished?" *English Journal* 21: 211–19.

Fabrizio, Ray, Edith Karas, and Ruth Menmuir, eds. 1970. The Rhetoric of No. New York: Holt, Rinehart and Winston.

Feinstein, Irving Norman. 1934. *The Growth and Development of the Study of the English Language and Literature at the College of the City of New York, 1847–1934.* Master's thesis, June. City College of New York Archives.

Fiellin, Alan. 1972. "Memo to Mina Shaughnessy." 10 July. City College of New York Archives.

Finnegan, Dorothy. 1993 "Segmentation in the Academic Labor Market: Hiring Cohorts in Comprehensive Universities." *Journal of Higher Education* 64: 621–56.

Flores, Juan. 1993. *Divided Borders: Essays on Puerto Rican Identity.* Houston: Arte Publico Press.

Flower, Linda. 1996. "Negotiating the Meaning of Difference." *Written Communication* 13: 44–92.

Fox, Helen. 1994. *Listening to the World: Cultural Issues in Academic Writing.* Urbana: NCTE.

Fox, Tom. 1990. "Basic Writing as Cultural Conflict." *Journal of Education* 172: 65–83.

———. 1999. *Defending Access: A Critique of Standards in Higher Education.* Portsmouth, N.H.: Boynton/Cook.

Frank, James. 1992. "City Colleges Battle: A Fight over 2R's." *Chicago Tribune* 2 February, 1, 1: 1.

———. 1993. "Some Alter Admissions Policy." *Chicago Tribune* 7 April, 2C 3: 1.

Freeman, Joshua. 2000. *Working-Class New York: Life and Labor since World War Two.* New York: The New Press.

Fusco, Coco. 1995. *English Is Broken Here.* New York: New Press.

Gallagher, Buell. 1968. "Letter to the Faculty." 30 April. City College of New York Archives.

Gay, Pamela. 1993. "Rereading Shaughnessy from a Postcolonial Perspective." *Journal of Basic Writing* 12: 29–40.

Gere, Anne. 1987. *Writing Groups: History, Theory, and Implications.* Carbondale: Southern Illinois University Press.

———. 1991. "Public Opinion and Teaching Writing." In *The Politics of Writing Instruction: Postsecondary.* Ed. Richard Bullock and John Trimbur. Portsmouth, N.H.: Boynton-Cook, 263–75.

Gilyard, Keith. 1991. *Voices of the Self: A Study of Language Competence.* Detroit: Wayne State University Press.

Glazer, Nathan. 1973. "City College." In *Academic Transformation: 17 Institutions under Pressure.* Ed. David Riesman and Verne Stadtman. New York: McGraw-Hill, 71–98.

———. 1994. "Unsentimental Education." *New Republic* 19 December: 38–41.

———. 1999. "What the CUNY-Bashers Overlook." *New York Times* 11 July: 4: 17.

———. 1999. "The Dilemma of Higher Education in the Inner City." *Chronicle of Higher Education* 3 December: 1–7.

Gleason, Barbara. 2000. "Evaluating Writing Programs in Real Time: The Politics of Remediation." *College Composition and Communication* 51: 560–88.

Gold, Emily. 1995. "Two, Four, Six, Eight: Can't Afford to Remediate?" *On Campus: American Federation of Teachers.* 15.13: 8–9, 14.

Goodburn, Amy. 1998. "It's a Question of Faith: Discourse of Fundamentalism and Critical Pedagogy in the Writing Classroom." *JAC: A Journal of Composition Theory* 18: 333–53.

Gould, Christopher, and John Heyda. 1986. "Literacy Education and the Basic Writer: A Survey of College Composition Courses." *Journal of Basic Writing* 5: 8–27.

Graff, Gerald. 1980. "The Politics of Composition: A Reply to John Rouse." *College English* 41: 851–56.

Graham, Ellen. 1994. "The Halls of Ivy Imitating Halls of Commerce." *Wall Street Journal* 10 October: B, 1: 2.

Gray-Rosendale, Laura. 1998. "Inessential Writings: Shaughnessy's Legacy in a Socially Constructed Landscape." *Journal of Basic Writing* 17: 43–75.

———. 2000. *Rethinking Basic Writing: Exploring Identity, Politics, and Community in Interaction.* Mahwah, N. J.: Lawrence Erlbaum.

Greenberg, Karen. 1993. "The Politics of Basic Writing." *Journal of Basic Writing* 12: 64–71.

Gross, Theodore. 1970–71. *Chairman's Report. City College of New York Department of English.* City College of New York Archives.

———. 1972. "Memo to Shaughnessy." 27 July. City College of New York Archives.

———. 1973. "Memo to David Dill, Assistant to the Provost." 14 September. City College of New York Archives.

———. 1980. *Academic Turmoil: The Reality and Promise of Open Education.* Garden City, N.Y.: Anchor Press.

Guillory, John. 1993. *Cultural Capital: The Problem of Literary Canon Formation.* Chicago: Chicago University Press.

Gunner, Jeanne. 1993. "The Status of Basic Writing Teachers: Do We Need A 'Maryland Resolution?'" *Journal of Basic Writing* 12 : 57–63

———. 1998. "Among the Composition People: The WPA as English Department Agent." *Journal of Advanced Composition* 18: 153–64.

——— 1998. "Iconic Discourse: The Troubling Legacy of Mina Shaughnessy." *Journal of Basic Writing* 17: 25–42.

Haas, Christina. 1994. "Learning to Read Biology: One Student's Rhetorical Development in College." *Written Communication* 11: 43–84.

Haefner, Joel. 1992. "Democracy, Pedagogy, and the Personal Essay." *College English* 54: 127–37.

Hall, Michael. 1987. "The Emergence of the Essay and the Idea of Discovery." In *Essays on the Essay: Redefining the Genre.* Ed. Alexander Butrym. Athens: University of Georgia Press, 73–91.

Halloran, Michael S. 1990. "From Rhetoric to Composition: The Teaching of Writing in America to 1900." In *A Short History of Writing Instruction.* Ed. James Murphy. Davis, Calif.: Hermagoras Press, 151–82.

Hamalian, Leon, and James V. Hatch. 1969–1970. "The City College Rebellion Revisited." *Changing Education* 4: 15–21.

Harkin, Patricia. 1991. "The Postdisciplinary Politics of Lore." In *Contending with*

Words: Composition and Rhetoric in a Postmodern Age. Ed. Patricia Harkin and John Schilb. New York: MLA, 124–38.

Harrington, Susanmarie, and Linda Adler-Kassner. 1998. "'The Dilemma That Still Counts': Basic Writing at a Political Crossroads." *Journal of Basic Writing* 17: 3–24.

Harris, Joseph. 1997. *A Teaching Subject: Composition since 1966.* Upper Saddle River, N.J.: Prentice Hall.

Harris, Wendell. 1996. "Reflections on the Peculiar Status of the Personal Essay." *College English* 58: 934–53.

Harvey, Gordon. 1994. "Presence in the Essay." *College English* 56: 642–55.

Hayden, Tom, and Connie Rice. 1995. "California Cracks Its Mortarboards." *Nation* 18 September: 265–66.

Healy, Patrick. 2000. "Can City College Restore Its Luster by Ending Open Admissions?" *Chronicle of Higher Education* 7 July: A24–26.

Heilker, Paul. 1996. *The Essay: Theory and Pedagogy for an Active Form.* Urbana: NCTE.

Heller, Louis. 1973. *The Death of the American University, with Special Reference to the Collapse of City College of New York.* New Rochelle, N.Y.: Arlington House.

Henning, Barbara. 1991. "The World Was Stone Cold: Basic Writing in an Urban University." *College English* 53: 674–85.

Herrnstein, Richard, and Charles Murray. 1994. *The Bell Curve: Intelligence and Class Structure in American Life.* New York: Free Press.

Herzberg, Bruce. 1991. "Composition and the Politics of Curriculum." In *The Politics of Writing Instruction: Postsecondary.* Ed. Richard Bullock and John Trimbur. Portsmouth, N.H.: Boynton/Cook, 97–117.

Hesse, Douglas. 1994. "The Recent Rise of Literary Nonfiction: A Cautionary Assay." In *Composition Theory for the Postmodern Classroom.* Ed. Gary Olson and Sidney Dobrin. Albany: State University of New York Press, 132–42.

Hints on the Writing of an Oration and General Instructions to all Students. May 1899. Department of English Language and Literature. City College of New York Archives.

Hoffman, Eva. 1989. *Lost in Translation: A Life in a New Language.* New York: Penguin.

Horner, Bruce, and Min-Zhan Lu. 1999. *Representing the 'Other': Basic Writers and the Teaching of Basic Writing.* Urbana: NCTE.

Hudson, Arthur Palmer. 1938. "The Perennial Problem of the Ill-Prepared." *English Journal* 27: 728–33.

Hughes, Merritt Y. 1938. "Freshman English at the University of Wisconsin." *English Journal* 27: 807–17.

Hunter, Paul. 1992. "'Waiting for an Aristotle': A Moment in the History of the Basic Writing Movement." *College English* 54: 914–27.

Hutcheon, Linda. 1985. *A Theory of Parody: The Teachings of Twentieth-Century Art Forms.* New York: Methuen.

Jefferson, B. L., S. E. Glenn, and Royal Gettmann. 1935. "Freshman Writing: September to February." *English Journal* 24: 28–38, coll. ed.

Jensen, George. 1988. "Bureaucracy and Basic Writing Programs; Or, Fallout from the Jan Kemp Trial." *Journal of Basic Writing* 7: 30–37.

Johnson, Paula. 1977. "The Politics of 'Back to the Basics.'" *ADE Bulletin* 53: 1–4.

Jones, Terry. 1998. "Proposition 209: Affirmative Action May Be Dying, but the Dream Lives on." *Academe* July–August: 23–28.

Jordan, Mary. 1992. "'Need-Blind' Admissions Policy at Top Private Colleges Losing Favor to Wealth." *Washington Post* 26 April, A1: 1.

Kachru, Braj, ed. 1982. *The Other Tongue: English across Cultures.* Oxford, England: Pergamon Press.

———. 1990. *The Alchemy of English: The Spread, Functions, and Models of Non-Native Englishes.* Urbana: University of Illinois Press.

Katz, Michael. 1993. "The Urban 'Underclass' as a Metaphor of Social Transformation." In *The "Underclass" Debate: Views from History.* Ed. Michael Katz. Princeton: Princeton University Press, 3–23.

Kerr, Clark. 1991. *The Great Transformation in Higher Education, 1960–1980.* Albany: State University of New York Press.

Kitzhaber, Albert R. 1962. "Freshman English: A Prognosis." *College English* 23: 476–83.

———. 1963. *Themes, Theories, and Therapy: The Teaching of Writing in College.* New York: McGraw-Hill.

———. 1990. (Ph.D. diss., Washington University, 1953). *Rhetoric in American Colleges, 1850–1900.* Dallas: Southern Methodist University Press.

Klaus, Carl. 1989. "Essayists on the Essay." In *Literary Nonfiction: Theory, Criticism, Pedagogy.* Ed. Chris Anderson. Carbondale: Southern Illinois University Press, 155–75.

Knopp, Linda. 1995. Remedial Education: An Undergraduate Student Profile. *American Council on Education Research Briefs* 6.8. Washington, D.C.

Kriegel, Leonard. 1968. "Headstart for College." *Nation* 26 February: 270–74.

Kutz, Eleanor. 1986. "Between Students' Language and Academic Discourse: Interlanguage as Middle Ground." *College English* 48: 385–96.

Kutz, Eleanor, Suzy Groden, and Vivian Zamel. 1993. *The Discovery of Competence: Teaching and Learning with Diverse Student Writers.* Portsmouth, N.H.: Boynton/Cook.

Laurence, Patricia. 1993. "The Vanishing Site of Mina Shaughnessy's Errors and Expectations." *Journal of Basic Writing* 12: 18–28.

Lauter, Paul. 1995. "'Political Correctness' and the Attack on American Colleges." In *Higher Education under Fire*. Ed. Michael Bérubé and Cary Nelson. New York: Routledge, 73–90.

Lavin, David, Richard Alba, and Richard Silberstein. 1981. *Right Versus Privilege: The Open-Admissions Experiment at the City University of New York*. New York: Free Press.

Lavin, David, and David Hyllegard. 1996. *Changing the Odds: Open Admissions and the Life Chances of the Disadvantaged*. New Haven: Yale University Press.

Lawlor, William. 1980. "The Politics of Rouse." *College English* 42: 195–99.

Leo, John. 1994. "A University's Sad Decline." *U.S. News & World Report* 15 August: 20.

Levine, David. 1986. *The American College and the Culture of Aspiration, 1915–1940*. Ithaca: Cornell University Press.

Lively, Kit. 1993. "States Step Up Efforts to End Remedial Courses at 4-Year Colleges." *Chronicle of Higher Education* 24 February 34: A28.

———. 1995. "Ready or Not." *Chronicle of Higher Education* 31 March: A23.

Lopate, Phillip, ed. 1998. *The Anchor Essay Annual: The Best of 1998*. New York: Anchor.

London, Howard. 1978. *The Culture of a Community College*. New York: Praeger.

Lu, Min-Zhan. 1987. "From Silence to Words: Writing as Struggle." *College English* 49: 437–48.

Lu, Min-Zhan, and Bruce Horner. 1998. "The Problematic of Experience: Redefining Critical Work in Ethnography and Pedagogy." *College English* 60: 257–77.

Lunsford, Andrea. 1977. *An Historical, Descriptive, and Evaluative Study of Remedial English at American Colleges and Universities*. Ph.D. diss., Ohio State University.

———. 1987. "Politics and Practices of Basic Writing." In *A Sourcebook for Basic Writing Teachers*. Ed. Theresa Enos. New York: Random House, 246–58.

Lyons, Robert. 1985. "Mina Shaughnessy." In *Traditions of Inquiry*. Ed. John Brereton. New York: Oxford University Press, 171–89.

Mac Donald, Heather. 1994. "Downward Mobility: The Failure of Open Admissions at City University." *City Journal* summer: 10–20.

———. 1995. "Why Johnny Can't Write." *Public Interest* 120: 3–13.

MacDonald, Susan Peck. 1994. *Professional Academic Writing in the Humanities and Social Sciences*. Carbondale: Southern Illinois University Press.

Mahala, Daniel, and Jody Swilky. 1996. "Telling Stories, Speaking Personally: Reconsidering the Place of Lived Experience in Composition." *JAC: A Journal of Composition Theory* 16: 363–89.

Maher, Jane. 1997. *Mina P. Shaughnessy: Her Life and Work*. Urbana: NCTE.

"Majority Need Remedial Help." 1995. *Gainesville Sun* 31 October: 1A, 9.

Marshak, Robert. 1973. *Problems and Prospects of an Urban University.* New York: City College of New York.

Mayhew, Lewis. 1977. *Legacy of the Seventies: Experiment, Economy, Equality and Expediency in American Higher Education.* San Francisco: Jossey-Bass.

McArthur, Tom. 1998. *The English Languages.* Cambridge: Cambridge University Press.

McCarthy, Lucille P. 1987. "A Stranger in Strange Lands: A College Student Writing across the Curriculum." *Research in the Teaching of English* 21: 233–65.

McGowan, William. 1993. "The Battle for City University." *Lingua Franca* January–February: 1, 24–62.

McKee, J. H. 1932. "Wherein They Improve." *English Journal* 21: 473–86.

———. 1936. "Portrait of a Department." *English Journal* 25: 752–59.

Mellix, Barbara. 1989. "From Outside, In." In *Essays on the Essay: Redefining the Genre.* Ed. Alexander Butrym. Athens: University of Georgia Press, 43–52.

Metzger, Walter P. 1987. "The Academic Profession in the United States." In *The Academic Profession: National, Disciplinary, and Institutional Settings.* Ed. Burton Clark. Berkeley: University of California Press, 123–28.

Mid-Term Reports, Fall 1970. Courtesy of Professor William Herman, City College of New York English Department.

Miller, Richard. 1994. "Fault Lines in the Contact Zone." *College English* 56: 389–408.

———. 1998. *As if Learning Mattered: Reforming Higher Education.* Ithaca: Cornell University Press.

Miller, Susan. 1990. "Two Comments on 'A Common Ground': The Essay in Academe." *College English* 52: 329–34.

———. 1991. *Textual Carnivals: The Politics of Composition.* Carbondale: Southern Illinois University Press.

Miller, Thomas. 1997. *The Formation of College English: Rhetoric and Belles Lettres in the British Cultural Provinces.* Pittsburgh: University of Pittsburgh Press.

Moran, Charles. 1991. "A Life in the Profession." In *An Introduction to Composition Studies.* Ed. Erika Lindemann and Gary Tate. New York: Oxford University Press, 160–82.

Morgan, Dan. 1998. "Opinion: Ethical Issues and Personal Writing." *College English* 60: 318–25.

Mutnick, Deborah. 1996. *Writing in an Alien World: Basic Writing and the Struggle for Equality in Higher Education.* Portsmouth, N.H.: Heinemann.

———. 2000. "The Strategic Value of Basic Writing: An Analysis of the Current Moment." *Journal of Basic Writing* 19: 69–83.

"National Council of Teachers of English, College Section." 1942. *English Journal* 3: 584–86.

Nazario, Sonia L. 1992. "Funding Cuts Take a Toll at University." *Wall Street Journal* 5 October: B1, 11.

Newt Davis Collective. 1974. *Crisis at CUNY.* New York: Manhattanville Station.

Norment, Nathaniel. *A Report of the Basic Writing Program 1985–1986.* City College of New York Writing Center.

North, Michael. 1994. *The Dialect of Modernism: Race, Language, and Twentieth-Century Literature.* New York: Oxford University Press.

O'Brien, Andrea. 2000. "Minority Enrollment at UC-Berkeley Plummets Post-Prop. 209." *Daily Californian* 1 December.

Ogbu, John. 1974. *The Next Generation: An Ethnography of Education in an Urban Neighborhood.* New York: Academic Press.

O'Hare, Frank. 1976. "Letter Re: Professors Trillin and Shaughnessy." 2 August. City College of New York Archives.

Ohmann, Richard. 1976. Rpt. 1996. *English in America: A Radical View of the Profession.* Hanover, N.H.: Wesleyan University Press.

————. 1987. *The Politics of Letters.* Middletown: Wesleyan University Press.

Penrose, Ann, and Cheryl Geisler. 1994. "Reading and Writing without Authority." *College Composition and Communication* 45: 505–20.

Perrin, P. G. 1933. "The Remedial Racket." *English Journal* 22: 382–88.

Portes, Alejandro, and Min Zhou. 1993. "The New Second Generation: Segmented Assimilation and Its Variants." *Annals of the American Academy of Political and Social Science:* 530. Philadelphia: Sage.

Recchio, Thomas. 1989. "A Dialogic Approach to the Essay." In *Essays on the Essay: Redefining the Genre.* Ed. Alexander Butrym. Athens: University of Georgia Press, 271–88.

"Remembering Mina Shaughnessy." 1994. *Journal of Basic Writing* 13: 91–102.

Rendón, Laura. 1992. "From the Barrio to the Academy: Revelations of a Mexican American 'Scholarship Girl.'" In *First-Generation Students: Confronting the Cultural Issues.* Ed. Steven Zwerling and Howard London. San Francisco: Jossey-Bass, 55–64.

Renfro, Sally, and Allison Armour-Garb. 1999. *Open Admissions and Remedial Education at the City University of New York.* Report Submitted to the Mayor's Advisory Task Force.
<http://www.ci.nyc.ny.us/html/cuny/home.html>

Rich, Adrienne. 1979. "Teaching Language in Open Admissions." In *On Lies, Secrets, and Silence: Selected Prose 1966–1978.* New York: W. W. Norton, 51–68.

Rich, Frank. 1995. "The Unkindest Cut." *New York Times* 12 May: 4: 15.

Ringnalda, Margaret. 1938. "One More Opinion." *English Journal* 27: 678–84.

Rodriguez, Richard. 1982. *Hunger of Memory: The Education of Richard Rodriguez.* New York: Bantam.

Rose, Mike. 1983. "Remedial Courses: A Critique and a Proposal." College English 45: 109–28.

————. 1985. "The Language of Exclusion." *College English* 47: 13–29.

————. 1989. *Lives on the Boundary: A Moving Account of the Struggles and Achievements of America's Educational Underclass.* New York: Free Press.

Rosenthal, A. M. 1994. "An American Promise." *New York Times Book Review* 2 October: 7: 7, 9.

Rouse, John. 1979. "The Politics of Composition." *College English* 41: 1–12.

————. 1980. "Feeling Our Way Along." *College English* 41: 868–75.

Roy, Alice. 1995. "The Grammar and Rhetoric of Inclusion." *College English* 57: 182–95.

Royster, Jacqueline Jones, and Rebecca Greenberg Taylor. 1997. "Constructing Teacher Identity in the Basic Writing Classroom." *Journal of Basic Writing* 16: 27–50.

Rubin, James H. 1995. "Colleges: Budget Cuts Will Hurt Minority Enrollment." *Boston Globe* 18 January: 12: 1.

Rudolph, Frederick. 1962. *The American College and University: A History.* New York: Alfred Knopf.

Rudy, Willis S. 1949. *The College of the City of New York: A History, 1847–1947.* New York: City College Press.

Rumbaut, Ruben. 1996. "The Crucible within: Ethnic Identity, Self-Esteem, and Segmented Assimilation among Children of Immigrants." In *The New Second Generation.* Ed. Alejandro Portes. New York: Russell Sage, 119–70.

Russell, David. 1992. *Writing in the Academic Disciplines: 1870–1990.* Carbondale: Southern Illinois University Press.

Schmidt, Benno, Herman Badillo, and Jacqueline Brady, et al. 1999. *The City University of New York: An Institution Adrift: Report of the Mayor's Advisory Task Force on CUNY.* <http://www.ci.nyc.ny.us/html/cuny/home.htm.>

Schrag, Peter. 1999. "End of the Second Chance? The Crusade against Remedial Education." *The American Prospect* 44: 68–74.

Schultz, Katherine. 1994. "'I Want to Be Good; I Just Don't Get It': A Fourth Grader's Entrance into a Literacy Community." *Written Communication* 11: 381–413.

Scott, Barbara Ann. 1983. *Crisis Management in American Higher Education.* New York: Praeger.

Selingo, Jeffrey. 2000. "Cal State Puts Remediation on an 'Or Else' Basis." *Chronicle of Higher Education* 4 August: A27.

Severino, Carol. 1992. "Where the Cultures of Basic Writers and Academia Intersect: Cultivating the Common Ground." *Journal of Basic Writing* 11: 4–15.

————. 1996. "An Urban University and Its Academic Support Program: Teaching Basic Writing in the Context of an 'Urban Mission.'" *Journal of Basic Writing* 15: 39–56.

Severino, Carol, Juan Guerra, and Johnnella Butler, eds. 1997. *Writing in Multicultural Settings.* New York: MLA.

Shaughnessy, Mina. 1967. "Memo to Edmond Volpe." 22 September. City College of New York Archives.

———. 1968. "Memo to Edmond Volpe." 4 January. City College of New York Archives.

———. 1970. "Memo to Professor Ted Gross Re: Progress Report on O.A. English Program." 3 September. City College of New York Archives.

———. 1971. "Memo to Teachers of Basic Writing 1 and 2, 3 and E.S.L." 18 October. City College of New York Archives.

———. *Report on the Basic Writing Program (Mid-term, Fall 1971).* City College of New York Writing Center.

———. 1972. "Research Proposal to The Carnegie Foundation: A Report on the Basic Writing Program at City College and on the Writing Problems of Its Students." Submitted Jointly by The City College and The City University Research Foundation of New York. City College of New York Archives.

———. 1973. "Memo to Saul Touster, Provost." 18 April. City College of New York Archives.

———. 1977. *Errors and Expectations.* New York: Oxford University Press.

———. 1970. Rpt. 1994. "Some New Approaches towards Teaching." *Journal of Basic Writing* 13: 103–16.

Shen, Fan. 1989. "The Classroom and the Wider Culture: Identity as a Key to Learning English Composition." *College Composition and Communication* 40: 459–66.

Shor, Ira. 1980. Rpt. 1987. *Critical Teaching and Everyday Life.* Chicago: Chicago University Press.

———. 1986. *Culture Wars: School and Society in the Conservative Restoration 1969–1984.* Boston: Routledge & Kegan Paul.

———. 1997. "Our Apartheid: Writing Instruction and Inequality." *Journal of Basic Writing* 16: 91–104.

———. 2000. "Illegal Literacy." *Journal of Basic Writing* 19: 100–112.

Sirc, Geoffrey. 1994. "The Autobiography of Malcolm X as a Basic Writing Text." *Journal of Basic Writing* 13: 50–77.

Skurnick, Blanche. *Report on the Basic Writing Program, 1972–73.* City College of New York Writing Center.

———. *Report on the Basic Writing Program, Fall 1975–Fall 1976.* City College of New York Writing Center.

Sledd, Andrew. 1988. "Readin' not Riotin': The Politics of Literacy." *College English* 50: 495–508.

Slevin, James. 1991. "Depoliticizing and Politicizing Composition Studies." In *The Politics of Writing Instruction: Postsecondary.* Ed. Richard Bullock and John Trimbur. Portsmouth, N.H.: Boynton-Cook, 1–21.

Smith, Ron. 1975. "The Composition Requirement Today: A Report on a Nationwide Survey of Four-Year Colleges and Universities." *College Composition and Communication* 25: 138–48.

Smitherman, Geneva. 1977. *Talkin and Testifyin: The Language of Black America.* Boston: Houghton Mifflin.

———. 1994. "'The Blacker the Berry, the Sweeter the Juice': African American Student Writers." In *The Need for Story: Cultural Diversity in Classroom and Community.* Ed. Anne H. Dyson and Celia Genish. Urbana: NCTE, 80–101.

Soliday, Mary. 1994. "Translating Self and Difference through Literacy Narratives." *College English* 56: 511–26.

———. 1996. "From the Margins to the Mainstream: Reconceiving Remediation." *College Composition and Communication* 47: 85–100.

———. 1997. "Towards a Consciousness of Language: A Language Pedagogy for Multicultural Classrooms." *Journal of Basic Writing* 16: 62–75.

Solomon, Alisa, with Deirdre Hussey. 1998. "Enemies of Public Education: Who Is Behind the Attacks on CUNY and SUNY?" *Village Voice Educational Supplement* 21 April: 1–5.

Sommers, Nancy. 1992. "Between the Drafts." *College Composition and Communication* 43: 23–31.

Spellmeyer, Kurt. 1993. *Common Ground: Dialogue, Understanding, and the Teaching of Composition.* Englewood Cliffs, N.J.: Prentice-Hall.

Stabile, Carol. 1995. "Another Brick in the Wall: (Re)contextualizing the Crisis." In *Higher Education under Fire: Politics, Economics, and the Crisis of the Humanities.* Ed. Michael Bérubé and Cary Nelson. New York: Routledge, 108–25.

Staples, Brent. 1998. "Blocking Promising Students from City University." *New York Times* 26 May: A20.

Sternglass, Marilyn. 1997. *Time to Know Them: A Longitudinal Study of Writing and Learning at the College Level.* Mahwah, N.J.: Lawrence Erlbaum.

Stewart, Donald. 1992. "Harvard's Influence in English Studies: Perceptions from Three Universities in the Early Twentieth Century." *College Composition and Communication* 43: 455–71.

Stewart, Jocelyn. 1995. "Remedial Cal State Students Blame School System." *Los Angeles Times* 8 January: B, 1: 2.

"Students' Right to Their Own Language." 1974. *College Composition and Communication Special Issue.* 25: 1–32.

Stygall, Gail. 1999. "Unraveling at Both Ends: Anti-Undergraduate Education, Anti-Affirmative Action, and Basic Writing at Research Schools." *Journal of Basic Writing* 18: 4–22.

"Symposium on Basic Writing." 1993. *College English* 55: 879–903.

Tan, Amy. 1990. Rpt. 2001. "Mother Tongue." In *The Best American Essays, College Edition.* Ed. Robert Atwan. Boston: Houghton Mifflin, 124–30.

Taylor, Warner. 1929. *A National Survey of Conditions in Freshman English.* Madison, Wisc.: University of Wisconsin Bureau of Educational Research Bulletin 11.

The *College of the City of New York, Annual Register.* 1895–1896. City College of New York Archives.

———. 1901–1902. City College of New York Archives.

———. 1927–1928. City College of New York Archives.

The *College of the City of New York, Bulletin.* 1940–41. City College of New York Archives.

———. 1960–1961. City College of New York Archives.

———. 1966–1967. City College of New York Archives.

The *Condition of Education, 1997.* The National Center for Education Statistics. <http: // nces.ed.gov/pubs/ce/index.html>

Thomson, Susan. 1992. "UM Proposes Harder Prep Course Load." *Saint-Louis Post-Dispatch* 2 May: A1.

———. 1992. "Missouri College Plan Promises Big Shake-Up." *Saint-Louis Post-Dispatch* 16 October: A1: 4.

Traschel, Mary. 1992. *Institutionalizing Literacy: The Historical Role of College Entrance Examinations in English.* Carbondale: Southern Illinois University Press.

Traub, James. 1994. "Class Struggle." New Yorker 19 September: 76–90.

———. 1994. *City on a Hill: Testing the American Dream at City College.* Reading, Mass.: Addison-Wesley.

Trimbur, John. 1991. "Literacy and the Discourse of Crisis." In *The Politics of Writing Instruction: Postsecondary.* Ed. Richard Bullock and John Trimbur. Portsmouth, N.H.: Boynton/Cook, 277–95.

Trimmer, Joseph. 1987. "Basic Skills, Basic Writing, Basic Research." *Journal of Basic Writing* 6: 3–9.

Troyka, Lynn Q. 1987. "Perspectives on Legacies and Literacy in the 1980s." In *A Sourcebook for Basic Writing Teachers.* Ed. Theresa Enos. New York: Random House, 16–26.

Trow, Martin. 1970. "Reflections on the Transition from Mass to Universal Higher Education." *Daedalus* 99: 1–40.

Valdes, Gina. 1994. "English con Salsa." In *Cool Salsa: Bilingual Poems on Growing Up Latino in the United States.* Ed. Lori Carlson. New York: Henry Holt, 4–5.

Vandenberg, Peter. 1999. "Taming Multiculturalism: The Will to Literacy in Composition Studies." *JAC: A Journal of Composition Theory* 19: 547–68.

Veysey, Laurence. 1965. *The Emergence of the American University.* Chicago: Chicago University Press.

Vobejda, Barbara. 1989. "Two-Year Colleges: Mixed Success as Vehicle of Upward Mobility." *Washington Post* 5 May: A16: 1.

Volpe, Edmond. 1967. "Memo to Mina Shaughnessy." 30 October. City College of New York Archives.

Yezierska, Anzia. 1923. Rpt. 1995. *Salome of the Tenements.* Urbana: University of Illinois Press.

———. 1925. Rpt. 1970. *Bread Givers.* New York: Persea.

———. 1950. Rpt. 1987. *Red Ribbon on a White Horse: My Story.* New York: Persea.

Wagner, Geoffrey. 1976. *The End of Education: Reflections of a City Teacher.* South Brunswick: A. S. Barnes.

Walker, Alice. 1984. "Looking for Zora." *In Search of Our Mothers' Gardens: Womanist Prose by Alice Walker.* San Diego: Harcourt Brace Jovanovich, 93–116.

Wallace, David, and Annissa Bell. 1999. "Being Black at a Predominantly White University." *College English* 61: 307–27.

Walters, Laurel Shaper. 1995. "Minorities in Higher Education." *Christian Science Monitor* 13 March: 13.

Washington, Charles, ed. 1994. *Higher Education Today: Facts in Brief.* Washington, D.C.: American Council on Education.

Waters, Mary C. 1996. "Ethnic and Racial Identities of Second-Generation Black Immigrants in New York City." In *The New Second Generation.* Ed. Alejandro Portes. New York: Russell Sage Foundation, 171–96.

Wechsler, Harold. 1977. *The Qualified Student: A History of Selective College Admission in America.* New York: John Wiley.

Weis, Lois. 1985. *Between Two Worlds: Black Students in an Urban Community College.* Boston: Routledge.

White, Edward. 1995. "The Importance of Placement and Basic Studies: Helping Students Succeed under the New Elitism." *Journal of Basic Writing* 14: 75–84.

Whitney, Norman J. 1924. "Ability Grouping at Syracuse." *English Journal* 13: 482–89.

———. 1928. "Ability Grouping Plus." English Journal 17: 559–65.

Wiener, Harvey. 1998. "The Attack on Basic Writing—and After." *Journal of Basic Writing* 17: 96–103.

Wilcox, Thomas. 1973. *Anatomy of English.* San Francisco: Jossey-Bass.

Wildavsky, Ben. 1995. "Hot Debate over CSU Standards." *San Francisco Chronicle* 2 January: A: 1.

———. 1995. "CSU Acts to Reduce Remedial Math and English Classes." *San Francisco Chronicle* 25 January: A, 17: 1.

Willis, Paul. 1977. *Learning to Labour: How Working-Class Kids Get Working-Class Jobs.* Westmead, England: Saxon House.

Winterowd, Ross. 1998. *The English Department: A Personal and Institutional History.* Carbondale: Southern Illinois University Press.

Woolley, Edwin C. 1914. "Admission to Freshman English in the University." *English Journal* 3: 238–44.

Wozniak, John. 1978. *English Composition in Eastern Colleges, 1850–1940.* Washington, D.C.: University Press of America.

"Writing within and against the Academy: What Do We Really Want Our Students to Do? A Symposium." 1990. *Journal of Education* 172: 15–37.

Wyatt, Monica. 1992. "The Past, Present, and Future Need for College Reading Courses in the U.S." *Journal of Reading* 36: 10–20.

Zamel, Vivian. 2000. "Engaging Students in Writing-to-Learn: Promoting Language and Literacy across the Curriculum." *Journal of Basic Writing* 19: 3–21.

Zwerling, Steven, and Howard B. London. 1992. *First-Generation Students: Confronting the Cultural Issues.* San Francisco: Jossey-Bass.

Index

academic success, barriers to, 8–9, 12–13, 85, 109, 117
access, 9, 11, 48, 180; to dominant languages, 151, 185; vs. excellence, 12, 40, 72, 105–6, 109, 116, 120; to four-year colleges, 69, 86, 98, 107, 123, 147, 182; to higher education, 2, 84, 104, 118, 140, 180, 189n3; to the liberal arts, 145, 184–85; for minorities, 61, 114, 123; reforms affecting, 8, 19, 67–68, 144, 181–82. *See also* open access; politics of access; selectivity, vs. access
acculturation, 13, 72, 129, 172, 184. *See also* Americanization; assimilation
activism, 95, 124–25, 141, 144, 150
Adler-Kassner, Linda, 142–43
admissions, 33, 45, 46
admissions, open, 3, 15, 63, 70, 79, 87, 96; alternatives to, 69; at CCNY, 87–88, 94, 124–25; criticism of, 22, 71, 98, 100–101, 190n9; at CUNY, 11, 60, 69–70, 118, 123, 126, 139; problems with, 102–3, 131; support for, 72, 94, 98, 103, 124–25
admissions requirements, 28, 38, 39–40, 49, 50, 123
admissions standards, 7, 12, 23, 24, 27–29, 32, 118; lowering of, 31, 123; raising of, 60, 107, 110, 112
affirmative action, 13, 25, 49, 59–60, 62, 124–25, 144; assault on, 111, 124

afrocentrism, 129–30, 192n6
Americanization, 155, 165, 169, 170. *See also* acculturation; assimilation
anti-intellectualism, 22, 129–30, 136, 149
Armour-Garb, Allison, 11, 45
assimilation, 17; to academic culture, 1, 145–46, 149, 157, 164, 169, 180; lack of, 138, 148; and language, 85, 163–64, 172; to mainstream cultures, 106, 147, 165, 170; resistance to, 129, 148. *See also* acculturation; Americanization
autobiography, 16–17, 19, 96, 153, 165, 192–93n7

Bartholomae, David, 63, 153–54, 190n4
Berlin, James, 92, 188n1
black studies, 89, 129, 147
Boyer, Ernest, 26, 27
Brown University, 38, 114–16
Buckley, David, 87–88, 98–99
budget crisis, 106, 118–19
budget cuts, 114, 116, 121–22, 144, 190n9. *See also* funding, insufficient

California, 69, 71, 72, 85, 110–11
California State University, 111, 123, 181
Cambridge University, 147–48
Carnegie Foundation, 23, 28, 33, 39, 89

CCNY (City College of New York),
85, 119; Basic Writing Program, 65,
78–80, 87–88, 90, 95–96, 100; Department of English, 20, 33–34, 44,
53–57, 87–89, 101, 190n9; faculty,
87, 94, 97, 98–99, 132–33; Institute
for Social History, 94–95, 184; intellectuals at, 146, 164; and open admissions, 87–88, 94, 124–25;
Pre-Baccalaureate program, 63, 65,
87, 89; preparatory programs at, 27,
30–31; and remediation, 10, 13,
20–22, 89–90, 102–3, 108, 119. See
also remediation, history of, at
CCNY; selectivity of, 46–47; Writing Center, 91, 96, 100; writing
teachers, 88–96, 102–3. See also
Shaughnessy, Mina; Traub, James,
City on a Hill
CCNY (City College of New York)
students, 17–19, 35, 71–72, 124–25,
135, 137, 139; and assimilation, 147,
170; and composition, 17–18,
144–47, 155–57, 168, 177; culture of,
17, 136, 140; narratives by, 149,
155–57, 159–64, 168–71, 173–78; and
outside work, 135, 140, 141–42; and
remediation, 20–21, 95–96
Chiseri-Strater, Elizabeth, 157–58
Chronicle of Higher Education, The,
105, 119, 181
Clark, Burton, 12–13, 15, 58, 106,
187n1, 189n3, 190n5
class difference, 106, 109, 132
class experience, 132, 134, 140
class mobility, 13, 71, 120, 147–48
class politics, 3, 16, 70, 122, 126, 136.
See also middle class; working class;
underclass
class stratification, 46, 112, 114–15
coalitions, 16, 126, 131, 144
college and university preparatory
programs, 4, 24, 27–31; at CCNY,
27, 30–31, 34, 63, 65, 89

college degree, value of, 126, 136
colleges, 136; community, 45, 71, 106,
111, 115, 122, 189n3; honors, 110, 119;
junior, 45, 50, 70, 115; teaching, 98;
vocational, 2, 7, 13, 70–71, 72, 112, 131.
See also vocationalism; vocational
programs
colleges and universities, 2, 9, 13, 52,
111; cost of, 107, 114, 115, 135; crisis
management of, 12, 48, 51, 58, 70,
105, 115; exclusivity of, 41, 47, 67, 113;
growth of, 25, 51–57, 125; needs of, 1,
2, 49, 62, 109, 125–26; politics of, 10,
65, 143; private, 13, 29, 32, 126, 133,
169, 187n1; public, 12–13, 15, 41, 70,
181, 187n1; public, defunding of, 6,
14; restratification of, 10, 14–15, 105,
106, 107, 108, 119; retention rates at,
106, 110, 144, 180; retiering of, 124,
144; tiering of, 71–72, 85, 107–8, 110,
112, 116. See also CCNY; CUNY;
SUNY; under names of specific
universities
colleges and universities, differentiation of, 13, 23, 24, 47, 70, 71, 125; by
curriculum, mission, and standards, 12; from secondary schools,
29–30; into tiers, 25, 57, 98. See also
stratification
colleges and universities, four-year,
38, 42, 45, 106, 114, 124, 136; access
to, 69, 84, 86, 98, 107, 123, 182; elite,
33, 46, 60, 107, 115, 147–48, 169; Ivy
League, 38, 39, 48, 114–16; liberal
arts, 7, 12, 13, 110, 114–15; remediation in, 4, 11, 110, 123, 192n5; research, 57–58, 106, 111. See also
Harvard; Yale
colleges and universities, missions of,
23, 49, 52, 99; differentiation of and
stratification by, 12, 106, 107, 111; research, 25, 29, 55, 56, 60, 87; vocational, 2, 13, 70, 72
colleges and universities, public com-

prehensive, 25, 54–55, 70, 87, 107;
and funding, 51–52, 98, 117; and research, 54–55
colleges and universities, two-year,
69, 107, 113, 125–26, 187*n1*, 190*n5*;
and remediation, 11, 110–12, 131,
189*n3*, 192*n5*; vocational mission of,
2, 13, 70, 72
Columbia University, 27–28, 31, 32,
44, 46, 114–15
composition, 24, 104
composition courses, 30, 33–34, 36,
40, 54, 144–45, 178; at CCNY,
17–18, 144–47, 155–57, 168, 177; as
crisis management tool, 48, 58; decline of, 52–53; goals of, 151, 185;
and nontraditional students, 61,
162–64, 173–75, 176–77; status of,
99, 188*n1*; and testing, 39
composition studies, 147–48, 150–53,
156, 177, 181
consciousness, individual, 83–84, 150,
153, 174, 184
Counihan, Beth, 136, 137, 138, 141
courses: basic skills, 117, 125; content,
82, 84, 89–90; elective, 36, 55, 56,
57, 116; honors, 32, 60; interdisciplinary, 89; liberal arts, 14, 59, 63, 136,
184. *See also* writing courses, basic
critical thought, 18, 150, 154, 157–58,
170, 183, 187*n1*
Crowley, Sharon, 1, 49, 61, 188*n1*
cultural alienation, 131–32, 137–38,
156, 157–58, 160, 182
cultural capital, 68, 148
cultural conflicts, 15, 18–19, 106, 134,
164
cultural crisis, 23
cultural deprivation, 15, 108
cultural identity, 4, 159, 170
cultural resistance, 181, 194*n6*
cultures, 140; ethnic, 159–60; mainstream, 1, 17, 127, 134, 138, 147, 178;
minority, 15, 128–30, 136, 179–80;

student, 16, 22, 109, 120, 128–31;
translation of, 165, 193*n2*; working-
class, 17, 108, 127, 130–31, 136
CUNY (City University of New
York), 72, 120, 180; Board of
Trustees, 111, 119, 127, 131; defunding
of, 116, 121–22, 144; faculty, 116, 118,
119, 126; intellectuals at, 16, 136; literacy crisis at, 121–22, 192*n6*; minorities at, 69, 189*n3*; open
admissions at, 3, 11, 60, 69–70, 118,
123–26, 139; and privatization, 107,
119, 141, 181; reforms at, 15, 86,
181–82; remediation at, 4, 10, 11,
14–15, 107, 117, 144; tiering at, 71–72,
107–8, 110, 112, 116, 119. *See also*
CCNY; Traub, James, *City on a Hill*
curricula, 3, 9, 12, 31, 51, 83, 104; classical, 24, 27, 51; development of, 6, 18;
goals of, 34–35, 84; and multiculturalism, 9, 119, 132, 153; reforms of, 6,
19, 83, 94, 105–6; shift in, 29, 82;
stratification by, 12, 51, 107, 111, 116,
124

demographics, 45–47, 126
disciplines, 65, 84, 106–7, 112, 120. *See
also* English departments; humanities
discourse, 17, 160, 162, 163, 164; academic, 13, 145, 148, 153, 157–58, 177,
193*n3*; critical, 75–76, 84; and
crossover, 175, 177, 184
diversity, 124, 127, 181
Dougherty, Kevin, 13, 125–26, 187*n1*,
189*n3*
downsizing, 6, 59, 142; advocates of,
10, 15, 17, 105, 108, 116, 128; of public
education, 15, 106, 108, 128, 181,
191–92*n4*; of remediation, 17, 181

economics, 7, 71, 121, 139. *See also*
budget crises; budget cuts; financial
aid; financial crises; tuition

educational organizations, 48, 90, 110, 115. *See also* NCTE
Ehrenreich, Barbara, 15, 108, 120–21
electives and elective system, 36, 55, 56, 57, 116
English departments, 41, 43, 51–57, 59, 67, 101, 120; and testing, 39, 49. *See also* CCNY, Department of English
English Journal, 21, 37, 39
enrollments, 49, 59, 115, 126; decline in, 31–32, 38–39, 48; increase in, 46, 50–52, 56, 57, 59, 61, 70; need to sustain, 23, 28, 41, 47, 59–60
equal opportunity, 25, 59–60, 72, 111, 114, 192*n5*
ESL (English as a Second Language), 117, 145
essays, familiar, 149, 152–57, 170–71, 179, 183; and languages, 146, 151, 154, 159–64, 173–75; and translation pedagogy, 17–19, 159, 176–77
ethnic conflict, 70, 94, 126
ethnic studies, 9, 128, 129, 147, 153
ethnography, 153, 185, 194*n6. See also* cultures, ethnic

faculty, 13, 54, 135, 145, 152, 157, 190*n5*; adjunct, 116, 138; at CCNY, 87, 94, 97, 98–99, 132–33; at CUNY, 116, 118, 119, 126, 144; full-time, 4–5, 50–51, 55, 101, 116, 124
financial aid, 46, 114, 117, 140, 141
financial crises, 13, 25, 58, 71, 94, 99–100, 103
Finnegan, Dorothy, 51–52, 55, 58, 87, 99, 101; Regional State University, 52, 99
Flores, Juan, 149–50
formalism, 66, 75–76, 85, 134, 135, 189–90*n4*
foundations, 23, 28, 33, 38, 39, 89. *See also* Carnegie Foundation

funding, 2, 6, 51–52, 103, 115, 119; federal, 13, 23, 52, 70, 114, 117; by foundations, 23, 47; insufficient, 14, 32, 98, 101, 116–17, 121–22, 144; private, 27, 52. *See also* budget crises; budget cuts; financial aid

Glazer, Nathan, 20–21, 69, 98, 118, 130–31, 192*n6*
Gonzalez, Sandra, 168–70, 171
Goodburn, Amy, 175–76
graduate education, 13, 51–52, 56, 58, 91, 98
graduation requirements, 41, 93
Gray-Rosendale, Laura, 4–5, 9–10
Great Society programs, 109, 122, 127
Gunner, Jeanne, 75, 84, 85, 97

Harkin, Patricia, 74–75
Harrington, Susanmarie, 142–43
Harris, Joseph, 70, 73
Harvard, 28, 32, 33, 36, 39, 188*n1*; and enrollments, 31, 47, 115; and literacy crisis, 60, 107, 121; and remediation, 26, 43, 44
Henning, Barbara, 134–35
Hesse, Douglas, 153–54
high school, 27, 29–30, 32–33, 40, 50, 160–61
Horner, Bruce, 3, 10, 97, 98, 127, 128; and critique of Shaughnessy, 63, 70–71, 73, 75–76, 97, 98
humanities, 101, 119. *See also* English departments
Hurston, Zora Neale, 17, 103, 169
Hyllegard, David, 69, 139, 140, 180

identity, 4, 17; class, 108, 122, 132; conflicts of, 5, 8, 140, 148, 168, 178; cultural, 4, 159, 170; ethnic, 16, 156, 170; middle-class, 109
identity politics, 6, 9, 16, 17–18, 84, 164

ideological conflicts, 1–2
illiteracy, 1, 40, 107
immigrants, 16, 126, 151, 165. *See also*
    students, immigrant
Indiana University, 29, 33
intellectuals, 16–17, 18, 109, 158, 164,
    170; and coalition-building, 108,
    127, 136, 144; at CUNY, 16, 136, 146;
    middle class, 113, 120, 133; minority,
    17, 108, 161, 164–68, 173; neoliberal,
    15, 127–31; and private literacies,
    151–52; progressive, 147–48, 180;
    right-wing, 122, 137–38; student,
    160, 169; working-class, 149

Jeffries, Leonard, 129–30, 192n6
Journal of Basic Writing, 65, 136, 190n4

Kachru, Braj, 171–72
Katz, Michael, 133–34
Kazin, Alfred, 148–49
Kerr, Clark, 61, 70, 101, 113, 190n9
Kitzhaber, Albert, 42–43, 47, 49–50,
    52–53, 56, 188n1
Knopp, Linda, 110, 111, 192n5
knowledge, 19, 180; local, 152; public,
    157; situated, 75; traditional, 17, 94,
    106, 181; transcreation of, 148,
    149–50, translation of, 147–48, 160,
    161, 166–68, 177
Kriegel, Leonard, 83, 164, 170

language, 146, 159–60; academic,
    8–9, 14, 68, 82–83, 155, 166; BEV
    (Black English Vernacular), 154,
    160–64, 169, 175–76; bilingualism,
    164, 168; dialects of, 159, 160, 161;
    dominant, 151, 161; and meaning,
    81–82, 88, 90, 97; nativization of,
    171–72, 173; politics of, 6–7, 9, 14,
    76, 83, 150, 182; and rap, 162–64;
    Spanglish, 171, 173–75; theories of,
    73–74, 76, 182; transcreation of, 173;

working-class, 17, 82
Latinos, 19, 89, 172. *See also* students,
    Latino
Lavin, David, 69, 123, 139, 140, 180
learning communities, 63, 90
Levine, David, 39, 46–47
liberal arts, 98–99; access to, 19, 68,
    72, 85, 96, 145, 187n1; courses, 14,
    59, 136, 184; institutions, 7, 12, 13,
    110
literacies, 5; private, 151–52, 158, 161,
    173, 179, 184; public, 179, 184
literacy crisis, 16, 44, 122, 127, 188n2,
    192n6; at elite institutions, 60, 107,
    121; as justification for downsizing,
    15, 106, 128; as justification for
    stratification, 10, 106, 107, 120–21;
    and remediation, 47, 124
literacy narratives, 151, 153
literary studies, 30, 31, 33, 34–36, 52,
    99
literature: ethnic, 89, 151, 153, 172;
    western, 59
Lu, Min-Zhan, 3, 10, 16, 97, 127, 151,
    164; and critique of Shaughnessy,
    73, 76–77, 80–82, 83–84, 190n4

Manhattan Institute, 131, 191n4
media, 20–21, 22, 121–22, 127–28,
    192n6; newspapers, 111, 115, 117, 118,
    124, 125, 131. *See also New York
    Times*
Mellix, Barbara, 154–55
middle class, 15, 109, 166, 178; exclu-
    sivity of, 3, 15; professional, 1, 13,
    120, 133, 134. *See also* students, mid-
    dle-class
Miller, Richard, 86–87, 96, 175, 178
Miller, Susan, 136–37, 154, 158
Miller, Thomas, 147–48
multiculturalism, 9, 16, 76, 169, 181,
    191n4; and curriculum, 19, 119, 132,
    153

Mutnick, Deborah, 134–35, 144

NCTE (National Council of Teachers
    of English), 38, 40, 41, 43, 47, 50
neoliberalism, 15, 127–31
New York City, 30, 120, 129, 137,
    162–64, 171, 179; cost of living in,
    117, 139, 141, 142; literacy crisis in,
    107. *See also* CCNY; CUNY
New York Post, 118, 125, 131
New York State, 15, 22, 30, 110, 116,
    117; Board of Higher Education,
    98–99; Board of Regents, 30, 119.
    See also SUNY
New York Times, 20, 22, 117, 128, 131

Ohio State University, 29, 38, 84
open access, 22, 25, 49, 52, 62, 66, 67;
    at CUNY, 3, 11, 60, 69–70, 118,
    123–26, 139; failure of, 108, 128, 132;
    struggle over, 103, 181; support for,
    116, 125–26, 139. *See also* admis-
    sions, open
oratory, 22, 34, 35, 54
"other," 1, 15, 108, 109, 133
Oxford University, 147–48

pedagogy: border, 180, 181, 182, 184;
    process, 4, 63; of translation, 17–19,
    149–51, 159, 176–77
politics of access, 8, 13, 16, 66, 84, 142,
    144; debates over, 105; definition of,
    5
politics of agency, 48, 106, 116, 127
politics of basic skills, 65–66, 68, 88,
    96, 103
politics of institutions, 10, 65, 143
politics of language, 6–7, 9, 14, 76, 83,
    150, 182
politics of meaning, 5, 7–8, 105. *See
    also* language, and meaning
politics of representation, 5, 6, 8, 16,
    65–66, 142, 144. *See also* remedia-
    tion; students

poststructuralism, 5, 8–9, 68, 72–73,
    75–76, 97, 153
poverty, 15, 117, 122, 134. *See also* stu-
    dents, low-income
privatization, 14, 16, 106, 114, 116–20,
    191n4; and CUNY, 107, 119, 141, 181
progressivism, 69, 73, 108, 133–34,
    165; and intellectuals, 7, 147–48,
    180; and teachers, 93, 96, 153, 176.
    See also under names of individuals

racism, 77, 111, 179–80. *See also* strati-
    fication, by race
Reagan years, 105, 112
recession, 71, 121
reforms, 4–5, 87, 142; affecting access,
    8, 19, 67–68, 144, 181–82; at CUNY
    and SUNY, 15, 86, 181–82; curricu-
    lar, 6, 19, 83, 94, 105–6
remediation, 70–71, 103, 118, 124, 151,
    153, 192n5; abolition of, 107, 110–11,
    123; backlash against, 4, 142, 144,
    181; at CCNY, 10, 13, 20–22, 89–90,
    95–96, 102–3, 119; college-wide, 89,
    94; and conditioning, 27, 32–33, 37,
    39, 42; conflicts over, 66–67, 122;
    costs of, 110, 118; criticism of, 4, 22,
    48–49, 105, 106, 131, 138; cultural
    arguments about, 105, 127; at
    CUNY, 11, 14–15, 117; decline of, 25,
    47–51, 100, 103, 115, 144; downsiz-
    ing of, 17, 181; failure of, 108, 118,
    128; at four-year colleges, 4, 11, 26,
    110, 123, 192n5; as a longitudinal
    process, 80, 93–94; and mathemat-
    ics, 26, 27, 28, 112, 124; for middle-
    and upper-income students, 2–3;
    and minorities, 13, 48–49, 103, 112,
    157, 181; quality of, 99–100, 116; rep-
    resentations of, 14–15, 109; scape-
    goating of, 116, 118; status of,
    109–10; and students of color, 60,
    65, 143; at two-year colleges, 11,
    110–12, 131, 189n3, 192n5. *See also*

writing, basic; writing courses,
basic
remediation, history of, 20–64; at
CCNY, 20, 25, 33–36, 46–47, 53–58,
61, 63; and conditioning, 27, 32–33,
37, 39, 42; and demographic
changes, 45–47; and enrollment increases, 50–52, 57, 59, 61; and the
forensic system, 24, 36–37; and
preparatory programs, 24, 27,
28–31; and testing, 37–42; for upper-
level students, 42–45, 49–50. *See
also* CCNY, Basic Writing Program; CCNY, Pre-Baccalaureate
program; CCNY, Writing Center;
Mina Shaughnessy
Renfro, Sally, 11, 45
research, 13, 14, 23, 25, 54–55, 98, 103;
vs. teaching, 40, 87, 98–99, 117
research and development, 2, 23
research institutions, 57–58, 106, 111
research missions, 25, 29, 55, 56, 60,
87
rhetoric, 22, 30, 33–36, 42, 54, 147–48,
188*n1*
Rich, Adrienne, 132–33, 134
Ringnalda, Margaret, 62–63
Rose, Mike, 3, 63, 151
Rouse, John, 74, 75, 189–90*n4*

Schmidt Report, 117–19, 122
Scott, Barbara Ann, 2, 12, 23–24, 50
SEEK (Search for Education, Excellence, and Knowledge) program,
89–90, 100
selectivity, 2, 13, 19, 31–32, 50, 70, 111;
vs. access, 40, 71, 181; at CCNY,
46–47; challenge to, 67–68, 69, 104,
180, 181; and remediation, 67
self, transcreation of, 168, 171
Shaughnessy, Mina, 8, 13–14, 21, 37,
54, 63–64, 189*n1*; and bureaucratic
struggle, 66, 85–89, 90–96, 182;

criticism of, 66, 70–71, 98, 190*n9*;
critiques of works of, 72–74, 75–77,
84; *Errors and Expectations,* 21,
72–78, 80–81, 88–89, 94, 97, 153;
formalism of, 66, 85, 189–90*n4*;
legacy of, 8, 64–66, 68, 76–77, 102,
104, 189–90*n4*; and reform, 67–68,
181–82
Shor, Ira, 7, 15, 107, 121, 187*n1*, 189*n3*
Slevin, James, 7, 90
Smith, Ron, 48, 49, 51
Smith College, 114–15
Solomon, Alisa, 191–92*n4*
Spellmeyer, Kurt, 153, 154, 155
standards, 11, 12, 41, 47, 91, 102; decline
of, 3, 106, 110, 118; for tenure and
promotion, 98–99, 101; writing, 1,
3, 24, 31, 55. *See also* admissions
standards
Sternglass, Marilyn, 8, 9, 63, 82,
139–41, 144–45, 157
stratification, 7, 12–13, 23–24, 40, 98,
143–44, 187*n1*; by admissions, 107;
among institutions, 22, 23, 61, 112;
class, 46, 112, 114–15; by curricula,
12, 51, 107, 111, 116, 124; of disciplines, 106; within institutions,
22–24, 32, 37–38, 41, 49, 51, 120; justified by literacy crisis, 10, 105, 106,
107, 120–21; by mission, 107, 111; by
race, 111–12, 114, 115, 128–30; support for, 142. *See also* colleges and
universities, restratification of; colleges and universities, retiering of;
colleges and universities, tiering of
student need, discourse of, 143; opposition to, 19; and remediation, 13,
49, 138, 151; and stratification, 105,
107
students, 1, 12, 124; Asian American,
111, 128, 137; bilingual, 141–42; culture of, 16, 109, 120, 128–31; deficits
of, 131–32; ethnicity of, 45, 46, 61,

students, *(cont.)*
71, 115; fundamentalist, 175–77; gender of, 45–46, 61; immigrant, 112,
128–29, 130, 141–42, 155–57, 164; international, 113; Jewish, 46, 126–27,
129, 137, 180; lower middle-class, 14,
45, 112, 189*n*3; low-income, 114, 115,
139; material needs of, 10, 108, 109,
120, 180; middle-class, 2–3, 13, 113,
114–15, 124, 136, 157; needs of, 1, 11,
19, 60, 106, 109; nontraditional, 61,
71, 96, 153, 181, 182; open admissions, 96, 100–101, 102–3, 123; and
parents, 135, 155–56, 159–60,
162–63, 168–71, 173–74, 176–77;
placement of, 91–93; representations of, 108–9, 138, 185; scapegoat-
ing of, 128–30; socioeconomic
status of, 2, 45, 61, 113; underclass,
16, 109, 130, 133, 136; upper-income,
2–3, 113, 115, 119; white, 111, 123–24,
128, 139, 157–58. *See also* CCNY
students
students, black, 65, 111, 124–25,
134–35, 160–62, 164; culture of, 22,
128–30
students, Latino, 19, 65, 111, 124, 125,
129–30, 137; and composition,
146–47, 162–64, 173–75, 176–77
students, minority, 69, 127, 189*n*3; access for, 61, 98, 114, 123; cultural difference of, 15, 108, 128, 129–30, 136;
and remediation, 13, 48–49, 103,
112, 157, 181
students, working-class, 14, 17, 45, 46,
61, 98, 166; barriers for, 12–13, 85,
109, 117; integration of, 13, 68,
69–70, 86, 104; and lower tiers, 112;
and remediation, 105, 112, 181; and
vocationalism, 107, 115
students of color, 1, 61, 69, 139, 180,
189*n*3; and remediation, 11, 13, 25,
60, 65, 112, 143
Stygall, Gail, 124, 144

SUNY (State University of New
York), 15, 86, 126, 181–82, 191*n*4. *See
also* CUNY
Syracuse University, 4, 41–42

Taylor, Warner, 38, 41
teachers, 14, 134, 144; hiring of, 5, 13,
50–51, 52, 99–100, 101; part-time,
99–100. *See also* writing teachers
teaching loads, 53–55, 91, 101
teaching vs. research, 13, 40, 87,
98–99, 117
testing, 49, 113, 139, 144; of basic
skills, 124; entrance, 123; mass assessment, 8, 41; placement, 40–42,
49, 100; proficiency, 3, 32, 37–39, 43,
93, 100
translation: cultural, 165, 193*n*2; of
knowledge, 147–48, 160, 161,
166–68, 177; pedagogy of, 17–19,
149–51, 159, 176–77; theory of, 177,
184–85, 193*n*2
Traub, James, 15, 135, 137, 138, 143, 150,
165; and afrocentrism, 192*n*6; *City
on a Hill,* 108, 122, 127–31, 136, 147,
148–49; and criticism of remediation, 17, 22
Trimbur, John, 15, 108, 122, 183, 188*n*2
Trimmer, Joseph, 48, 49, 105
tuition, 33, 126, 180; increases in, 114,
116, 117, 119, 139, 140–41

underclass, 108–9, 132–35, 138, 149
University of California, 62, 115
University of Illinois, 29, 31, 42, 60
University of Massachusetts, 59,
110–11
University of Michigan, 29, 31, 33, 46,
60
University of Minnesota, 29, 31, 42
University of New Hampshire, 157–58
University of North Carolina, 31, 42,
43
University of Pennsylvania, 26, 31

University of Utah, 136–37, 158
University of Wisconsin, 21–22, 28, 39–40, 41

values, 138, 158, 167, 175, 176, 177, 178
Veysey, Laurence, 32, 39, 57
vocationalism, 2, 59, 107, 129, 136, 187*n1*, 189*n3*
vocational programs, 115, 119. *See also* colleges, vocational

Wagner, Geoffrey, 101, 190*n9*
Wellesley College, 26, 33
Wesleyan, 114–15
Wilcox, Thomas, 47–48, 49, 66
women's studies, 9, 94
Woolley, Edwin, 21, 38, 39
working class, 72, 94–95, 126, 127, 128, 149; culture of, 130–31, 136; and identity, 17; language of, 17, 82. *See also* students, working-class
Wozniak, John, 26, 36, 38

WPAs (Writing Program Administrators), 8, 14, 85, 144, 181
writing, 150, 175; standards for, 1, 3, 24, 31, 55
writing, basic, 5–6, 17–18, 20, 30, 34, 37, 42, 44, 56, 76–77, 77, 92, 96; tutorials for, 3, 24, 37, 43, 44–45, 92, 100. *See also* essays, familiar
writing centers and clinics, 3, 37, 38, 43, 44, 91, 111. *See also* under CCNY
writing courses, basic, 48, 60, 63, 82, 104, 131; agency of, 1, 22; status of, 1, 90, 96, 103. *See also* remediation; politics of basic skills; under CCNY
writing teachers, 88–94, 102–3, 145, 154, 160, 175, 182; evaluations by, 91–93; progressive, 93, 96, 153, 176; quality of, 95–96; status of, 88, 91

Yale, 32, 43–44, 47, 60
Yezierska, Anzia, 16–17, 148, 151, 165–68, 169